There and Back

There and Back
Twelve of the Great Routes of Human History

STEWART GORDON

OXFORD
UNIVERSITY PRESS

OXFORD
UNIVERSITY PRESS

Oxford University Press is a department of the University of Oxford.
It furthers the University's objective of excellence in research, scholarship,
and education by publishing worldwide. Oxford is a registered trademark of
Oxford University Press in the UK and in certain other countries.

Published in India by
Oxford University Press
22 Workspace, 2nd Floor, 1/22 Asaf Ali Road, New Delhi 110 002, India

© Oxford University Press 2018

The moral rights of the author have been asserted.

First Edition published in 2018

ISBN-13 (print edition): 978-0-19-947645-9
ISBN-10 (print edition): 0-19-947645-4

ISBN-13 (eBook): 978-0-19-909356-4
ISBN-10 (eBook): 0-19-909356-3

Typeset in Arno Pro 10.5/14.5
by Tranistics Data Technologies, Kolkata 700 091
Printed and bound in India at Repro India Ltd., Mumbai

The maps in this book do not represent authentic international boundaries.
The maps are not to scale and are provided for illustrative purposes only.

Contents

Contents

Part IV Trade Routes

Introduction

Throughout human history, routes concentrated, funnelled, and mixed human experience. On these routes moved books, scrolls, and art, in addition to armies, ambassadorial entourages, slaves, brides, and pilgrims. The interaction of people on routes generated surprising innovations in ideas, religions, art, technology, and cuisine. Slavery, piracy, government taxation and control, medicinal plants, military expeditions, the interaction between competing religions, the processing of goods along the way, and networks of credit, trust, and information that often spanned continents— routes have witnessed all this and more.

Yearly patterns of travel set by ecology and climate are typical of routes and form part of the mental expectations about them. The thousands of boats that carried grain north on the Grand Canal were limited to one passage a year, after the harvest and before the level of the Yangtze and Yellow rivers dropped so low that the grain boats could not cross them. Similarly, grain from Egypt to Rome had to be harvested, the ships loaded, and the fleet reach Brindisi before the winter storms beset the Mediterranean.

Travellers knew these constraints of physical conditions and ignored them at their peril. No one wanted to be on the Silk Road in winter. Fodder was unavailable. Snow closed the passes and the cold was lethal. Travellers sought a town, a warm fire, and the coming of spring. Summer on the trans-Sahara route was equally lethal. Whole caravans disappeared into waterless heat. In spite of these constraints, for centuries routes provided the best way across an ocean or over a mountain range to connect a supply of salt to a market or to accomplish a pilgrimage.

Strong governments have always influenced the appearance of land routes with characteristic boundaries, material, and markers. Routes were an expression of the power and reach of empires such as the Inka kingdom with its government-built guardhouses, way stations, and government-sponsored colonies. Yet, governments might protect only part of a route, perhaps the most dangerous portion. Travelling groups often hired a military escort, as did those on the Hajj in fourteenth-century North Africa. Many routes had a myriad of rulers and taxes along the way, such as on the Rhine River.

Routes were not merely influenced by kingdoms and rulers; they typically exerted profound influence on regions and cities along the way. The route itself made possible the transportation of raw materials and the shipping of value-added commodities. Those associated with a route knew that water transport was many times cheaper than overland. On the Nile, hewn stone blocks moved downstream for millennia. On the Erie Canal, towns like Rochester processed cattle into preserved meats for shipment via New York to Europe. Canals worked particularly well for fragile items, such as porcelain in China or the light bulbs produced by the General Electric Company at Schenectady, New York.

A route's commodities forced traders to ask hard questions that were also part of mental expectations and cognitive geography. Were his goods the right colour or weight to find buyers at the end of the trip? How high were transit tolls? Was there war along the way? Would buyers and sellers find an acceptable common currency? Would they share a common language? Was there a way to enforce legal contracts? These were the hopes and fears discussed in caravan stops and port towns. Was the road safe enough to get there at all? Any route had people bent on stealing the goods and enslaving or ransoming the travellers. Bandits and pirates lurked near vulnerable portions of the route—mountains, forests, coasts with many isolated coves, the open ocean, and deserts—all places beyond government protection. The pirate or bandit leader had mental expectations about the route as well. He needed to know what sort of traveller would be found on which route at what season of the year.

Travellers on routes were seldom alone. Pilgrims travelled with other pilgrims, usually identified by distinctive clothes or a certain kind of staff. Brides and ambassadors travelled in entourages. Slaves bound for Baghdad trudged together shackled and guarded. Travellers sought out others from their country or those who spoke their language and shared a culture of the road, whether through their attire, cuisine, alcohol, entertainment, stories, boasts, and jokes. These face-to-face networks facilitated exchange of information about other travellers, courts, and cities, and reinforced mental expectations of the route. Government bureaucrats, ship captains, pilgrims, sailors, caravan leaders, traders, itinerant preachers, skilled tradesmen, professional entertainers, poets, and philosophers all needed to know the character of potential employers, the current politics of courts, and possible contacts along the way. These discussions affected a man's reputation, which was crucial to trust, credit, useful information, and hospitality.

The flow of information along a route was generally dense, specialized, and varied among different types of travellers. Traders wrote letters to members of their network, which conveyed up-to-date information on markets, the larger politics of transit regions, and personal news of family and friends. Letters of introduction, which identified trustworthy people along the way and at the destination, were equally important to the trader, the pilgrim, and the scholar. Roman routes had a formal, government-paid system of couriers, including post stations, seals, and procedures. In contrast, the exchange of information between riverboat pilots on the Mississippi was more informal. They left letters on current river conditions in simple boxes for pilots guiding boats in the opposite direction.

These routes can largely be divided into four categories—river, pilgrimage, tribute, and trade—and I have divided the book into these four sections. The arrangement is based on cognitive geography rather than technological or physical differences. The Rhine is not a river route because there is water flowing between two banks. Rather, it is a river route because of the songs and fairy tales about it and its long history as a political boundary. Pilgrimage routes are treated together, regardless of religion, because of the similar expectations and experiences of pilgrims, just as routes of imperial tribute rest primarily on the expectations of local officials, transporters, military guards, and marauders hoping to steal goods. Trade routes foreground markets, commodities, and professional traders.

I have chosen specific routes based on four criteria. First, the route must have had name and fame, important enough that it was known in song and story. Second, I wanted a very wide geographic spread and deep historical connections in order to show that the features of these four types of routes were part of common human experience. Third, each route needed a memoir or other intimate documentation to approach the mental expectations of those on the route. And finally, I wanted routes with archaeological evidence to supplement the memoirs and letters. I have chosen only those sea routes whose documentary evidence is so rich that a compelling case could be made without archaeological evidence.

The book rests on the theory of cognitive geography, a body of research which found that mental expectations about space and landscape predicted how people navigated far more accurately than maps of actual distance and proximity.[1] Each chapter is based on an actual memoir of a man or woman who followed a route, allowing us to experience their expectations, their hopes and fears, their trials and triumphs. Throughout the book I have chosen routes that were treated as a function of season and place, government infrastructure, movement of commodities, technology and human networks, and as the mental expectations, the cognitive geography of the featured traveller. Let us then set out with the hopes of pilgrims, the fears of traders, the expectations of bureaucrats and explore some of the great routes of human history.

Note

1. The theoretical underpinnings of this book revisit a subfield of geography known as cognitive geography, behavioural geography, or mental mapping, whose roots go back to the 1940s, though the most active and creative period was during the 1970s and 1980s. Its central insight, which seems just as valid today, is that people's perception of concepts like near and far, long and short journeys, and significant and insignificant landmarks were strikingly different from what was portrayed on maps or even what an outsider might see on the ground. The early studies, such as Kevin Lynch, *The Image of the*

City (Cambridge, Mass: Technology Press, 1960) attempted to redraw cities as people actually perceived and navigated them. See also Douglas Pocock and Ray Hudson, *Images of the Urban Environment* (London: Macmillan, 1978). Through the 1970s and 1980s, geographers attempted to generalize these urban insights into a wider perspective, namely that individuals or at most small local groups had their own valid ways of understanding and organizing space, and that these micro-geographies were worth studying, even if the usual methods of geographic research were difficult to apply. See, for example, John Wright and David Lowenthal (eds), *Geographies of the Mind* (New York: Oxford University Press, 1976); Roger M. Downs and David Stea (eds), *Image and Environment: Cognitive Mapping and Spatial Behavior* (Chicago: Aldine Pub. Co, 1973); Peter Gould and Rodney White, *Mental Maps* (Harmondworth, England: Penguin, 1974); and Yi-Fu Tuan, 'Images and Mental Maps', *Annals of the Association of American Geographers*, vol. 65 (1975). Useful interchange with both game theory and cognitive psychology ensued. The movement seemed to attract more proponents in Europe, especially in France. The field of cognitive geography and mental mapping received much criticism, such as Trudi E. Bunting and Leonard Guelke, 'Behavioral and Perceptual Geography: A Critical Appraisal', in *Annals of the American Geographers*, vol. 69, no. 3 (September 1979), pp. 448–62, which centred on the approach's failure to produce significant data-driven scientifically testable hypotheses. By the 1980s 'mental mapping' was largely subsumed by a movement broadly known as 'humanistic' geography, which sought to break down the positivistic bias of previous geographic thought through local fieldwork and textual studies. See, for example, Toms Mels (ed.), *Reanimating Places: A Geography of Rhythms* (Aldershot, England: Ashgate, 2004).

The idea of mental maps has, however, gained some popularity in history and anthropology owing to lesser demands than geography for statistically provable hypotheses. Pivotal to this was the popularity of Hayden White's ideas of imagined community. See, for example, Dennis Cosgrove (ed.), *Geography and Vision: Seeing, Imagining and Representing the World* (London: I.B. Tauris, 2008), which brought together scholars to examine large-scale ancient indigenous worldviews. An imagined continent is central to Sumathi Ramaswamy's *The Lost Land of Lemuria: Fabulous Geographies, Catastrophic Histories* (Berkeley: University of California Press, 2004). See also Kurt A. Raaflaub and Richard J.A. Talbert (eds), *Geography and Ethnography: Perception of the World in Pre-Modern Societies* (Chichester, England: Wiley-Blackwell, 2010).

My use of mental mapping is part of this 'softer' mental mapping venture. I have found ideas from cognitive geography useful in conceptualizing how people on the same road could have quite different experiences based on their focus and mental expectations. For this 'mental' side of routes, the reader will notice that I have used a variety of terms, some, such as 'ethos', quite broad, and others, such as 'mental expectations' or 'reputation', quite specific. This messiness is by choice. It is relatively easy to specify the directly observable features of a route, such as the climate, goods traded, human networks, and technology. It is much more difficult to access the interior perceptions of people centuries or millennia ago. My assumption is that the best a historian can do is utilize what travellers documented, including songs and stories from the route and the created visual record, to form some rough approximation of these interior mental states. I further assume that, like all culture, a single ethos for a route was never wholly accepted. Images and expectations about a route were fragmented among groups in competition, connected to political and military power, and changed over time. I have, therefore, in the various chapters used the term that seems the most appropriate cognitive side of the route considered.

Acknowledgements

A book of this scope depends on the expertise of colleagues. I wish to acknowledge colleagues who discussed aspects of or formally critiqued chapters: Richard Eaton, Collin Ganio, Juan Cole, Patrick Manning, Stephen Morillo, and Lee Schlessinger. I appreciate the chance to present the substance of the book in public lectures at the University of Pittsburgh, the Center for South Asian Studies at the University of Michigan, and at the American Geographic Society Archives in Milwaukee. I wish to thank Karl Longstreth and Tim Utter of the University of Michigan Map Collection, the curators and staffs of the University of Michigan Rare Book Room, the Cleveland Public Library, the St. Louis Public Library, the Cincinnati Public Library, the Library of Congress Prints and Photographs Department, the Newberry Library, the American Geographical Society Collection at the University of Wisconsin-Madison, and the Erie Canal Museum. I would especially like to thank Stephen Allee, Curator of East Asian Painting and Calligraphy at the Freer Gallery for the opportunity to examine their wonderful eighteenth-century scroll painting of the Grand Canal. The anonymous reviewers assisted in the intellectual development of the book and my agent, Roger Williams, helped the business side of the book. I greatly appreciate Linda Stanley's copy-editing of an early draft.

I served as historical consultant to the Delta Queen Steamboat Company for several years and learned much of the history of the Mississippi while on their boats and in the libraries of their ports. Consulting with the History Channel on two series about the Mughal Empire helped me think about the Silk Road. The financial support of the Helen and John S. Best Fellowship assisted in the research. I would also like to acknowledge Peter Gottschalk whose fine photos accompany the Compostela chapter. I would also like thank my brother, Roy Gordon, for the opportunity to see and walk a small portion of the great Inka route.

PART I

RIVER ROUTES

Introduction

L arge rivers and their tributaries were some of man's first routes. They inevitably connected ecologically different regions, such as the highlands of the headwaters, the tributaries of the middle reaches, and the coastal plain and delta. From the earliest human record, for example the northern migration from southern Africa, archaeologists know that such movements followed rivers, as did small amounts of hand-to-hand trade. Much later in human history man developed canals around dangerous portions of the river. Many rivers were difficult to cross and became boundaries as well as routes.

The limitations of rivers as routes remained unchanged for millennia, the most fundamental of which was that the river went only exactly where it went. Irrigation from the river made adjacent farmland particularly valuable, while good agricultural land well away from a river suffered because of the high costs of overland transportation to reach it. Rivers were primarily one-way routes. They basically carried commodities from the heartland downstream to the mouth of the river. It was brutally difficult to row, pole, paddle, or drag boats upstream. Many rivers also had only a single place to trade goods, invariably the city at the mouth, such as Cairo, New Orleans, or Rotterdam. These large cities exported across oceans and connected the heartland commodities with both the vagaries and opportunities of a world market.

Rivers were also subject to climatic limitations. Northern rivers froze and became impassable half the year or more. All rivers rose and fell with seasonal rains, the effect most pronounced in monsoonal rivers, such as the Nile, Yangtze, and the Indus. After the seasonal rains produced flood conditions, the water level of the rivers fell. Low water and dangerous rocks prevailed the rest of the year. A river, as a route, needed as much water as possible to make it navigable through more months of the year. Other uses, however, competed for the water, such as irrigation, mills, and cities. Low water meant that large trade expeditions were limited on many rivers to a single traverse each year.

Rivers, especially those with a powerful current, shifted course frequently in stretches without the confines of high bluffs or gorges. For the river as a route, up-to-date information was essential—islands and channels appeared and disappeared, and channels shifted as well. In fact, until the late nineteenth century, channels remained unmarked on maps. Boatmen and pilots, as professionals, therefore, tended to exchange information at every opportunity.

Attempts to politically control the entire length of a large river rarely succeeded. Invaders from the lowlands could not control the highlands and vice versa. The multitude of river tolls often reflected the fragmentation of political control along rivers. Political control also determined whether a far-away government or local nobles marshalled the slaves, local peasants, or free labour for the yearly toil of dredging the main river channels and side irrigation channels. There was also political and military competition to control both banks of rivers. Indeed, the political currents along rivers often proved just as dangerous as the shifting channels.

People along various stretches of a large river had different languages, myths, ethnicities, and religions. The variety of peoples along the river created trading opportunities, but also produced a confluence of cuisine and fashion, a jostling of religions and ideas, and the appearing of the river itself in myth, poem, and story.

Venture capital and credit often followed rivers. Entrepreneurs have, for millennia, opened new land or introduced new crops along rivers, such as grapes along the Rhine and cotton along the Nile and the Mississippi. Businessmen in towns along rivers developed small industries for processing local commodities into higher-value goods. Their networks often connected upriver towns and farms with the large city at the mouth of the river. The more populated and integrated the towns along a river, the more likely that they became a vector for periodic outbreaks of serious disease, such as cholera, malaria, and yellow fever.

Steam technology in the nineteenth century fundamentally changed large rivers as routes, substantially lowering both upstream and down-stream costs of transportation. This new technology thereby promoted both bulk transport of commodities and the development of national markets for manufactured items such as soap, stoves, and shoes. By providing comfortable accommodations and regular schedules, steamboats made many large rivers into tourist routes. The infrastructure of travel agents, hotels, tour guides, and restaurants followed. Steamboats also allowed, for the first time, the rapid deployment of government troops upriver.

Today, large rivers are workhorses of heavy industry. Barge traffic exploits the fundamentally lower cost of water transport over land transport, moving heavy, bulky items, such as stone, sand and gravel, coal, oil, and chemical precursors. Tourists, private boaters, and armchair travellers still find rivers an irresistible way to travel.

All of these features, from the annual rhythm of a river to the lore of its boatmen, from the fame of its commodities to its periodic epidemics, form portions of the cognitive geography, the mental expectations, of its travellers. Let us then accompany a famous author on the Rhine in search of nature, sail the Nile with a Victorian woman in search of health, and tag along with a colourful St Louis family on vacation on a Mississippi steamboat.

The Rhine

In July 1839, Victor Hugo set off from his home in Paris to tour the Rhine. At 37, he was already a famous poet and had written eight novels, including the financially successful and politically influential *Hunchback of Notre Dame*. Only two years after his Rhine journey, the French Academy would make him a member, and the king would make him a peer of the realm with a royal pension. Hugo's Rhine journal opens with an explanation of why he travelled.

> … renovation of ideas and sensation is the object of my journey, rather than mere adventure: for which purpose a succession of new objects suffices me. I am easily contented. Provided I have vegetation around me, and air above—a road in view and a road in my rear—I have nothing to complain of. If the country be flat, the broad horizon delights me; if mountainous, I rejoice in the unexpected openings of landscape: and at the summit of every hill I am sure to find an extant prospect truly delightful.[1]

Hugo bought a seat on a public coach headed east. He carried a tourist guidebook, a set of Cassini maps, and books by Tacitus, the Roman historian. Victor Hugo liked inns, particularly old, clean, and well-appointed ones.

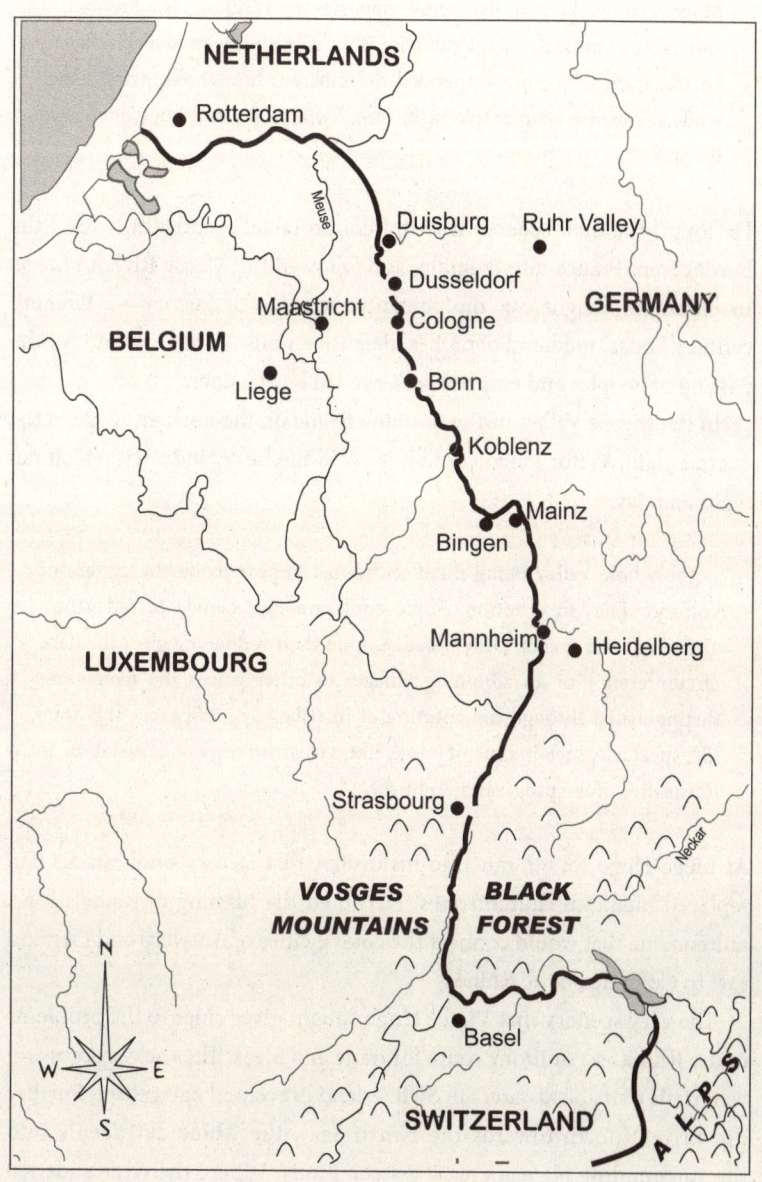

Rhine River

The Kitchen of the Hotel de Metz is a kitchen worth speaking of; being an immense hall, one side of which is decorated with rows of saucepans, the other with crockery. In the centre, opposite the windows, is a fireplace, a vast cavern, containing a splendid fire. The ceiling is traversed by blackened beams, from which are suspended the different household instruments: while the centre is an ample rack, stored with hams and huge flitches of bacon.[2]

He found the mail coaches fast and comfortable, eventually crossed the border from France into Belgium, and followed the Meuse River to Liège. In cities, he sought out the romantic remains of history—a fifteenth century house, medieval churches, defensive walls—even evidence of the passing of peoples and empires preserved in local names.[3]

In the Meuse Valley, just west of the Rhine on the northern edge of the coastal plain, Victor Hugo could not avoid the heavy industry, which ran night and day.

...the whole valley being filled with what appear to be the craters of volcanos [sic] in eruption. Some emit immense clouds of red vapor, glittering with sparks. Others define upon their reddening glow the dark circumference of an adjoining village; in other places the flames are distinguished through the aperture of mis-shapely edifice. ... This war-like spectacle, seen in time of peace, like a frightful copy of devastation, is illustrative of the progress of industry...[4]

At Liège Hugo found, much to his dislike, that factory smokestacks had replaced medieval church spires. He noted the blasting of tunnels for a railroad line that would connect the coastal cities of Antwerp and Osstend east to Cologne on the Rhine.[5]

The very scenery that Victor Hugo sought gives clues to the problems of the Rhine as a unifying route for trade and ideas. The rocky gorges and waterfalls of its headwaters in Switzerland prevented navigation. Further downriver (north towards the North Sea), the Rhine cut deeply into the surrounding plateau creating steep bluffs. Where the river widened into a valley (above and below Strasbourg), the floodplain was stony and relatively unproductive. In this valley, the river frequently changed course and inundated the land, so that towns were sited well away from the Rhine in side valleys. The surrounding plateau on both sides of the river was heavily forested. It was only within a hundred miles of the ocean that the Rhine entered a broad coastal plain on which grain grew. The Rhine delta, today's Netherlands, became productive only through the enormous human effort of channelling and draining. The people at the source of the Rhine in Switzerland and at the mouth in Holland spoke different languages, while several dialects of German and French were spoken in between.[6]

The Rhine, in spite of these disadvantages, became a true river route and, for more than two thousand years, has been central to the trade and politics of Europe. It has spawned more thriving towns along its length than any comparable river in the world. The river is at the heart of folklore and legends, such as Lohengrin and Grimm's fairy tales. As a boundary, competing empires have fought over the river century after century, most recently in World War II. Rotterdam, the busiest port in Europe, lies in the Rhine delta.

The earliest evidence of the Rhine as a river route centres on a high-value, hand-to-hand trade in Baltic amber. That mysterious, warm, transparent fossilized resin of ancient larch trees, worked into beads and jewellery, appears in Neolithic burials (c. 3000 BCE) from Spain to the shores of the Caspian Sea. Amber was picked up on the shores of the North Sea, traded south along the Rhine, then east along the Danube, west along the Moselle, and south over the Alps into modern-day Italy.[7]

More than two thousand years later, in 58 BCE, Julius Caesar and four veteran legions invaded what is today France. In his famous book, *Gallic Wars*, Caesar defined the Rhine as the eastern extremity of the civilized world. Beyond it was a land of endless dark forest with no towns and no knowable rivers, inhabited by non-humans—wild tribes that ate raw flesh and loved to kill, in addition to giants and all manner of fabulous beasts. Caesar judged it worth neither trading with nor conquering.[8]

Rome for the next four centuries defined the Rhine as the defensive edge of the empire. It was a militarized boundary with fortified legion camps on the west bank, many of which grew to be important cities. Augusta became Basel, Argentina became Strasbourg, Moguntiacun became Mainz, Confluentia became Koblenz, Colonia Agrippa became Cologne, and Trajectum-ad-Mosam became Maestricht.

This chain of fortified camps created and promoted a common Roman culture up and down the river, from the mountains of Switzerland to the Netherlands. Recent research on micro-remains at Roman sites along the Rhine has established some elements of that culture: Roman officers ate well. Their diet included wine from the Mediterranean, tropical spices such as pepper, and imported almonds, figs, dates, rice, pine nuts, pistachios, and pomegranates. The four centuries of Roman rule also introduced a variety of foods and herbs into the Rhine Valley for the first time; these were cultivated long after the collapse of Roman authority, and included fruits such as peach, cherry, plum, cultivated apple, chestnut, and walnut trees, and herbs such as dill, coriander, anise, celery, summer savory, and fennel. The most economically important Roman imported plant was the grapevine.[9] Wine became the main crop of the steep banks and side valleys of the central portions of the Rhine region. This movement of new commercial plants along river routes was typical.

The Romans brought much more than new foods. Their roads and bridges were certainly the most sophisticated and standardized construction the region had ever seen. Roman town architecture included many standard features—baths, government buildings, a public place to stroll, and villas. Christianity moved upriver as the state religion.

The momentum of the Roman Empire pushed east of the Rhine, establishing two new provinces in the valleys of the Neckar and the Mainz Rivers. By 200 CE, however, the empire began to collapse. Its borders were too long to defend, the military too expensive, and the will to conquer gone. The Rhine boundary became more and more porous. At first Rome merely recruited many Germanic soldiers from beyond the frontier. In the fourth and fifth centuries, however, peoples from east of the Rhine invaded Roman France and eventually the heartland of Italy.[10] Roman roads crumbled; forts and baths were abandoned. Christianity, the official Roman religion, largely disappeared from the Rhine Valley, as did imported luxury foods. The introduced plants remained, as did the Rhine's position as a disputed political boundary.[11]

In the millennium after the Roman period, the towns of the northern reaches on the Rhine (present-day Switzerland) formed a defensive union. The economy of the region was originally herding but, by the Middle Ages, skilled processing of imported raw materials, such as flax to linen and steel to instruments, was the basis of the economy of its towns.

The central portions of the river produced no single dominant city like Paris or London, but rather a host of medium-sized cities that competed for trade. Politically, the central regions of the Rhine consisted of a myriad of small feudal states, usually centred on a single castle overlooking the river. These tiny kingdoms were generally established by war, banditry, and conquest, and demanded river tolls while providing no services, as suggested by this ancient ditty, originally in German:

> The bishop and the king divide
> Stronghold and abbey, church and town,
> The Rhine can count more tolls than miles
> And knight and priest grind us down.[12]

Bishops of nearby towns, as suggested by the song, directly controlled some of these small states.[13] A few larger towns throttled trade by successfully asserting their right to have all river-transported goods unloaded, taxed, offered for sale in town markets, and reloaded if not sold.[14]

The return of Christianity to the Rhine began with the arrival of monks and missionaries from Ireland and England in the reign of Charlemagne (ruled 768–814 CE). Monks and clerics slowly converted the tribes living near the river. By the middle of the ninth century, a chain of monasteries had been constructed along the Rhine, typically in side valleys. The most famous of the clerics along the Rhine was Abbess Hildegard von Bingen (1098–1179 CE), known for her visions, writings, and especially her musical compositions.[15]

The central portions of the river typically consisted of a walled city along the riverbank (dense with docks, winding streets, and churches), a nearby side valley with a stone monastery surrounded by terraced fields, and a brooding crenelated castle on the cliffs overlooking the river. Grapes were processed into wine for large-scale export. From the central part of the river came two other important exports—stone for the seawalls of the Netherlands and wood for the costal shipbuilding industry.

About a hundred miles north of the sea, the Rhine entered a broad coastal plain, where the principal crop was grain for export. The people of the Rhine delta were oriented towards the sea. Fishing was the central occupation, but they also engaged in long-distance trade, such as importing wool from England.[16] This region was the first in Europe to reject feudalism for trade-based free cities.

By 1650, the river was sharply divided on the basis of religion. Switzerland and Holland were centres of Protestantism, while the states along the central river remained staunchly Catholic. During the wars of religion, the Netherlands simply cut off trade upriver to the Catholic states on the Rhine. This pattern of different cultures and beliefs upriver and downriver was also typical of the Mississippi. The issue was slavery rather than religion, but the war was deadlier than the religious wars in Europe.

The beginning of the nineteenth century profoundly changed the Rhine. Napoleon swept through and conquered the length of the river from the Netherlands to Switzerland. He ordered wholesale destruction of castles along the Rhine and seized the small states, leaving a legacy of only two powers on the Rhine: France and an emerging Germany, with the two watching each other suspiciously across the river, and both claiming it as part of their heartland. Immediately after the defeat of Napoleon, the Treaty of Vienna set up a multistate Rhine River commission, whose stated purpose was to free the river of onerous tolls and allow equal access to all nations. It took sixteen years to produce the Rhine Navigation Treaty of 1831, which dramatically reduced the number of tolls, eliminated boatmen's guilds, and ended any town's demand to unload and sell cargo. The treaty also established, for the first time in history, a permanent multistate commission to finance improvements, oversee trade, and promote safety along the entire river.[17] The Rhine thus gained a special trans-state legal status.

This was around the same time as Victor Hugo's journey on the Rhine. However, Hugo's mental map of the river only makes sense in the context of a movement known as Romanticism. It began in the 1750s and 1760s in England and the many states of a fragmented Germany. The context was a mid-century worldwide war between France and England, fought on four continents, which made many doubt that the prevailing beliefs in science and rationality could ever bring peace, insight, or happiness. Writers, musicians, and artists turned away from the idea of sophisticated urban life as the ideal. Rather than the broad generalities of science, the Romantic Movement celebrated the unique beliefs and history of a people, as embodied in the customs, stories, and music of country folk. For Romantics, urban life only corrupted. True individual insight depended on communion with Nature. The movement generally had a melancholic tone and a strong element of nostalgia for a time uncorrupted by modern life. For inspiration, Romantics looked to the medieval period and its chivalry, 'noble savages', and the world of folk tales. Romantics often incorporated elements of gothic horror and the supernatural into their art, music, and writing. The Romantic Movement came to France only after Napoleon's downfall in 1815 and, therefore, was still quite new and controversial when Victor Hugo set off for the Rhine.[18]

Arriving at the Rhine, Hugo spent only 48 hours in Cologne, just enough time to walk across the bridge, appreciate his inn, and wander a few streets. The city fulfilled his Romantic ideals of medieval architecture and music. He explored the cathedral, which produced an added thrill of the juxtaposition of religious music and the sounds of construction.

> To the left there are four or five windows admitting a brilliant light, which reaches from the wooden arch to the pavement: to the right are ladders, pulleys, windlasses, trowels, and squares. At the farther extremity, the chanting, grave voices of the choiristers and prebends, the beautiful Latin of the Psalms floating through the church, the clouds of incense, the organ weeping with expressive suavity, and from the works above, the biting of saws, the moanings of cranes, and the deadened blows of the hammer on wood…[19]

Had Victor Hugo headed downriver from Cologne for 30 miles, he would have reached the junction where the Ruhr tributary met the Rhine. There, his romantic sensibilities would truly have been offended. At about the time of his trip, Ruhr Valley miners discovered coal at a depth of 2,000 feet. Within a decade of Hugo's trip, entrepreneurs developed large-scale mining, and the population grew rapidly. Huge factories followed and the valley evolved into the iron and steel centre of Germany, fabricating a variety of products from cast iron pipe to steel cutlery and weapons. As a route, the Rhine took on critical importance

Illustration 1 *Burg Rheinstein,* by W. Leo Arndt. Note the Romantic ruin and the steamboat in this nineteenth century etching. Public Domain. Courtesy of Library of Congress.

for transporting raw materials and the finished products of the emerging German industrial economy.

Victor Hugo, in fact, headed upriver to the central potions of the Rhine, an epicentre of the Romantic experience of exploring medieval ruins and contemplating nature. With some sense of irony, Hugo boarded a steamboat, the most modern means of transportation. The steamboat era on the Rhine began in the 1830s and made upriver transportation far quicker, much more reliable, and cut costs by three-quarters. They made downriver transport of goods speedy and predictable. They gave tourists travel schedules and comfort.

In towns along the central Rhine, Hugo listened to and wrote down folk stories and observed customs, agriculture, and medieval architecture. He wrote of ancient and recent historical events. At Andernach, 50 miles above Cologne, he realized that many places along the river layered historic events centuries apart. Caesar's first crossing of the Rhine and the tomb of a French general who invaded the region in the late eighteenth century were within a mile of each other.[20]

Victor Hugo synthesized a grand history of the Rhine river region while staying at St Goar, halfway between Koblenz and Bingen. He divided the river's history into four epochs. The Rhine's first epoch included the geological history of the Alps, the German tribes, and Roman conquest. The river's second epoch, which Hugo termed the 'epoch of the supernatural', took place after the area passed out of Roman control. The Rhine became a force and a character in song and story. The many folk stories from the Rhine region have their own particular darkness, featuring a malevolent river that had to be recognized and appeased. Across the world, one of the ways that people who lived on the banks of rivers psychologically survived its dangers was to personify the river as a god or a spirit who could be propitiated.

Victor Hugo thus listed some of the famous characters in the folk tales from the Rhine:

> Undines, who took to the rivers; Gnomes, who were said to dwell in the bowels of the earth; the Striker, or Sprite of the Rocks; the Black huntsman, riding over the thicket, mounted on a sixteen-horned stag; ... and Sigfreid, the horned, who attacked dragons in their dens.[21]

Hugo was familiar with these tales because, as part and parcel of the Romantic Movement, only a few decades before his Rhine journey, the Grimm brothers had assembled and published their folk tales. The collections were wildly successful and translated into most European languages. They precipitated a search for folklore in many countries. The collections yielded not only stories of giants and fairies, but also widely believed stories of heroes such as Charlemagne and Roland, as well as long-told stories of Christian saints.[22]

According to Hugo, the third epoch of the Rhine, from about the mid-1300s CE to the 1600s CE, was characterized by a myriad of small states, held by nobles, bishops, Teutonic Knights, the Knights of Rhodes, and the Templars.[23] The fourth epoch of the river began with the Reformation (c. 1600 CE) and continued into the nineteenth century.

For Victor Hugo the reason for dividing the Rhine's history into these four epochs was to highlight the three times that France controlled both banks of the river—under Pepin, Charlemagne, and Napoleon. Hugo marshalled these three brief episodes of French control to argue that

Illustration 2 *The Old Rhine Bridge near Laufenburg,* by Alexander M. Liebmann, c. 1875. Public Domain. Courtesy of Library of Congress.

France's destiny was to destroy the small states along the Rhine during the Napoleonic wars and to control both banks of the river.[24] 'Geography, in its inflexible distribution of territory, according to the landmarks of hill, valley, and stream, which all the Congresses in the world will never suffice to suppress, manifestly assigns the left bank of the Rhine to France.'[25] The Romantic Movement fed the glorification of the nation and patriotic nationalism.[26]

By the 1830s, the time of Victor Hugo, the gloomy towers and medieval towns of the Rhine had been incorporated into a well-developed tourist industry. Hugo regularly met hordes of other tourists at historic sites. Inns were equipped for large numbers of tourists. Illustrated guidebooks to the Rhine began around 1800; hundreds were printed in French, German, and English in the nineteenth century.[27] Woodcuts and etchings of sites along the river were available as souvenirs. Professional guides served tourists. Most guides simply showed visitors around and explained the history in several languages, but other guides, for example, demonstrated whirlpools by throwing in logs for a fee. Many castles and churches kept visitor registers. Scheduled steamboat passenger services served the Rhine as far as Manheim. Shopkeepers casually quoted prices in kreutzers, Prussian dollars, or French francs. Hugo noted that the owner of a ruined castle at Bingen chose to keep it a well-maintained ruin rather than rebuilding it. Tourists were more willing to pay to see a ruin: 'I visited the square donjon of Rüdesheim, now belonging to an intelligent proprietor, who fully understands that, in order to remain a palace, it must remain a ruin.'[28]

Victor Hugo continued his trip upstream by steamboat, regularly disembarking to explore medieval villages, pursue the location of tales of kings and giants, traverse 'wild and lonely' stretches between villages, and climb to ruined castles. In a moment of self-awareness, Hugo realized that, to his reader, one ruin might seem much like another: 'An antiquary, who describes a ruin much as a lover draws the portrait of his mistress, while he delights himself, is likely to weary other people.'[29]

Late in August, Victor Hugo reached Bingen, about 80 miles above his starting point at Cologne, which fulfilled his romantic imagination.

> To repose on the summit of Klopp, about the approach of sunset, and gaze upon the city beneath and the immense horizon around you, ... when the air is genial, the season mild, and the day fine, is an exquisite and inexpressible sensation, replete with a mysterious charm, derived at once from the grandeur of the scenery, and the depth of the contemplation it engenders.[30]

Romantic etchings and woodcuts of this portion of the Rhine circulated widely in the early nineteenth century. They helped people who had never actually seen the river form a mental map of it. One such woodcut, directly from his childhood, influenced how Victor Hugo thought about the Rhine.

> In my childhood there was an old woodcut suspended near my bed, hung up there by an old German nurse, which represented an ancient, moulding, isolated ruin, amidst fogs and mountains. The sky was charged with black and threatening clouds, and every evening, after offering up my prayers, and previous to closing my eyes, I used to gaze til [sic] the last moment upon the woodcut. In the night I saw it in my dreams, and connected it with terrible ideas.[31]

The woodcut pictured the Mouse Tower near Bingen. At night, on an island in the river, he found a 'black tower of hideous form' out of which spewed 'by fits and starts, a reddened nebulosity.'[32] The tower housed a forge.

The Mouse Tower had all the age, decay, and stories of terrible violence necessary to fire Hugo's romantic imagination. The story is set long ago in a time of famine. The rich and powerful Hatto, Archbishop of Mainz, possessed great stores of food in his granary but refused to share them with the poor people of his domain. As the famine worsened, he sent word that the people should assemble in one of his barns to receive grain. Many came at the appointed time. Evil Hatto, rather than distributing grain, locked the people in the barn and burned it down. The rats that lived in this barn and all the other rats of Mainz pursued Hatto first to his castle in Mainz, then to a lonely tower in the middle of the Rhine. He barricaded the doors, sealed the window, and retreated to the top floor. Inexorably a tide of rats crossed the water and assaulted the tower. In the story's gruesome ending the rats finally climbed the tower and ate Hatto alive. This folk story has many typical elements: poor people suffering from the evils of the rich, a powerful person breaking a promise, and swift and gruesome retribution by non-human forces.

At Mainz, Hugo sought out the medieval cathedral but realized that the character of the current city was commerce and trade: 'Thanks to the Rhine, a degree of activity, issuing from its waters prevails in the city. She is not less crowded with ships and merchandize, nor is there less bustle of trade, than at Cologne. They walk, talk, push, drag, buy, sell, cry, and sing in every street.'[33]

The whole Rhine trip had been less satisfyingly Romantic than Hugo hoped. There was just too much progress and too much commerce.

> Oh noble towers! Oh poor old paralytic giants! Oh defeated knights! Behold! A steamer crowded with shopkeepers and their traffic spouts out its fumes into your faces, and ye have neither an arm nor a voice to uplift in self-defense.[34]

In the fall of 1739, Victor Hugo returned to Paris and developed his letters and notes into a book. Over the course of his life, Hugo moved further and further away from his conservative and Catholic roots. In 1851, thoroughly anti-Catholic and favouring a republican form of government, Hugo denounced the French king as a tyrant and fled into exile to the Jersey Islands. His greatest novel, *Les Miserable*, came out in 1862. He stayed in exile the remainder of his life, producing novels, operas, and commentary on French politics and economics.

Much change occurred along the Rhine shortly after Hugo's trip. Navigation of the river was professionalized in the nineteenth century. The multistate commission issued licences to pilots and captains. It installed beacons and markers and dredged channels. Special courts adjudicated legal issues of river maintenance and traffic.[35]

By the 1860s, railroads spread over the lower valley of the Rhine and much of the upper river. The logic of the railroads was inexorable. They connected mines and farms directly with factories and cities. They ran all year around and did not have to follow the winding course of the river. The Rhine steadily lost tonnage to the railroads from 1860 to 1900.[36] In the twentieth century, unable to compete with the railroads for passenger traffic or general freight, Rhine shipping became limited to barge traffic carrying heavy materials such as iron, coal, sand and gravel, and stone.

Particularly important among the bulk goods carried on the Rhine were chemicals, pharmaceuticals, steel, and the raw material used in the technology of electricity generation. In the 1870s, Germany had established state-of-the-art technical schools and leapfrogged England in the new sciences of chemistry and electricity. These new studies catalysed manufacturing industries along the lower Rhine. By 1900, the Rhine valley was producing ninety per cent of the chemical dyes used across the world. Consequently, during the early decades of the twentieth century, the Rhine became one of the most polluted rivers in the world. Its heavy industry, crucial railroads, and bridges made it a target for heavy bombing in World War II.[37]

Nevertheless, some of the charm that Hugo sought remained throughout the following century and a half. Rhine cruises to the wild towers and quaint cities are just as popular today as they were in Victor Hugo's time.

Over its long history what, then, made the Rhine a route rather than just a river? Trade had unified the Rhine's upriver and downriver regions for millennia. Raw materials and products came out of the heartland—wine from the Rhine Valley and side valleys, timber from the upriver forests, granite, and stone from the canyons and side streams.

Central to the mental image of the Rhine as a route, rather than merely a river running between banks, was the sheer human effort invested in the river. Starting in the late medieval period, there had been efforts to clear rocks and improve channels. Development accelerated in the nineteenth century with the invention of dynamite to remove rocks and a multistate river commission to coordinate efforts to make the river safer and more efficient by, for example, straightening the meandering river in the rift valley to a single channel. The multistate commission articulated and lobbied for the image of the Rhine as a unified route from source to mouth. Its improvements made the image a reality. By the beginning of the twentieth century, the river was navigable by large crafts as far upriver as Manheim, which became a significant port for overseas trade. In the same period the Netherlands completely changed the course of the Rhine by dredging and constructing dikes, investing in the creation of Europe's busiest deep-water port.

Europe, especially France and Germany, cultivated the image of the Rhine as a much-disputed, bloody political boundary. The conflict between Germany and France intensified in the nineteenth century, and generated popular patriotic songs on both sides, none more evocative or powerful than the 'Watch on the Rhine' (1870). In translation it reads:

> Our oath resounds, the river flows,
> In golden light our banner glows;
> Our hearts will guard thy stream divine:
> The Rhine, the Rhine, the German Rhine!
> Dear Fatherland, no danger thine;
> Firm stand thy sons to watch the Rhine![38]

For Victor Hugo, the dominant cognitive geography of the Rhine was its Romantic character, its gloomy towers, medieval towns, and wooded pathways. This set of mental expectations was reinforced by the many folk stories, ballads, and sagas set in the Rhine region, featuring a mixture of historic and supernatural figures, and a generally cruel river. The stories included the evil Archbishop of Mainz and his Mouse Tower;

Charlemagne and the river serpent; Lohengrin and the swan boat; the Lorelei Rock; and the Siegfried saga, made famous as an opera by Wagner. Many of these stories were printed in illustrated versions, which became part of a shared image of the Rhine across Europe. The Romantic Rhine represents only a portion of its complexity as a route today, with its intertwining of history and nationalism, folk stories and opera, religion and war, romanticism and science, technology and industry.

Notes

1. Victor Hugo, *The Rhine*, translated by D.M. Ard (New York: Wiley and Putnam, 1845), p. 24.
2. Hugo, *The Rhine*, p. 17.
3. Hugo, *The Rhine*, pp. 43–4.
4. Hugo, *The Rhine*, p. 47.
5. See the assessment by the American author E.D. Howard, *The Cause and Extent of the Recent Industrial Progress of Germany* (London: Archibald Constable & Co. Ltd., 1907).
6. See Halford J. Mackinder, *The Rhine* (New York: Dodd, Mead and Company, 1908), pp. 10–34. A better modern overview of the Rhine, including its history and myths, is Horst Johannes Tümmers' *Der Rhein: Ein europäischer Fluss und seine Geschichte* (München: Verlag C.H. Beck, 1984).
7. See Arnold Spekke, *The Ancient Amber Routes and the Geographical Discovery of the Eastern Baltic* (Stokholm: M. Goppers, 1957) for Greek and Roman textual sources. For the archaeological evidence, see the special issue on Baltic amber, *Journal of Baltic Studies*, vol. 16, no. 3 (1985).
8. Caesar's description of Germania was self-serving. He had to justify to the senate his failure to conquer the region. His simple answer was that it was not worth the life of a single legionnaire. At the same time he claimed that there was nothing worth trading with Germania, his information about the region came from traders who travelled there regularly. See Christopher B. Krebs, '"Imaginary Geography" in Caesar's Bellum Gallicum', in *American Journal of Philology*, vol. 127, no. 1 (Spring 2006), pp. 111–36.
9. Corrie Bakels and Stefanie Jacomet, 'Access to Luxury Foods in Central Europe in the Roman Period: The Archaeobotanical Evidence', *World Archaeology*, vol. 34, no. 3 (2003), pp. 552–4. See also André Tchernia, 'Italian Wine in Gaul at the end of the Republic', in Peter Garnsey, Keith Hopkins, and

C.R. Whittaker (eds), *Trade in the Ancient Economy* (Berkeley: University of California Press, 1983), pp. 87–104.

10. See Herwig Wolfram, *The Roman Empire and Its Germanic Peoples*, translated by Thomas Dunlap (Berkeley: University of California Press, 1990). Also, Thomas A. Burns, *A History of the Ostrogoths* (Bloomington: Indiana University Press, 1984).

11. For a general idea of the cultural changes in Europe after the fall of Rome, see Julia H.M. Smith, *Europe after Rome: A New Cultural History, 500–1000* (Oxford: Oxford University Press, 2005).

12. Edwin J. Clapp, *The Navigable Rhine: The Development of Its Shipping, the Basis of the Prosperity of Its Commerce and Its Traffic in 1907* (Boston: Houghton Mifflin Company), p. 7.

13. See Tom Scott, *Regional Identity and Economic Change: The Upper Rhine, 1450–1600* (Oxford: Clarendon Press, 1997).

14. Clapp, *The Navigable Rhine*, p. 9.

15. Goronwy Rees, *The Rhine* (New York: G.P. Putnam's Sons, 1967), p. 135.

16. See William H. TeBrake, 'Taming the Waterwolf: Hydraulic Engineering and Water Management in the Netherlands during the Middle Ages', in *Technology and Culture*, vol. 43, no. 3 (July 2002), pp. 475–99.

17. See Dale S. Collinson, 'The Rhine Regime in Transition–Relations between the European Communities and the Central Commission for Rhine Navigation', in *Columbia Law Review*, vol. 72, no. 3 (March 1972), pp. 485–516. See also, Clapp, *The Navigable Rhine*, pp. 13–14.

18. These broad-brush generalities cannot do justice to the complexity of the Romantic Movement, its regional variations, or its internal contradictions. The movement has generated an enormous scholarly literature. A useful introduction to all aspects of the Romantic Movement is found in *Encyclopedia of the Romantic Era, 1760–1850*, edited by Christopher Murray (New York: Fitzroy Dearborn, 2004).

19. Hugo, *The Rhine*, p. 76.

20. Hugo, *The Rhine*, pp. 110–11.

21. Hugo, *The Rhine*, p. 110.

22. Some Charlemagne and Roland stories were also central to the Compostela pilgrimage. For a full discussion of the Rhine in myth, see Gertrude Cepl-Kaufmann and Antje Johannig, *Mythos Rhein: Zur Kulturgeschichte eines Stromes* (Frankfurt: Primus Verlag, 2003).

23. Hugo, *The Rhine*, p. 114.

24. Hugo, *The Rhine*, p. 250.

25. Hugo, *The Rhine*, p. 117.

26. Both French and German Romantics generally supported the Franco-Prussian War of 1880. Romantic themes fed into the nationalist movements at the intellectual centre of both World War I and World War II.

27. See the bibliography of this Rhine genre. Michael Schmitt, *Die Illustrierten Rhein-Beschreibungen: Dokumentation der Werke und Ansichten von der Romantik bis zun ende des 19. Jahrhunders* (Köln: Böhlau Verlag GmbH & Cie, 1996).

28. Hugo, *The Rhine*, pp. 96–7, 108, 132–3, 161, 172, 240, 243.

29. Hugo, *The Rhine*, p. 154.

30. Hugo, *The Rhine*, p. 238.

31. Hugo, *The Rhine*, pp. 172–3.

32. Hugo, *The Rhine*, pp. 177–8.

33. Hugo, *The Rhine*, p. 256.

34. Hugo, *The Rhine*, p. 291.

35. Clapp, *The Navigable Rhine*, pp. 16–17.

36. Clapp, *The Navigable Rhine*, pp. 26–30.

37. See Clapp, *The Navigable Rhine*, pp. 33–4.

38. Eva March Tappan (ed.), *The World's Story: A History of the World in Story, Song and Art*, 14 vols, vol. 7, *Germany, The Netherlands, and Switzerland* (Boston: Houghton Mifflin, 1914), pp. 249–50.

The Nile

In November 1862, an upper-class British woman named Lucy Duff Gordon rented a sailing houseboat, fitted it out, and headed upriver on the Nile. She might have been part of the large, politically powerful British expatriate community in Cairo at the time or one of hundreds of wealthy Europeans who came to Egypt as 'archaeological tourists', but she was not.[1] Lucy Duff Gordon's reasons for travelling the Nile were more serious and sombre. At the age of forty-one, she already had advanced tuberculosis, and had come from England betting her life on the fact that Egypt's hot, dry climate would cure her.

For seven years in Egypt, through recurrent bouts of coughing and weakness, she remained a remarkable observer, curious about and sympathetic to all 'natives' around her, and an inveterate letter writer to her husband, children, and mother. She encountered and wrote about all that tied the upper and lower river together as a route—ecological rhythms and constraints, human networks, labour, trade, slavery, religions, technology and transportation, and disease.

As an important human route, the Nile is breathtakingly old. Between 200,000 and 100,000 years ago, the ancestors of humans made their first tentative long-distance migrations. They left southeastern Africa, moved north through the Rift Valley, and followed the Nile north. The climate was wetter then, savannah with stands of trees, not so different from their

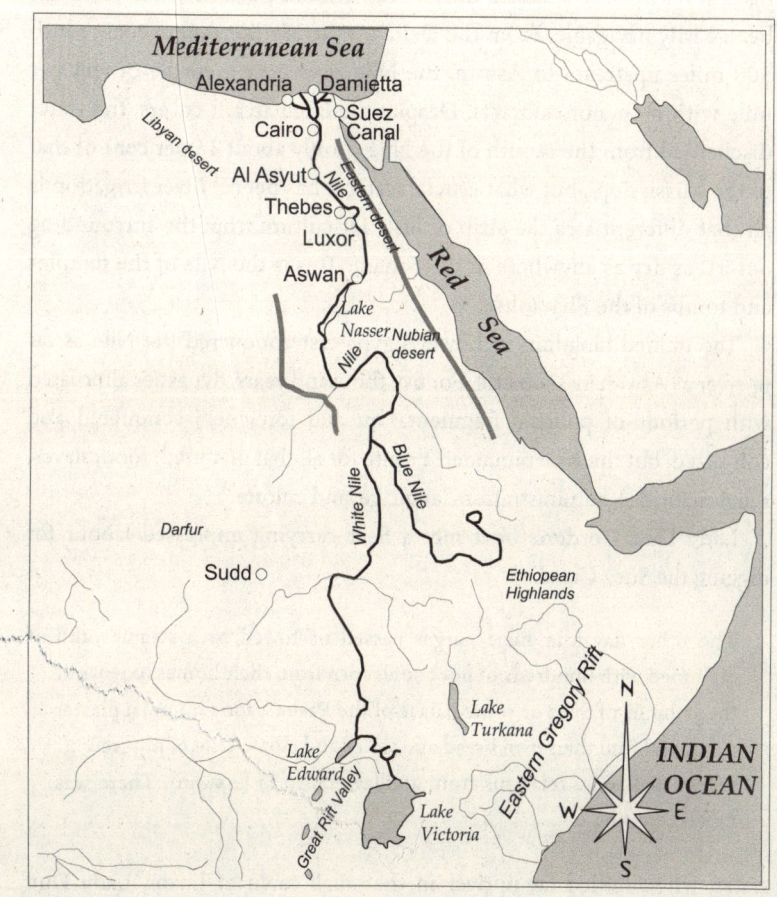

Nile River

homeland. Archaeologists have found their bones and remains in current-day Israel. A second wave of migration 80,000 to 60,000 years ago also followed the Nile and spread humans across Europe and Asia.[2]

The modern Nile found its current route only about 18,000 years ago, when the climate was wetter and the raging river broke through natural barriers. In historic times, only a small portion of the river has been easily navigable. From the Delta on the Mediterranean coast south 500 miles upstream to Aswan, the Nile rises only a couple of feet per mile with no major cataracts. Despite the large area it covers, the water discharged from the mouth of the Nile is only about 15 per cent of that of the Mississippi, but what crucial water it has been.[3] River irrigation is all that differentiates the strip of lush agriculture from the surrounding desert, as dry as anywhere in the Sahara. This is the Nile of the temples and tombs of the Pharaohs.

The unified kingdom in Lower Egypt first conquered the Nile as far upriver as Aswan in 3200 BCE. For five thousand years, dynasties alternated with periods of political fragmentation and foreigners conquered and colonized, but the Nile remained a route for all that mattered: food, slaves, religion, brides, administration, language, and culture.[4]

Lady Duff Gordon's boat met a fleet carrying impressed labour for digging the Suez Canal.

> The other day four huge barges passed us towed by a steamer and crammed with hundreds of poor souls torn from their homes to work at the Isthmus of Suez or some palace of the Pasha's, for a nominal piaster a day, and find their own bread and water and cloak. One of my crew ... recognized some relations from a village close to [Aswan]. There was much shouting...[5]

Later, when settled far upriver in the small town of Luxor, Lady Duff Gordon wrote of the suffering caused by impressed labour.[6] There were no remaining men for cultivating the fields, tending the flocks, or driving irrigation oxen. The practice of rounding up rural men for impressed labour was very old. They were part of the work force for the big tomb and temple building projects from the Old Kingdom (ca. 3000 BCE) to the end of the New Kingdom (ca. 1000 BCE). In later periods, they cleared irrigation channels. Part of what defined the Nile as a route, rather than just a river,

CAIRO. Dahabeah or Nile Boat.

Illustration 3 *A Dahabeah of the type Lady Duff Gordon used to Travel the Nile River*, c. 1880. Public Domain. Courtesy of Library of Congress.

was the expectations of impressed labour, both by officials who used it and peasants who provided it.[7]

As Lady Duff Gordon's boat travelled slowly upriver by sail and oar, it averaged about 10 miles a day. Her crew of a dozen men was largely from far upriver 'mostly men from near the first Cataract above ... [Aswan], sleek-skinned, gentle, patient, merry black fellows'.[8] The rest of the crew was of 'various colours' and lived as far north as Cairo. The crew shared a common stock of stories, jokes, and songs. Like other rivers, such as the Rhine, boatmen on the Nile had their own culture and it extended the whole length of the river.

Lady Duff Gordon next wrote from Al-Asyut, about 175 miles south of Cairo, where she stopped to see a sugar-processing factory owned by a Turk. Like all routes, venture capital had long followed the river and its opportunities. Developers opened irrigated farmland in biblical times. Jews started sugar plantations in the twelfth century. Ismail Pasha, head of the government of Egypt in Lady Duff Gordon's time, gave out non-irrigated land for development.[9] Europeans funded steamship lines in the 1860s.

What sort of commodities had moved along the Nile? The most visible were the great building blocks, used in pyramids and tombs, brought to their sites by barges on the Nile. Egyptian mines near the Nile produced marble used in Roman villas.[10] Foodstuffs were, of course, what made sophisticated Egyptian civilization possible. Wheat moved from south to north to feed successive capitols as well as Rome in its heyday. Taxes on grain constituted the bulk of every Egyptian empire's income. Cattle, sheep, and goats were transported for meat and leather.

Towns along the Nile specialized in processing raw materials into higher-value commodities, just as they did along the Rhine. On the Nile, beehives were turned into honey, cane juice into sugar, flax into linen, wool into fabrics.[11] These processing towns had long been a part of the culture of the Nile. Five centuries before Lady Duff Gordon's journey up the Nile, Ibn Battuta, the most widely travelled man of the Middle Ages, was astonished by the sheer number of trading vessels: 'It is said ... that on the Nile there are thirty-six thousand vessels belonging to the Sultan and his subjects, which sail upstream to Upper Egypt and downstream to Alexandria and Damietta, laden with goods and commodities of all kinds.'[12]

A month after departing from Cairo, Lady Duff Gordon moored her boat at Thebes. She enjoyed the hospitality of the indigenous Christian Copt community.

I can't describe the kindness of the Copts. The men I met at a party in Cairo wrote to all their friends and relations to be civil to me. Wassef's attentions consisted first in lending me his superb donkey and accompanying me about all day. Next morning arrived ... a live sheep, a huge basket of the most delicious bread, a pile of cricket-balls of creamy butter, a large copper caldron and a cage of poultry.[13]

The Nile had been a conduit for religions for millennia and a certain mixing and jostling of religions was part of its ethos as a route. Lady Duff Gordon saw a few remaining traces of worship of the ancient Egyptian gods.

Among gods, Amun Ra, the sun-god and serpent-killer, calls himself Mar Girgis (St George), and is worshipped by Christians and Muslims in the same churches, and Osiris holds his festivals as riotously as ever at Tanta in the Delta, under the name of Seyd el Bedawee. The Fellah women offer

sacrifices to the Nile.[14]

29

The Nile

Islam came early to the lower Nile, in the first wave of conquest in around 640 CE. The Arab invaders settled in a new city named Fustat ('encampment' in Arabic) that became Cairo (about 400 miles downstream from Aswan). Missionaries and armies sailed upriver. Below Aswan mosques and administration rapidly followed. The conquest stopped, however, just above Aswan. In two major battles the famed Christian archers of Nubia decisively defeated the Arab cavalry. Nubia remained outside the sphere of Islam for six centuries.[15] Ethiopia, more distant and less accessible than Nubia, remained Christian. Cairo evolved into one of the world's great centres of Islam, attracting men from all over the Islamic world. In the fourteenth century, for example, Ibn Battuta saw many Persian practitioners of Sufism residing in Cairo.

It is unclear just when Cairo and Baghdad first became the two main staging points for the Hajj, but the professional outfitting and assembly of pilgrims was certainly in full swing by the thirteenth century. Every year a wave of Islamic pilgrims assembled at Cairo and the expectation of this Hajj caravan formed an important part of the ethos of the Nile as a route. In a single specialized bazaar, tens of thousands of pilgrims bought everything they needed for the trip. The yearly route from Cairo started by boat up the Nile, went overland to the Red Sea well north of Luxor where Lucy Duff Gordon lived, sailed across the Red Sea to Jeddah, and assembled into a massive caravan to Mecca.

In the spring of 1863 Lady Duff Gordon returned slowly down the Nile. Above Bellianeh, one of her boatmen asked her to stop and see a famous Muslim ascetic. She found an old man, 'utterly naked, with the skin of a rhinoceros all cracked with the weather, [who] sat there, and had sat day and night, winter and summer, motionless for twenty years. He never prays, he never washes, he does not keep Ramadan, and yet he is a saint.' Lady Duff Gordon expected that he would curse her as a non-believer, but quite to the contrary 'he was delighted with my visit, asked me to sit down, ordered his servant to bring me sugar-cane, asked my name ... and was quite talkative and full of jokes and compliments, and took no notice of anyone else'.[16] This ascetic was known and supported by the boatmen. His reputation extended up and down the navigable portion of the Nile.

Jewish presence on the Nile, if Exodus has any historical truth, goes back to around 1500 BCE. Archaeologists have located some later but more concrete evidence, excavating a Jewish fort and settlement, occupied from about 750 BCE to about 550 BCE, on Elephantine Island near Aswan. There is, however, no archaeological evidence of Jewish settlements further upriver in Nubia.[17] Throughout the Islamic centuries (after 640 CE) Judaism centred on synagogues in Cairo and a trade network that extended far beyond, into the Middle East, the Mediterranean, and India.[18]

At Aswan Lady Duff Gordon met a party of slave merchants returning to their homes far upriver in Sudan. They had sold the slaves they captured on the borders of Sudan in the Cairo slave market and purchased a variety of goods for trade in Sudan. She enjoyed their hospitality: 'Oh! How delicious it felt to sit on a mat among the camels and strange bales of goods and eat the hot tough bread, sour milk and dates, offered with such stately courtesy.'[19] In this encounter she focused on their romantic caravan life and seems not to have considered the human suffering that underlay this trade.

Slave labour had been a defining feature of the Nile as a route since early Dynastic Egypt (c. 3000 BCE). Many tomb and temple paintings of subsequent centuries feature war captives from upriver marching off to slavery. Slavers were specialized professionals. They knew how and where to seize slaves, the costs and difficulties of transport north to Aswan, and the food necessary to keep the slaves in moderately good condition on the river route to Cairo. They knew the likely market prices for various categories of slaves. The slave trade formed a portion of the ethos of the Nile.

By the 1860s, the time of Lady Duff Gordon, slavery had been illegal in Britain and its colonies for three decades, but it continued up and down the Nile. Every upper-class household, whether Turkish, Copt, or Arabic, had dozens of slaves.[20] Europeans in Cairo also regularly kept household slaves. Lady Duff Gordon was rather caught in a dilemma. She claimed to abhor slavery, but within six months of arriving in Egypt she herself owned a slave. The American Consul-General had received the young girl as a

present, but Lady Duff Gordon asked to take her after seeing the household   31
staff beating her.

The Nile

> I have a black slave—a real one. I looked at her little ears wondering they had
> not been bored for rings. She fancied I wished them bored (she was sitting
> on the floor close to my side), and in a minute she stood up and showed
> me her ear with a great pin through it: 'Is it well lady?' The creature is eight
> years old.[21]

The relationship began with the slave girl 'as happy as possible and sings
quaint, soft little Kordofan songs all day'.[22] A few months later Lady Duff
Gordon left the girl with the American Consul in Alexandria. When Lady
Duff Gordon took her into her temporary residence in Cairo, the relationship went steadily downhill.

> Zeynab, after behaving very well for three weeks, has turned quietly sullen
> and displays great religious intolerance ... As she evidently does not like
> us I will offer her to Mrs. Hakekian Bey, and if she does not do there, in a
> household of black Mussulman slaves, they must pass her on to a Turkish
> house. She is clever and I am sorry, but to keep a sullen face about me is
> more than I can endure, as I have shown her every possible kindness.[23]

The flow of slaves, south from Sudan to the Cairo slave market, was one
of the Nile's most predictable features. The slave dealers travelling to the
Cairo market used desert tracks in Sudan, west of the Nile, to avoid a vast
swamp known as the Sudd. Located in northern Sudan, the swamp formed
because the land was virtually flat and the Nile's run-off to the north happened very slowly. During the rainy season, the Sudd could spread to a size
equal to all of England. In the long history of the Nile, whoever controlled
the fertile Nile Delta and the lower reaches of the river aspired to extend
control upriver. For millennia, imperial ambitions ended at the impen-
etrable Sudd. It regularly decimated expeditions that tried to cross it. In
1869 and 1870, however, the head of the Egyptian government ordered
a large expedition to conquer the Sudd. An Englishman named Samuel
White Baker headed the project. Using steamboats, and at huge human
and financial cost, the expedition finally succeeded in cutting a canal across
the swamp.[24] Even with annual vegetation-cutting expeditions, the canal

was frequently closed and was never a paying proposition. Today's national boundaries reflect the impossibility of sustaining imperial control south of the great swamps of the Nile.

Settled at Luxor, Lucy Duff Gordon watched trade and people pass up and down the river. She only slowly came to understand the central place of personal networks in the Nile as a route. The legal institutions that were supposed to regulate trade were weak and slow. Credit was a personal matter, dependent on the reputation and family name of the borrower. Upriver commodities were consigned to downriver family members or long-time business associates. These human networks were essential to travel, hospitality, and marriage. She came to understand that even the hospitality of the Copts that she had received when she first arrived in Egypt had a practical side for individuals in the community. Any skimping on hospitality would have affected upriver Copts' reputation within their community, both locally and in the eyes of their Cairo brethren. Feeding Lady Duff Gordon was part of the hospitality given to travelling community members passing upriver and downriver, which influenced far larger issues of credit, character, and possible marriage matches for children of upriver traders.

Over time, Lady Duff Gordon became part of upriver and downriver networks. She actively passed information to her Turkish friends and Europeans. She advised Europeans on outfitters, guides, hotels, boat owners, and restaurants. At towns along the river, such as Luxor, Europeans compared notes about archaeologists, people's health, doctors, and local magnates. Europeans' letters, which moved swiftly up and down the river, were central to the maintenance of this human network. In Lady Duff Gordon's time, runners brought the post upriver from Cairo to Luxor within three weeks.[25] She witnessed the installation of the telegraph, which, while costly, cut that time to minutes.

Every community, including the Europeans, speculated when the Nile would 'rise'. This yearly 'rise' was recorded on rocks and riverside buildings from the earliest of Egypt's dynasties.[26] Speculations of natural and supernatural causes went on for millennia. The prosperity of agriculture depended on the river overflowing its banks, which it did in June with stunning regularity. Year after year, century after century, the overflow brought silt and nutrients from far upriver to fertilize and water the fields

Illustration 4   *Ancient Stone Device to Measure the Nile's Rise, Near the First Cataract.* Stereo Card, 1904. Public Domain. Courtesy of Library of Congress.

in the lower Nile. Agriculture was utterly dependent on it. The river's yearly rise was one of the most central features of the mental expectations of the Nile as a route, as were the January and February winds from the north, which assisted travel upriver (downstream traffic in grain and other commodities moved at any time of the year slowly on the sluggish current).

It was not until the late nineteenth century that European explorers provided observations that solved the riddle of the Nile's rise. A vast monsoon weather pattern dominates the yearly pattern of Africa's weather. Onshore, easterly winds in early June bring clouds and moisture from the Atlantic to the heart of the continent. Heavy rain falls in the Nile's upland watersheds, current-day Kenya, Uganda, and Tanzania. This additional water formed the 'rise' of life-giving waters to the lower Nile.[27]

The Nile carried not just silt and nutrients, but also disease, which also formed a prominent part of its ethos as a route. The river has been the vector for epidemics such as dengue, bubonic plague, and various forms of water-borne parasites.[28] In 1863, there was an exceptionally high Nile rise and much flooding. Serious disease, known as 'cattle murrain', followed. Lady Duff Gordon wrote that friends in Cairo lost whole herds. 'Hekekenian's wife had seventy head of cattle on her farm—one wretched bullock is left; and, of seven to water the house in Cairo, also one left, and that expected to die.'[29]

Over the next year, the epidemic got worse, much worse. Herds of cattle died in towns and villages up and down the Nile. Thousands of animals were buried and thousands more floated down the river. The disease spread to humans, some of whom had only serious inflammation of the digestive tract, while others died within days of infection. Lady Duff Gordon dispensed what medicines she had, begged more from passing Europeans, and gained a reputation as a healer.[30]

Today there is a name for and considerable scientific research on what Lady Duff Gordon knew as 'cattle murrain'. Rift Valley Fever, its centre far south in Kenya and Tanzania, is a haemorrhagic disease related to Ebola that attacks organs and connective tissue, and kills by massive internal and external bleeding. Survivors often have liver or eye damage. Mosquitoes, hatching from long-standing water, propagate the disease to both animals and humans. As a modern research article noted, 'Localized heavy rainfall is seldom sufficient to create conditions for an outbreak'.[31] Rift Valley Fever was a disease of the Nile and reached epidemic proportions only following a particularly high Nile summertime rise and flooding. Shared disease, its myths of supernatural origin, and stories of suffering and magical cures contributed to the culture of the route.

After a stay in Cairo, Lady Duff Gordon travelled upriver from Cairo to Luxor in a steamboat, which had been introduced to the Nile only about twenty years earlier. The first Nile steamboats were part of a serious British strategic concern—swift communication between England and India, its prized colony. Peninsular Steam won the first contracts by a private firm to carry overseas mail to Egypt in 1840. The company (which became the famous P&O Line) provided the most luxurious and up-to-date transport in the Mediterranean during the middle decades of the nineteenth century. Its ships soon also carried mail and passengers from the Red Sea to Bombay (now Mumbai). The Suez Canal had not yet been built, so that travellers from Europe, as they had for centuries, had first to pass from Alexandria up the Nile to Cairo. By steamboat, this trip took only twelve hours, rather than several days. Most travellers stayed a few days at Sheppard's Hotel. From Cairo, passengers followed the same route as the Hajj, upstream almost 300 miles and 18 hours, east across 80 miles of desert for 36 hours, and onto a Bombay-bound steamer.[32]

By the 1860s, steamboats had fundamentally changed the Nile as a route, just as they had on the Rhine. They made river travel safer, less expensive, and much faster. Steamboats made upriver travel possible at any time of the year. They brought supplies and small luxuries to upriver towns. They also changed upriver political control by the Cairo government, which could quickly bring troops if there was trouble. The first Mahdi revolt in 1865 destroyed four villages upriver from Luxor. A major military force from Cairo arrived within a week.[33] Lady Duff Gordon first heard that 500 rebels were hanged, later that 1,400 had been executed.[34] The army bivouacked near Luxor and oppressed the locals. The steamboat was equally important to moving troops for British colonial adventures in the Sudan two decades later.

As on the Rhine, steamboats also made upriver sites readily accessible. In the cold season, tourists inundated Luxor—usually rich Europeans 'doing Egypt'. The Nile and its architecture must be one of the oldest tourist destinations on earth. Herodotus, writing in the fifth century BCE, produced Egypt's first guidebook. Centuries of tourists included Greeks, Persians, Romans, Muslims from North Africa, Ottomans, the French after Napoleon, and British and Germans in the nineteenth century. Seeing the sites formed an important part of the ethos of the river and continues right down to our time.

What, then, made the Nile through the millennia a route, rather than just a river flowing between banks? There was an interweaving of physical, institutional, and mental features. The lower river from Aswan to the

Mediterranean flowed gently and was easily navigable. The agriculture along its whole length depended on the same summer rise and the same forms of irrigation. Similar cattle and crops—dates, flax, cotton, and wheat—were grown. The wheat harvest determined whether it would be a good year or a bad year, whether Egypt was ruled from Rome, Cairo, or Constantinople. Politically, there were repeated attempts, often successful, by a kingdom in the lower river to conquer upstream. A unified Nile kingdom was the long-term ideal. When this occurred there was a unified tax collection structure and military presence up and down the river. The Nile figured prominently in the ancient religions, and the river's importance still figured in folk ceremonies of Lady Duff Gordon's time.

Many groups—Jews, Copts, Turks, Europeans—embedded in their own networks, travelled up and down the Nile. Reputations were made or ruined. Each community had a stereotype of other communities, reinforced by stories and homilies. Friendships crosscut these stereotypes. Each community prayed for a good summer rise of the river and a good harvest. All feared flood and consequent disease.

Sudanese traders brought slaves to the Cairo market. Impressed labour built the impressive architecture along the Nile. Their shared suffering found its way into songs and stories. Brides and members of elite administrative families moved up and down the river. So did pilgrims on the Hajj to Mecca. Soldiers went to war in the south. Emissaries came and went to the Sudan. Tourists explored the ruins and painted pictures. Archaeologists mounted expeditions. Developers opened new land or started processing industries. Political rumour, family gossip, trading information, and news of a new archaeological discovery moved quickly up and down the river. All of these features of the Nile formed part of the mental expectations of people along the river, making it a route rich in associations, history, and culture.

Since the time of Lucy Duff Gordon the Nile has changed much. With the opening of the Suez Canal in 1869, pilgrims travelled by ship directly to Jeddah on the Red Sea, rather than down the Nile and overland to the Red Sea. The old spice trade from India was no longer offloaded about halfway along the Red Sea for transport down the Nile to Cairo. Instead, the spices went directly to ports in the Nile Delta. Much of the inland traffic that formerly went by riverboat moved to the railroad in the last three decades of the nineteenth century. The river, however, remains an important inland waterway and the heart of an active tourism industry upriver as far as Aswan.

The Nile also no longer has its yearly rise. Completed in the 1950s, the Aswan High Dam has stopped the annual floods, but also held back the fertile silt far upriver. In many respects, however, the Nile remains as central to the daily life of Egypt as it has for millennia, furnishing the water that makes the desert bloom.

And what of Lady Lucy Duff Gordon? She returned to England for a few months in 1865 but, after that, she would not see England or her husband again. She stayed in her house in Luxor, entertained friends, visited nearby sites, and wrote letters when she could. There were good days and bad days, but slowly the tuberculosis took her. In the summer of 1869 Lady Duff Gordon said goodbye to her friends and set off by boat north to Cairo. Before she died on her riverboat near Cairo, she wrote to her husband, 'Do not think of coming here. Indeed it would be almost too painful to me to part from you again; and as it is, I can patiently wait for the end among people who are kind and loving enough to be comfortable, without feeling the pain of parting.'[35]

Notes

1. In the half century before Lucy Duff Gordon's arrival, Britain had played a larger and larger political and economic role in Egypt. By the 1860s, British administrative 'advisers' controlled much of what went on in the country, and there was a large resident British community in Cairo.

2. Peter Forster, 'Ice Ages and the Mitochondrial DNA Chronology of Human Dispersals: A Review', *The Royal Society: Philosophical Transactions: Biological Sciences*, vol. 359, no. 1442, *The Evolutionary Legacy of the Ice Ages* (20 February 2004), pp. 255–64.

3. Bonnie M. Sampsell, *The Geology of Egypt: A Traveler's Handbook* (Cairo: American University in Cairo Press, 2014).

4. See L. Casson, *Ships and Seamanship in the Ancient World* (New Haven: Princeton University Press, 1971). For other roads in Egypt in the Roman period, see Colin Adams, '"There and Back Again": Getting around in Roman Egypt' in Colin Adams and Ray Laurence (eds), *Travel and Geography in the Roman Empire* (London: Routledge, 2001), pp. 138–66.

5. Lucy Duff Gordon, *Letters from Egypt* (Reprinted edition; London: Virago Press, 1983), p. 32.

6. Poor peasants were also gathered up for the Pasha's army. Duff Gordon, *Letters from Egypt*, p. 96.

7. The seizing of labour was not without resistance. Lady Duff Gordon heard of a woman who travelled to a downriver city to confront personally the official who drafted her only son. See Duff Gordon, *Letters from Egypt*, p. 154. In 1865, 200 men were drafted from Luxor for 60 days' service, including Lady Duff Gordon's own house servants. She bribed their freedom. See Duff Gordon, *Letters from Egypt*, pp. 230–1, 233, 242.

8. Duff Gordon, *Letters from Egypt*, p. 27.

9. Duff Gordon, *Letters from Egypt*, p. 64.

10. See Pliny, *Natural History*, translated by D.E. Eichholz, The Loeb Classical Library (Cambridge Massachusetts: 1962), vol. X, pp. 43–7. See also, Steven E. Sidebotham, Ronald E. Zitterkopf, and John A. Riley, 'Survey of the Abu Sha'ar–Nile Road', *American Journal of Archaeology*, vol. 95, no. 4 (October 1991), pp. 571–622. Lady Duff Gordon found an active granite quarry at Aswan, still shipping building material to cities and towns. See Duff Gordon, *Letters from Egypt*, p. 37.

11. See Ibn Battuta, *The Travels of Ibn Battuta, A.D. 1325–1354*, translated by H.A.R. Gibb (first Indian edition; New Delhi: Munshiram Manoharlal, 1993) vol. 1, pp. 59–68.

12. Battuta, *The Travels of Ibn Battuta*, p. 42.

13. Duff Gordon, *Letters from Egypt*, p. 35. The history of the Coptic Christian community is long and complex. Readers wishing to explore the early period may consult Stephen J. Davis, *The Early Coptic Papacy: The Egyptian Church and Its Leadership in Late Antiquity* (Cairo; New York: American University in Cairo Press, 2004). For the later period, see Mark Swanson, *The Coptic Papacy in Islamic Egypt (641–1517)* (Cairo; New York: American University in Cairo Press, 2010).

14. Duff Gordon, *Letters from Egypt*, p. 57. See also pp. 11, 67.

15. David Ayalon, 'The Spread of Islam and the Nubian Dam', in Haggai Erlich and Israel Gershoni (eds), *The Nile: Histories, Culture, and Myths* (Boulder: Lynne Reinner Publishers, 2000), pp. 17–23.

16. Duff Gordon, *Letters from Egypt*, p. 45.

17. Steven Kaplan, 'Did Jewish Influence Reach Ethiopia via the Nile?' in Haggai Erlich and Israel Gershoni (eds), *The Nile: Histories, Culture, and Myths* (Boulder: Lynne Reinner Publishers, 2000), pp. 58–9.

18. See, for example, Shlomo Goitein, 'Portrait of a Medieval Indian Trader: Three letters from the Cairo Geniza', *Bulletin of the School of Oriental and African Studies*, vol. 50, no. 3 (1987), pp. 449–50. See also Shlomo Goitein, *Studies in Islamic History and Institutions* (Leiden, Holland: E.J. Brill, 1966), p. 344.

19. Duff Gordon, *Letters from Egypt*, p. 37.

20. Duff Gordon, *Letters from Egypt*, p. 49.

21. Duff Gordon, *Letters from Egypt*, p. 51.

22. Duff Gordon, *Letters from Egypt*, p. 53.

23. Duff Gordon, *Letters from Egypt*, pp. 82–3.

24. Collins, *The Nile*, p. 55. For the full story, see Robert O. Collins, *The Waters of the Nile: Hydropolitics and the Jonglei Canal, 1900–1988* (Oxford: Clarendon Press, 1990).

25. Duff Gordon, *Letters from Egypt*, p. 120.

26. Barbara Bell, 'The Oldest Records of the Nile Floods', *The Geographical Journal*, vol. 136, no. 4 (December 1970), pp. 569–73.

27. Collins, *The Nile*, pp. 14–15.

28. See H. Kamal, 'The 1927 Epidemic of Dengue in Egypt', *The British Medical Journal*, vol. 1, no. 3521 (30 June 1928), pp. 1104–06. See also, G.F. Petrie, Ronald E. Todd, Riad Skander, and Fouad Hilmy, 'A Report on Plague Investigations in Egypt', *The Journal of Hygiene*, vol. 23, no. 2 (November 1924), pp. 117–50.

29. Duff Gordon, *Letters from Egypt*, p. 78.

30. Duff Gordon, *Letters from Egypt*, pp. 163, 179, 184, 234. Lady Duff Gordon disparaged the local Muslim doctors and was perfectly willing to displace their practices. This sort of medical competition and entrepreneurship is typical of a route, whether along the Buddhist monasteries in Central Asia in the seventh century or on the Camino Real in California in the eighteenth century. A reputation for successful healing travelled as fast as any trade goods.

31. See G.H. Gerdes, 'Rift Valley Fever', in *Revue Scientifique et Technique de L'Office International des Epizooties*, vol. 23, no. 2 (August 2004), pp. 613–23.

32. See Sarah Searight, *Steaming East: the Forging of Steamship and Rail Links Between Europe and Asia* (London: Bodley Head, 1991), pp. 74–84.

33. The first major use of steamboats for the moving of troops was on the British side in the Crimean War of 1854. They had worked extremely well.

34. Duff Gordon, *Letters from Egypt*, p. 220.

35. Duff Gordon, *Letters from Egypt*, p. 381.

The Mississippi

In August 1910 two brothers, Alfred and Charles Spink, took their wives and Alfred's daughter on a vacation on a traditional Mississippi steamboat. The brothers were from a colourful and wealthy St Louis family, which owned a newspaper, racetracks, and a baseball team. The trip in itself was not uncommon, as thousands of passengers used the boats for business and personal travel. The Spinks' trip was unique because one of the brothers and a woman friend named Miss Copley, who also went on the trip, carried 'Brownies'. Kodak had only a few years before introduced this rugged and simple fixed-focus box camera, which opened up travel photography to the amateur.[1] It is literally through the eyes of Al Spink and Miss Copley that we shall see the Mississippi River and how it functioned as a route.[2]

The first glimmerings of the Mississippi as a route, a conduit for goods and ideas, come from tantalizing archaeological evidence. Around 2000 BCE, Indians buried more than a thousand of their dead at a site known as Indian Knoll in Kentucky. A few of these burials contain objects that suggest a small hand-to-hand trade in high-value items along the river. From the mouth of the Mississippi came seashells, and from Lake Superior came copper and red iron ore, used as paint.[3]

Archaeologists have unearthed considerable evidence of river-borne trade from the Mississippian culture (600–1300 CE), centred near present-day St Louis. Farms and large villages of 1,000 to 10,000 inhabitants

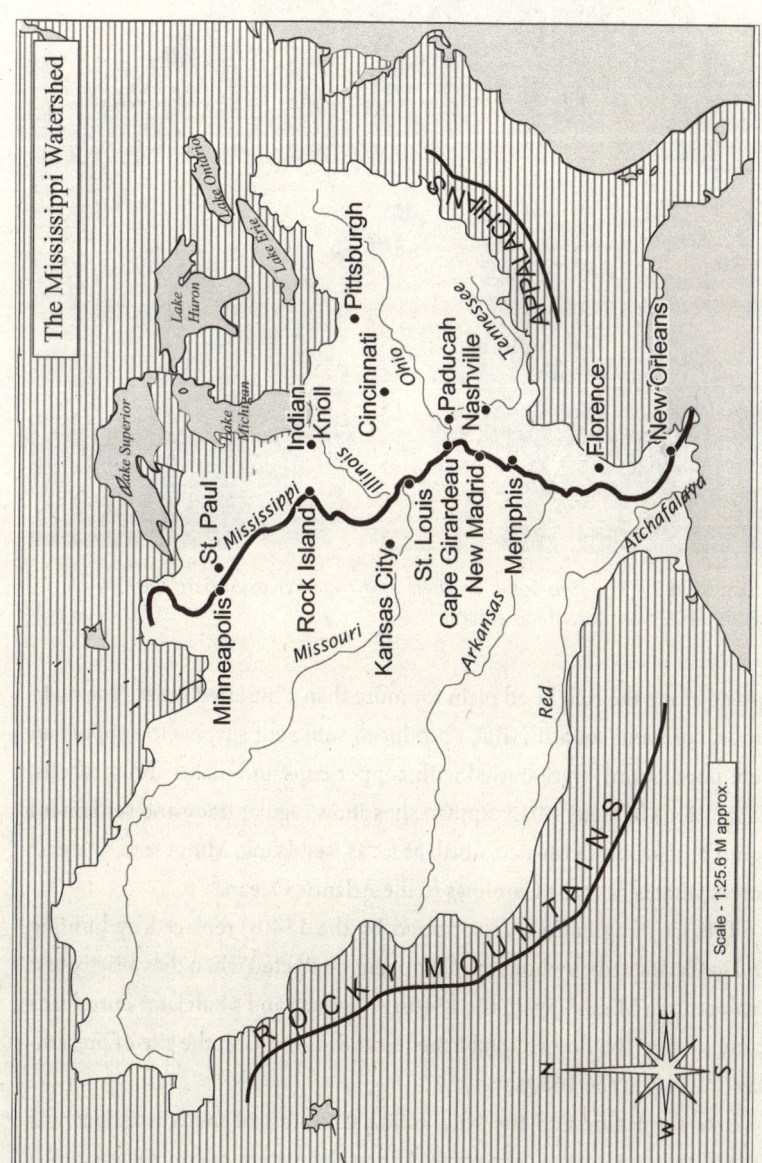

The Mississippi Watershed

Scale - 1:25.6 M approx.

Mississippi River

Illustration 5 *The Two Spink Brothers and Their Wives Aboard the* City of Savannah. Collection of the author.

spread along the rich flood plain for more than a hundred miles. The main crops, corn and squash (which produced sufficient surplus to support an elite population), were buried with copper cups and plates and seashells. Excavations of many Mississippian sites show regular trade and settlement south to the Gulf of Mexico, north as far as Red Wing, Minnesota, and east across what is now the Carolinas to the Atlantic Ocean.[4]

This far-flung culture disappeared by the 1540s, replaced by hunting and gathering tribes whom the Europeans contacted when they briefly first explored the Mississippi in the 1540s. A century and a half later Europeans came to stay. The French established Fort St George on the site of present-day St Louis in the 1680s.

Like the Rhine and the Nile, military control of the Mississippi was central to its emergence as a route. At first the pattern of control was much like the Nile: military contingents pushed upriver from New Orleans and established forts. In the middle and later eighteenth century, however, fierce competition and warfare broke out between the French, the English, and their respective Native American allies for control of the river. Each side attacked the other's forts and trading posts. After the United States bought the Mississippi and its western watershed in the Louisiana Purchase of 1803, the military, if anything, was even more of a presence on the river. Increasing European settlement meant constant warfare with and displacement of tribes along the river. The United States Army first secured the lower and middle Mississippi and placed forts, such as Fort Orange near present-day Kansas City, on the main tributaries. In 1825 a military detachment completed Fort Snelling in Minnesota as the hub of control over the upper river.[5]

From the first French fur traders of the eighteenth century, until the arrival of steamboats in the early decades of the nineteenth century, the Mississippi remained mainly a one-way route. The heartland produced raw materials and shipped them south to New Orleans. Furs, corn, cotton, salt, sugar, wheat, preserved pork, lead, and timber first came downriver on simple rafts. Boatyards along the river rapidly developed two specialized craft to ride the Mississippi downstream—the flatboat and the keelboat. Low water in the summer on the Mississippi dictated no more than a four-foot draft. The boats had to be narrow enough to pass between rocks and utilize deeper water channels, and long enough to carry 40–60 tonnes of cargo. Returning a boat upstream was a backbreaking business. Where they could, the crew pushed long poles into the muddy river bottom and, yard by yard, pushed the boat forward. Sometimes they stayed close to the shore, grabbed overhanging branches, and pulled the boat along. In stronger currents, the crew tied a stout rope to an upriver tree and pulled the boat. The captain frequently guided the boat across the river to avoid powerful currents and find calmer waters.[6] All rafts and most boats were simply broken up in New Orleans and sold for the wood. The crew rode a horse or walked north on the famous Natchez Trace.[7]

Working the flatboats, keelboats, and rafts was a rough, dangerous life, but one of relative freedom, as reflected in romantic paintings of the period. Perhaps the most famous of these paintings was Caleb Bingham's 'The Jolly Floatboatmen' series from the 1830s, which visually define the river as a place of hard work and freedom. The series portrays riverboat men dancing to a fiddle on a flatboat and contemplatively smoking as the boat drifts downstream, with the broad Mississippi ahead. In subsequent decades, this image was sold in inexpensive reproductions all over the country.[8]

Romantic popular songs in the first half of the nineteenth century portrayed a cognitive geography of the Mississippi that consisted of promise and danger in equal parts.

> Sweet Mississippi, pride of the west
> How often I sail in the stream I love best,
> The wealth of the world now floats on thy tide
> And gladly I sing as onward I ride
> The song of the boatman falls on my ears
> And our pilot steers unconscious of fears
> Sweet Mississippi, sweet Mississippi
> Pride of the west.[9]

This is the ethos popularized by the writings of Mark Twain, so intimately described in *The Adventures of Tom Sawyer*, *The Adventures of Huckleberry Finn*, and *Life on the Mississippi*. The Mississippi was profoundly dangerous. It changed course every year, uprooting masses of trees. The trees floated downstream, were trapped underwater, and formed snags that could rip open the bottom of a boat. Rocks lurked just below the surface. Eddies and rapids flung boats onto rocks. The lower river snaked back and forth in sinuous curves that created fast-running channels and slower shallows. The current carved new islands and channels every season. Sandbars appeared and disappeared in days. The river had no markers, buoys, or channel lights.

Just as on the Nile and the Rhine, steamboats, when introduced to the Mississippi in the 1830s, brought remarkable changes. For starters, they dramatically cut upriver travel time. Earlier, keelboats often took months for the journey from New Orleans to St Louis; steamboats did it in 12 days. The price of upriver freight dropped by three-quarters, and the volume of downriver freight sharply increased as the price of transporting goods downstream to New Orleans dropped.

The basic design of Mississippi steamboats evolved well before the Civil War and remained unchanged when Charles Spink photographed them in 1910. The river determined the draft and width of the boats. Too deep in the water and the boat would not clear the sandbars. Too wide and it would not fit through the channels. Years of practical experience proved that longer and narrower boats handled better in most situations. Mississippi riverboats generally had three decks. The lowest deck carried freight and the boilers. Above that was a deck with cabins, an outside promenade, and a dining room. Above that were crew quarters and, at the very top, the pilothouse.

One of the first pictures in the Spink photograph album shows the *City at Savannah* waiting at its wharf in St Louis. It would be their home for the three weeks of their vacation. The boat had a six-foot draft, was 200 feet long, and 36 feet wide. Roustabouts loaded goods from a warehouse and passengers boarded. The steamboat's route, posted on board above the gangway, was south from St Louis on the Mississippi to Cairo, Illinois, then east up the Ohio River to Paducah, Kentucky. The boat then proceeded south on the Tennessee to end the trip at Florence, Mississippi.[10] Above Florence were the treacherous Muscle Shoals rapids, a climb of 134 feet over 37 miles, which even the smallest river boats could traverse only during the rainiest weeks of the year.

The Mississippi, like all routes, had a yearly rhythm. Summer traffic, such as the Spinks' vacation (probably taken during September), depended on rains across the entire centre of the continental United States. In good

Illustration 6 *Unloading Freight at a Farm.* Collection of the author.

years, the Mississippi and its tributaries produced adequate draft. More often, boats were plagued by low water, and even shallow draft riverboats could not clear the rocks and sandbars for weeks at a time. Fall usually brought more rain across the Mississippi basin, which allowed traffic on the river to resume.

In late October, boats on the upper river made their final run south to St Louis. Owners and captains knew that the river would freeze solid from Rock Island to St Paul, trapping and crushing boats. Several of the northern tributaries also froze, including the upper Ohio, Arkansas, and Missouri rivers. From long experience, boat captains knew that St Louis stayed ice free. They were occasionally wrong. In 1878 the river froze at St Louis and destroyed more than 200 riverboats. The spring season began with groaning, creaking, and thunderous booms as the locked river ice broke up and floated downstream. The melting of the upriver ice and snow produced the highest water and the fastest and most dangerous currents of the year.

By the 1860s, the river had a complement of trained professional captains and pilots. The apprenticeship of a riverboat pilot was formal, lengthy, and rigorous. To steer the correct course, pilots scrupulously memorized landmarks on shore and the necessary course adjustments. The pilots thus carried a full mental map of the river, even to the length of time they should hold a course from a particular landmark. This oral teaching and commitment of crucial information to memory is one of the most universal features of the professionals who lived by navigating routes. As we shall see, sailors on the east coast of Africa chanted their landmarks and star headings in rhymed verses.

As Mark Twain observed, when pilots got together, they discussed particularly tricky passages:

'Jim, how did you run Plum Point, coming up?'

'It was in the night, there, and I ran it the way one of the boys on the "*Diana*" told me; started out about fifty yards above the wood pile on the false point, and held on the cabin under Plum Point till I raised the reef—quarter less twain—then straightened up for the middle bar till I got well abreast the old one-limbed cotton-wood in the bend, then got my stem on the cotton-wood and head on the low place above the point, and came through a-booming—nine and a half.'[11]

All pilots, new and old, were periodically tested and licensed for sections of the rivers they navigated. The exams consisted of 'singing' a section of the river, that is, visualizing and describing its twists and turns, sandbars, currents, obstructions, islands, bridges, tributaries, and the appropriate course changes, before a group of experienced pilots and captains.

A widely held perception that steamboat travel was safe was, in fact, quite untrue. The two dozen boats owned by the company that ran the *City of Savannah* averaged somewhat less than ten years of service before burning, colliding, or snagging and sinking. This level of risk was known and accepted by riverboat companies because riverboats paid off their initial investment in five years. Just a year after the Spinks' vacation, the *City of Savannah* sank and was lost in the Mississippi at Dog Tooth Bend, about 22 miles north of Cairo, Illinois.

Just like the Nile, the Mississippi, too, was a vector for disease. Poor sanitation and polluted water supplies up and down the river promoted cholera, which poisoned the intestines, produced severe diarrhoea, and resulted in rapid death in as much as half of those infected. The swift upriver travel of steamboats spread epidemics much more quickly. By 1830, for example, there had been several serious cholera epidemics that moved up from New Orleans to St Louis. Some even reached Minnesota.[12] In 1802, a smallpox epidemic killed 1,500 children in New Orleans—the total population at the time was only 10,000—before spreading upriver. Yellow fever recurred throughout the lower river. In 1867, an epidemic in New Orleans killed 3,200 of a population of 41,000. In spite of boycotts of riverboat traffic from New Orleans, the epidemic spread upriver. In Memphis, 6,000 people died in a population of 20,000.[13] The very real dangers of epidemic formed part of a shared set of mental expectations up and down the river.

In spite of the unifying effects of the steamboats, the economic, political, and social realities of slavery sharply divided the broader ethos of the lower river from that of the upper river. By the eighteenth century it was clear that the only profitable agricultural products that could be grown on the lower river were sugarcane and cotton. Both were labour intensive. Planters first tried to encourage European immigrants to meet their needs for labour, but immediately ran into problems. French law forbade settlement in its colonies by Jews or Protestants. More significantly, word circulated in Europe that New Orleans and the lower river had rampant malaria,

yellow fever, floods, and chronic food shortages. Europeans refused to
emigrate. Enslaving Native Americans, such as the nearby Tunica, Natchez,
or Quapaws tribes, also failed. They either died or, sensibly, fled.

To meet the labour requirements of cotton and sugarcane, white planters
along the lower Mississippi tapped the already developed world of Atlantic
slavery. By the middle decades of the eighteenth century there was a population of about 5,000 slaves and 1,000 free blacks—compared to the 4,000
whites—in Louisiana. For at least 200 miles upriver from New Orleans,
vast swamps surrounded the Mississippi. The river constantly carved new
channels through these bottomlands and deposited massive amounts of
silt. Turning these rich bottomlands into cotton plantations meant draining the swamps and controlling the Mississippi. The process proved just as
dicey as farming the lower reaches of major rivers everywhere—the Yellow,
Yangtze, Mekong, and the Nile. Across the world and over the centuries,
peasants and governments have built dikes to confine a river to a single
course. Such control has always been a solution that comes with terrible
costs and dangers. Year by year, the Mississippi deposited silt and raised the
bed of the river, forcing the building of yet higher levees. As in other rivers
from China to Holland, soon the water level of the river was well above
the surrounding farmland. Any break in the levees produced calamitous
inundation. Levees, by necessity, were collectively maintained. One failure
flooded everyone. Fear of flood and enforced collective levee maintenance
were part of the shared ethos of all river routes. On the Mississippi, slave
labour maintained the levees—work as crucial to the plantation economy
as planting, weeding, and harvesting.

During the Civil War (1861–65), the Union and the Confederacy well
understood the crucial importance of the Mississippi as a route, as a trade
lifeline, and as an important symbol of the unity of the country. The two
sides fought at Shiloh on the Tennessee River, a tributary of the Mississippi.
An uncle of the Spink brothers who belonged to an Illinois regiment survived the battle. And so the vacationers spent a day at the Shiloh battlefield.
Al Spink photographed the monument honouring the Illinois troops and
the 'Hornet's Nest', fought over in repeated attacks. The bucolic scene gives
no hint of the violence and destruction of Shiloh.

The campaign began with a serious Confederate loss near Somerset in
southern Kentucky in late January 1862. Fort Henry, which protected the

mouth of the Tennessee River where it joined the Ohio River, was also lost, as was Nashville a short time later. The pace of the campaign accelerated in the second week of March, when a large Union force commandeered riverboats, passed into the Tennessee River, and raced south (recall that only a few years later, steamboats rapidly moved troops up the Nile to crush the Mahdi Rebellion). The Union and Confederate armies fought near the Tennessee River at Shiloh on the first day of April 1862. The Union forces received reinforcements through the following night and defeated the Confederate army the next day.

The carnage at the Battle of Shiloh appalled both sides. At the end of the two days, 23,000 Union and Confederate soldiers had been killed or seriously wounded. There were more casualties at Shiloh than in all prior wars involving the United States.[14] The wounded on both sides overran medical facilities to such an extent, that every house and shelter in the area was full. Riverboats immediately ferried wounded Union soldiers upriver to any city that could take them.

The results of the Battle of Shiloh were immediate. Confederate troops on the Mississippi knew they would receive no reinforcements. Union ironclads ran past the heavily firing Confederate stronghold on Island 10 and supported Union land troops approaching the Confederates at New Madrid, Missouri. Both New Madrid and the 7000-man Confederate force at Island 10 surrendered. Memphis fell. David Farragut's forces took New Orleans.[15]

Both the national and international situation changed with Union control of the Mississippi. At the time of the Civil War, American cotton from plantations along the Mississippi was the largest single supply of the commodity for the entire world. The Union control of the Mississippi River and New Orleans meant that cotton exports from the South simply ceased. The plantation economy collapsed. Overseas buyers scrambled to find supplies for the world demand for cotton, provoking cotton booms in places where it was grown, such as India and Egypt. After the Civil War, the plantation economy of the South never recovered.

With the end of slavery, small farms became the dominant form of agriculture on the lower Mississippi, as it had been for much of the rest of the Mississippi and its tributaries. Steamboats on these rivers were the lifeblood of small farms. Boats like the *City of Savannah* carried supplies in and brought out produce. Captains and pilots knew farm families all along their route. For pickup of a passenger or freight, someone stood on the bank and either hailed the boat or waved a handkerchief. To alert a farm of a delivery, the boat would blow its whistle, then nose in, so that the deck crew could drop the landing stage. Several photos in the Spink album show just such loading and unloading at farms and small towns. All steamboats transported animals up and down the river. The photographs suggest that the *City of Savannah* handled relatively little of this trade. Some boats, known as 'hucksters', were floating animal pens, picking up and delivering cows, pigs, goats, and chickens.

In the decades after the Civil War many freed slaves went to work on the Mississippi. The Spink album contains a telling photograph of roustabouts, raggedy men who loaded the boat and carried the goods ashore.[16] Their work on the river was only slightly more profitable than sharecropping. Roustabouts received meals, were on call at all hours, and earned a dollar day, payable when the boat returned to its homeport. Irish immigrants first took these jobs, followed by Germans, Eastern Europeans, and freed slaves. Lack of education and pervasive racism meant that African-Americans could serve on riverboats as roustabouts, cooks, waiters, or engine room stokers, but could never be engineers, mates, pilots, or captains.

Illustration 7 *Crew of the City of Savannah Unloading Freight at a Farm on the Tennessee River.* Collection of the author.

By the later decades of the nineteenth century, simple shipping of goods was not enough to sustain cities along the Mississippi and its tributaries, such as St Louis, Cincinnati, Kansas City, Pittsburgh, Minneapolis, and New Orleans. Like cities along the Rhine and the Nile, and as we shall see along the Silk Road and the Erie Canal, cities along the Mississippi turned from shipping goods to processing and manufacture. The waterfalls at Minneapolis proved ideal for the milling of grain from the western prairies. General Mills, Pillsbury, and Robin Hood Flour became national brands. Cincinnati and Kansas City became meat-processing centres.

St Louis developed from a city that supplied settlers heading further west into a major manufacturing city. Typical of this development is the story of the Hamilton Brown Shoe Company. J.M. Hamilton and Alanson D. Brown were jobbers for New England shoe manufacturers. During the 1880s and 1890s, Hamilton-Brown steadily expanded their shoe business, graduating to general and dry goods stores in the Mississippi valley and the western plains. Around 1900, Hamilton-Brown decided that producing shoes locally in St Louis would be more profitable than bringing them from New England. Within a decade, Hamilton-Brown was arguably the largest shoe manufacturer and distributor in the world. Several crates of Hamilton-Brown shoes were in transit from the St Louis factory to Tennessee and Alabama aboard the *City of Savannah*. They too appear in the background of the Spink photographs.

Smaller cities along the river also shifted to manufacturing in the later decades of the nineteenth century. Al Spink photographed Cape Girardeau, located where the Ohio River met the Mississippi. The town had originally supplied settlers headed west. Its manufactures were limited to barrels for flour and meat. By 1910, the town included several brick kilns utilizing clay from the surrounding region, a foundry making agricultural implements, a woollen factory, a factory fabricating doors and windows, several large flourmills, a shoe factory, and a rail line.[17]

At the turn of the twentieth century, factories along the Mississippi cities were generally competitive, because they were new compared to those in cities of Europe or the Eastern United States and used sophisticated machines which required cheaper labour than older, craft-based manufacturing methods. They were also closer to markets as settlers moved into the land beyond the Mississippi. In much of the newly settled land farming was profitable and the market for windows, side tables, shoes, and store-bought clothes developed apace. The 'go-ahead' image of these river towns was part of the ethos of the Mississippi and its tributaries in the early decades of the twentieth century, and this cognitive geography seems to be reflected in several of the Spink photos.

In this same period (1890–1910), the United States government passed legislation removing control and maintenance of the Mississippi from the hands of the adjoining states and assigning it to the Army Corps of Engineers. They began a programme, much like the multistate commission of the Rhine at the same time, which included locks and dams, cutting off shallow ox-bow channels, constructing wing dams to convert shallow, wide channels to narrower, deeper channels, dredging, and channel lights and markers. The government committed to a six-foot channel the length of the Mississippi in 1907 and a nine-foot channel in the 1930s. In 1910 Charles Spink photographed a US government dredge working to maintain the channel.

There are, today, more than 100 dams and locks on the Mississippi's tributaries and 27 on the main river between St Paul, Minnesota, and Cairo, Illinois. In spite of this massive work by the Army Corps of Engineers, the intrinsic problems of the Mississippi as a route remain. Control of the river is just not humanly possible as the flow is much too powerful. There are still disastrous floods. The steady draining and building on surrounding natural wetlands has exacerbated the problem. As hurricane Katrina proved, channels that provide easy access for river traffic can also rapidly raise water levels.

A more basic problem was that the Mississippi runs north to south, but the country's main supply lines needed to go east to west. Entrepreneurs well understood the problem and, after the Civil War, built railroads. Railroads went to the mines and fields and carried the raw materials to processing centres. They took the finished products to wholesale distribution locations. Unlike the river, railroads did not have to cope with the problems of low water or floods. They ran in the winter while the riverboats sat idle in St Louis. By the 1870s, thirteen bridges crossed the Mississippi.

Just as on the Rhine, by 1900, steamboat traffic was reduced to a tiny fraction of rail traffic. The boats, however, still had a cachet for people along the river. Pilots and other riverboat officers held the highest prestige jobs

on the river. Captain William Tippitt was a boy of ten in Cairo, Illinois, 53
when the *City of Savannah* arrived with the Spink family.

The Mississippi

> I was born June the 8th, 1900 and down there every kid in the neighbor-
> hood ... could tell you the name—especially the boys—of practically every
> packet boat that landed in Cairo by the time they was five years old because
> that was, well, you might say the most exciting place for a small boy to be is
> on the levee looking down that long slope to the wharf boat and looking at
> all these steamboats come in, the people on them. The people coming off
> and the labor working there, carrying the freight off. They lived down there
> in our neighborhood, so us boys knew all of the steamboatmen. And another
> reason we knew them, they was the richest folks in town. They always had
> money and they was liberal, too, with it. They'd give a kid a penny anytime
> for a piece of candy or something, and they all had diamonds. You see a man
> goin' down, has a great big diamond in his shirt stud, big gold watch across
> that overport stomach of his, and big gold pilot wheel on there about the
> size of a fifty-dollar gold piece shinin' there—why all duded up. That man
> was something, when he walked down the street! And every kid wanted to
> be a steamboatman.[18]

Steamboats were practically gone by the 1920s. Popular music reflected
this change with songs of nostalgia for the romantic days of the steamboat.

> Don't you hear those whistles blowing
> There's going to be a jubilee down where the Mississippi's flowing
> They searched the country until they found
> All those old time steamboat racers of great renown
> Grand old boats with all their beauty
> Gray-haired captains still on duty.[19]

What, then, made the Mississippi a route rather than merely a large river?
Much of the cognitive geography of the river remained the same for centuries, such as the yearly rhythm of the river. Winter ice closed the northern
portions of the river and summer's low water limited traffic. The river
functioned first as a one-way route bringing goods from the heartland
downstream to markets.

It was new technology that fundamentally changed this pattern. By
the 1830s steamboats cut transportation costs and made upstream traffic

feasible. This two-way traffic fostered new sorts of networks—pilots and captains, riverboat labour, and gamblers. Steamboats brought the salesmen to general stores along the river with new merchandise, such as shoes, flour, stoves, furniture, cloth, and buttons. Each group saw the river, its dangers, and opportunities, from their own viewpoint. Along these human networks that followed the river, a good reputation was just as important for a steamboat captain as it was for salesman of cast iron cookware.

The Spink photographs suggest their cognitive geography of the Mississippi River system. The family, after all, lived along the Mississippi at St Louis. Their photos of the captain and pilot suggest that they well understood them as professionals and essential to the functioning of the river. The shots of the roustabouts suggest the gulf between the black lower class and the white upper class was part of their mental landscape. A photo of the black section of Cairo, Illinois, has a note that it was shot from a streetcar, not a place to be visited according to their mental map.

About other aspects of the Spink's cognitive geography of the river we have only clues. They took a picture of a government dredge boat and must have been aware that the Army Corps of Engineers had jurisdiction over the river's locks, dams, markers, lights, and levees. The family, after all, was in the newspaper business. Both brothers were reporters and must have covered year-by-year ups and downs of business along the river. Growing up in St Louis, they may have heard songs and stories of the river. The photographs show that they certainly knew the role of the Mississippi in the Civil War and their uncle's role in it.

Today, the Mississippi River handles mainly heavy goods in flotillas of 15–25 barges pushed by tugs. Standard barges are 120–200 feet long and 30–40 feet wide. The Mississippi carries more than 300 million tonnes of cargo each year, such as grain, coal, petrochemicals, sand and gravel, and chemicals.[20] The Army Corps of Engineers have made the river now perhaps as safe as humanly possible for barges and tourist boats. The mighty Mississippi will, however, never be fully tamed. The route is still at heart a river with equal parts danger and promise.[21]

Notes

1. The photograph album of the Spinks' steamboat vacation is in the collection of the author. The window of opportunity for taking such photographs was

small. Paper film, in widespread use only for a decade prior to the vacation, 55
was much faster than the older glass plates. Subjects did not have to pose and
the photographer did not have to carry a heavy tripod. Working river steamboats were in sharp decline by 1910 and would virtually disappear within
a decade of the Spinks' vacation. Other experts agree with my assessment
that this is the only known photographic record of a vacation on a working
steam riverboat. Amateur photography was so new at the time that there was
a kind of innocence for both photographer and subject. Anyone and everyone
allowed the photographers to shoot them while continuing with their jobs or
posing willingly.

2. In the absence of a memoir or letters it might seem difficult to tease out the
   Spinks' cognitive geography. The visual record, however, provides substantial
   clues. What they found interesting enough to photograph, how subjects were
   grouped and posed, even the short captions written below the photos in the
   album suggest much about their expectations and preconceptions about the
   Mississippi, Ohio, and Tennessee rivers.
3. George S. Pabis, *Daily Life Along the Mississippi* (Westport, Conn.: Greenwood,
   2007), p. 13.
4. Pabis, *Daily Life Along the Mississippi*, 19–23.
5. Pabis, *Daily Life Along the Mississippi*, 40–9.
6. Timothy Flint, *Recollections of the Last Ten Years*, edited by C. Hartley Grattan
   (New York: A.A. Knopf, 1932), p. 26.
7. See Flint, *Recollections of the Last Ten Years*, pp. 20–2. The author was on the
   Mississippi River and its tributaries, from Pittsburgh to the Missouri River,
   from 1815 to 1825.
8. Caleb Bingham's, 'Jolly Floatboatmen' series is still popular and readily
   accessible via an internet image search under the painter's name.
9. J.H. Kavanach, 'Sweet Mississippi' (1853). Available at the American Memory
   Project of the Library of Congress, original bound volumes. Ma A12v vd.53.
   Folk music, written by those who worked and lived along the river, presented
   a rather earthier viewpoint. Titles included 'Mississippi Baby', 'Mississippi
   Bottom Blues', 'Mississippi Boll Weevil Blues', 'Mississippi Flood', 'Mississippi
   Heavy Water Blues', 'Mississippi Moan', 'Mississippi Mud', 'Mississippi Snag',
   'The Flood of 1927', and 'Mississippi River Man'. See www.ibiblio.org/
   folkindex/kwframe.htm
10. The route is visible in the photograph on the signboard above the gangway.
    The captions to the photographs confirm the route.
11. Mark Twain, *Life on the Mississippi* (New York: Harper and Brothers
    Publishers, 1901), p. 50.

12. Pabis, *Daily Life Along the Mississippi*, p. 78.

13. Pabis, *Daily Life Along the Mississippi*, pp. 112–13, 148–9.

14. For the events and effects of the Battle of Shiloh, I have generally followed Larry J. Daniel, *Shiloh: The Battle That Changed the Civil War* (New York: Simon & Schuster, 1997).

15. See Daniel, *Shiloh*.

16. The origin of the term 'roustabout' is not clear. It perhaps comes for the verb 'rouse' and 'about', and might refer to labour that could be roused for work at any hour. The word may also connect to old British usage meaning 'shaggy' or 'unkempt'. In any case, the term was in use on the Mississippi in the 1850s and spread to unskilled labour in circuses, fairs, and oil fields. See www. etymonline.com. The grouping, the clothes, and the framing of this shot all suggest that the men were a bit embarrassed by being photographed. Both photographer and subject must have been all too aware of the gulf of class and race that separated them. This gulf formed part of the cognitive geography of the river for both groups.

17. *Wilson's History and Directory of Southeastern Missouri Southern Illinois* (St Louis, 1876).

18. Quoted in Jane Curry, *The River's in My Blood: Riverboat Pilots Tell Their Stories* (Lincoln, Nebraska: University of Nebraska, 1983).

19. See Joe Kelsey and Charley Straight, *See Those Mississippi Steamboats on Parade* (New York: Jerome H. Remick & Co., 1916).

20. The early coal transport was rather more exciting than today's barge traffic. In the last three decades of the nineteenth century, coal from the hills of western Pennsylvania moved on barges that could only clear the rocks in the Ohio River at a brief moment of the year. The boats waited in Pittsburgh, their captains watching for the rise. The moment the water was deep enough, the coal fleet of several thousand boats raced downriver to deliver the year's coal to all downstream cities and towns. Thus, the rise of the Ohio was critical, just as the rise of the Nile was to Egyptian agriculture.

21. The subsequent history of the Spink brothers was one of economic decline. Within a few years of the vacation, the family lost its racetracks, newspaper, and baseball team. They moved to Chicago and their father became a famous sports reporter. Al and Charles were involved with theatres.

PART II

PILGRIMAGE ROUTES

Introduction

Pilgrimage was, and still denotes, travel to a special, sacred place to receive the blessings of a god, a holy man or woman (or from their remains, if they are no longer alive) associated with the site. Pilgrimage routes differed from river routes in several basic ways. They did not, except incidentally, follow a natural feature such as a river. Rather, they followed a spiritual imperative that dictated crossing dangerous and difficult terrain in the pilgrim's quest. Even the overall shape of pilgrimage routes was different from river routes. Rivers were linear, transporting the commodities of an upstream heartland to downstream markets. Pilgrimage routes, in contrast, had a distinctive shape, perhaps easiest to visualize as a bush. Pilgrims started out on the twig that was their local village, and moved down towards a larger branch, which eventually joined one of a few large trunks relatively close to the site. Pilgrims usually travelled with others from their village or town. The regular and predictable meeting up with other pilgrims headed to the sacred site strengthened the will and commitment of all and reinforced the spiritual and emotional flow towards the shrine. River routes were profoundly affected by changes in technology. Steamboats made upstream transport efficient. Dynamite made the clearing of rocks possible. Governments built canals around rapids and dredged channels. In contrast, pilgrimage routes, until the twentieth century, were little affected by changes in technology. The difficulty of walking to the site was part of the commitment of the pilgrim and an integral part of the spiritual experience.

A pilgrimage begins long before the pilgrim sets out for the sacred site. He or she needs a deep conviction that the spiritual and physical benefits are worth the costs, risks, dangers, and difficulties of the venture. Pilgrims have mental expectations about the trip based on their familiarity with the ceremonies of departing, the joyous return, and the recounted stories of the trip to the site, its power, and miracles observed there. He or she might even gain local respect—a new name, a distinctive article of clothing, or a privileged seat in the local house of worship.

All routes repeat their yearly pattern of the best time to travel. So it is with pilgrimages: each route having an optimum time to start out.[1] In earlier times, when pilgrims set off, the local people recognized their special status. They were usually blessed by a local cleric and donned special pilgrim clothes, such as a cloak or a hat, and carried a distinctive staff, prayer rug, or bowl. In many cases, this remains true today. They might also carry a document designating them as pilgrims, specifying their vows, obligations, or medical conditions that impelled them to set out on their pilgrimage in the first place.

Like any travellers, pilgrims need shelter, warmth, and food. Special institutions existed to support the sacred journey. Kings and nobles built rest houses and garrisons, provided food, and planted trees. Some of the wealthy financed poor pilgrims, who then prayed at the shrine for their sponsors' salvation. Patrons supported monasteries, madrasas, and subsidiary sites at which pilgrims prayed to keep up their resolve on the journey. These institutions became part of a sacred landscape that was central to a pilgrim route and irrelevant for secular travellers. For the pilgrim, there are deep spiritual resonances with the places the Buddha taught, Muhammad preached, or Roland fought. At a deeper spiritual level are stories of the direct intercession of the holiness and power of the shrine to protect pilgrims from dangers along the route.

Within this sacred landscape, pilgrims also entered a non-normal sacred time. By throwing a stone at the same place that the Companions of Muhammad did, pilgrims recreate that event and merge the present with the sacred past. This special merging of past and present is freshly recreated for each pilgrim and each pilgrimage.

Even today, as before, pilgrimage routes have a distinctive set of human networks, including the suppliers of pilgrim garb and equipment, and professional leaders and organizers of pilgrimages. Back then, networks of bandits and pirates hoped to capture and ransom wealthy pilgrims. Monasteries along the route were interconnected, exchanging texts and artwork, hosting monks from each other's monasteries, and often providing shelter for pilgrims. Networks and friendships grew among pilgrims from distant places. They got to know one another and exchanged stories and songs on the long trek. Clerics at the site had their own networks. To attract pilgrims, they sought funds from kings and nobles for impressive architecture and furnishings suitable to the importance and power of the site.

Their vows fulfilled, their blessings received, pilgrims returned along the route, carrying a suitable symbol of the pilgrimage—a shell, a text, or a picture. Groups said goodbye to each other as their routes branched and diverged.

Pilgrimage routes, like all routes, have their own history. Over the centuries, sacred sites gained and lost popularity and patronage. Some went into decline only to experience rebirth much later.

Let us then travel the routes with three pilgrims, one setting forth from China on the Silk Road, one undertaking the Hajj to Mecca, and one seeking the blessing of St James at Compostela in Spain.

Note

1. The reader might recall that the prologue to Geoffrey Chaucer's *Canterbury Tales* declares that April, with its warmth and bursting buds, is the right time for the pilgrimage to Canterbury.

The Silk Road

By Land and Sea

In the year 399 CE seven monks set out from their monastery in China on the Silk Road. Theirs was to be a long, cold, dangerous pilgrimage overland to India. They sought to experience the power of the relics of the Buddha, walk in the places that he lived and taught, study in the most ancient monasteries, and obtain true copies of sacred texts from the Indian heartland of Buddhism. Three turned back, two died, one stayed in India, and only one, Fa Xian, returned fourteen years later, by sea, to China to record his experiences and deliver the precious texts.[1]

The Silk Road, one of the most fabled and studied routes of human history, began in China, skirted the Taklamakan Desert, and followed the northern foothills of the Himalayas into Persia and the Middle East. The route crossed some of the most difficult terrain on Earth, with steep mountain passes and intense cold. Less well known is the maritime complement to the Silk Road, which led from the south coast of China through the seas of Southeast Asia and around India to the Middle East. The sea route also had its dangers, such as shallows and rocks, long sailings out of sight of land, and violent storms. Nevertheless, year in and year out, caravans arrived at Middle Eastern cities and the spice fleet brought its wares to Cairo, the Egyptian terminus of the maritime route.

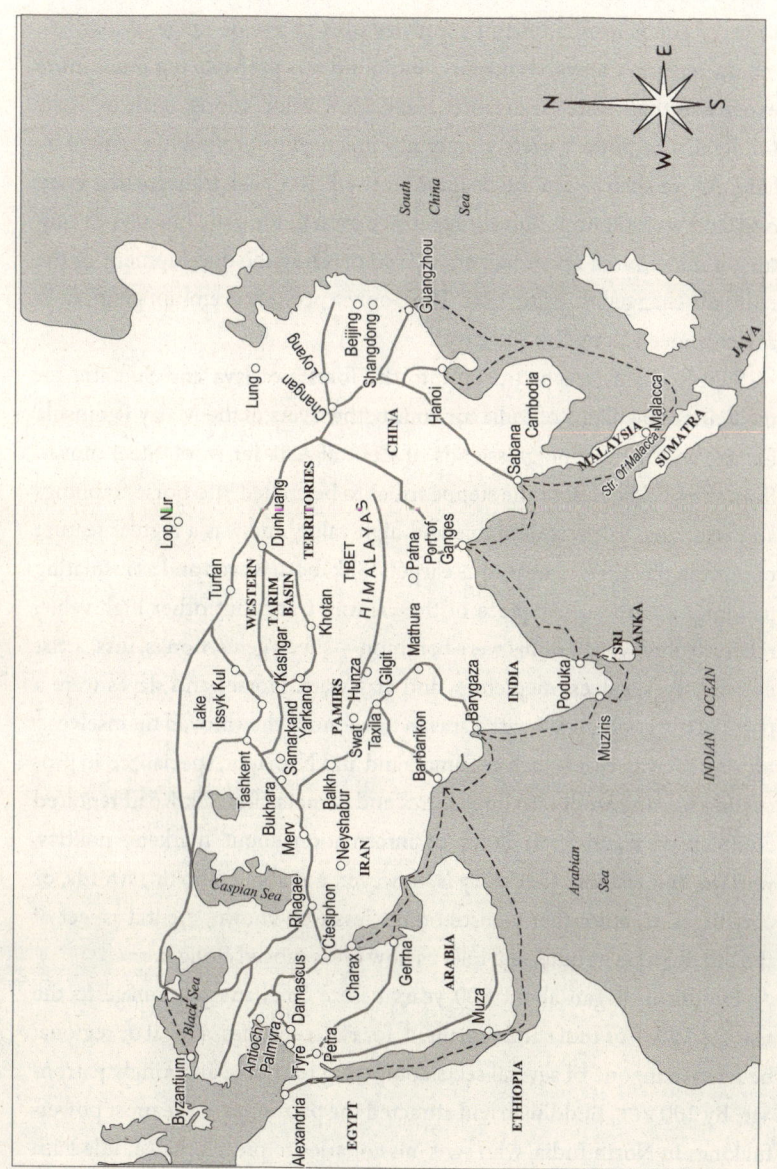

Silk Road

The common view that the Silk Road connected China and the Mediterranean is erroneous. The Silk Road and its maritime complement were developed not to meet the demands of the Mediterranean region, but to carry goods from a host of supply centres to a wide range of markets, mainly in Asia. Caravan transport per pound was probably ten times more expensive than water transport. Heavy, low-value goods, such as basic foodgrains or pottery, were simply not practical or profitable to move by land. As we shall see in the chapter on the Erie Canal, transporting grain overland was still prohibitively expensive even in the early nineteenth century, a millennium and a half after Fa Xian. Only the development of the railroads changed this situation. Thus, only a prestige premium grain, such as rice, moved along the Silk Road.

Supply chains reached deep into the forests of Java and Sumatra for medicines, the plains of India for cotton, the rivers of the Malay Peninsula for tin, and the steppe grasslands of Central Asia for wool. Steel moved from the Middle East to the steppe tribes to be crafted into horse trappings and weapons. Salt was desirable and high-value, and was a regular feature of caravan trade. Wool moved as carpets. Silk, both woven and as insulating padding, was the centrepiece of the caravan trade, but other high-value, relatively low-weight items were common—silver, gems, books, furs, artist colours, dyes, spices, medicines, and glassware. Horses and slaves were a particularly good match with caravan travel since they moved themselves.[2] Storied caravan cities, such as Samarkand and Nishapur, specialized in processing silk and wool into fine fabrics and carpets. The Silk Road required complex back-and-forth flows of information about markets, politics, warfare, and fashion. Our story is, however, not about silk, tin, swords, or cooking pots, but rather focuses on the less well-known, mental aspect of the Silk Road as a route, and tells us how ideas moved along it.

Buddhism began about 800 years before Fa Xian's pilgrimage to the Ganges Valley of India and remained, for two centuries, a local or regional belief system, one of several sects competing for noble and kingly patronage. By 200 BCE, Buddhism had attracted the patronage of the most powerful kings in North India, who sent missionaries to preach the Middle Path along the trade routes up and down the Ganges Valley, north into Kashmir, and south and west into Central India. By 100 BCE, Buddhism had spread along the trade routes to western India, south to Sri Lanka, and north into Afghanistan and Central Asia. As one of many competing religions, Buddhism appealed to kings in search of a wider-than-local legitimacy for their rule. Traders welcomed the protection of a deity known along the routes, whose monasteries were the repositories of medical knowledge. Buddhism also appealed to low-caste and hill people who were generally excluded from Hindu ceremonies officiated by Brahmins.[3]

In the first century CE, Buddhist monks and texts travelled to China, both on the Silk Road and by sea through Southeast Asia. Modern scholars have speculated that Buddhism's preaching of individual enlightenment was a welcome alternative to well-established Confucianism, with its emphasis on good government and collective responsibility. Existing Taoist meditation practices and goals were similar enough to Buddhist ones that many early converts saw Buddhism as a branch of Taoism. In China, Buddhism spread from a handful of monasteries in the north and one in the south, probably staffed by foreign monks, to many monasteries across much of China, staffed by local converts.[4] In this early period, Buddhism shifted to accommodate existing beliefs in China. For example, in Indian Buddhist belief everything was impermanent. There was no immortal soul. In China, the strong existing belief in an immortal soul could not be displaced and became a central tenet of Buddhism.

    Fa Xian, in about 370 CE, had entered his monastery in the capital of Chang'an as a young boy. He grew up there and took full orders around the age of twenty. Soon, he began to worry that errors of misinterpretation had crept into Buddhist texts in China through translation and copying. He thought that accurate texts from Buddhism's Indian heartland might cleanse Chinese Buddhism of harmful and incorrect practices, and decided on a pilgrimage to India in search of such texts. Fa Xian and his fellow monks departed in the spring of 399 CE and walked west and north to the city of Lung in current-day western Shensi Province.

    The monks were in no sense explorers. They followed the well-established Silk Road west from China.[5] Even before the beginning of their trek, however, mental expectations permeated the expedition. The monks well knew that Buddhism had come by the Silk Road and that monks before them had undertaken the long pilgrimage back to India along this route. They likely had a good idea that they would find Buddhist kings and Buddhist monasteries already established along the way. For Fa Xian and his small party, the Silk Road was not a trade route. It was a pilgrimage route, each step bringing them closer to a sacred and holy land.

The abbot of their monastery blessed their venture. Soon after they set out, still well within the Great Wall, Fa Xian and his companions encountered a region so 'disturbed that traveling on the roads was impossible'.[6] The monks' pilgrimage took place towards the end of a period of Chinese history known as the Sixteen Kingdoms (265–420 CE). There was little central authority and the land was controlled by a multitude of local and regional dynasties. Warfare and banditry were chronic.

A local Buddhist king offered the monks housing and food and they stayed nearly a year.[7] When travelling conditions improved, five monks joined the original seven pilgrims. This boost in numbers to their party along the way bolstered everyone's strength and resolve. In this early period, however, the route to India was so long, cold, and dangerous that, in spite of Buddhist institutional support along the way, few monks undertook the pilgrimage, although many shared the desire to go.

The pilgrims passed around the western end of the Great Wall and reached Dunhuang, which would not receive its famous Buddhist caves and shrines for another two centuries. A local Buddhist king gave the monks supplies and equipment to traverse the southern rim of the Taklamakan Desert. It is difficult today to imagine the brutal travelling conditions on this enormous sea of sand. Fa Xian's memoir is generally laconic on the difficulties of the road, but not about this area:

...the desert, in which there are many evil demons and hot winds. [Travellers] who encounter them perish all to a man. There is not a bird to be seen in the air above, nor an animal on the ground below. Though you look all around most earnestly to find where you can cross, you know not where to make your choice, the only mark and indication being the dry bones of the dead.[8]

The group pushed hard. If the memoir is accurate, they walked 15 miles a day for seventeen straight days and reached a city south of a lake with the modern name of Lop Nor, one of the few places for hundreds of miles with a consistent source of water.

At Lop Nor, the monks found not just a friendly king, but also a large, functioning Buddhist monastery with 4,000 monks in residence. This was the pattern of Fa Xian's experience on the land route west from China to

India. At caravan city after caravan city for 3,000 miles, the monk found the institutional support of Buddhist monasteries and kings who supported them. Another aspect of the mental side of the pilgrim's experience, as Fa Xian described, was that all monks studied Sanskrit in order to read the Buddhist texts. It was a common, shared language, regardless of their original tongue.

The section of the pilgrimage route westward from Lop Nor to the caravan city of Khotan was a difficult 300 miles, in part because the tight-fisted folk of Lop Nor had not given the monks enough supplies. The Silk Road had no mile markers, no rest stops for the midday meal, no stations where officials and couriers changed mounts, and certainly no inns. Between cities the caravan followed a track that might disappear with shifting sand and was dependent on the skill of the leader to find the track again.

They [the travellers] found the country uninhabited as they went along. The difficulties which they encountered in crossing the streams and on route, and the sufferings which they endured, were unparalleled in human experience, but in the course of a month and five days they succeeded in reaching Yu-teen [current day Hotan].[9]

Illustration 8 *The Remains of the Ancient City of Turfan, along the Silk Road.* Courtesy of Gretchen Hall.

Modern-day Hotan is in the Xinjian Province of far western China and was was, at the time of Fa Xian, a flourishing caravan city with four great monasteries and many small ones. The pilgrims stayed at the Gomati Monastery, where 3,000 monks were in residence. The king was Buddhist and actively patronized all the monasteries in the area. Fa Xian witnessed a ceremony in which the various monasteries brought out their images in a great and colourful procession. The cognitive geography that Fa Xian described was not one of trade, it was rather a special, sacred landscape of Buddhist monasteries and the veneration of their ritual objects. In this aspect, Fa Xian's memoir is similar, as we shall see, to the pilgrim *Guide* to Compostela or Ibn Battuta's writing on the Hajj.

The pilgrims proceeded west in a caravan from Hotan and eventually turned south into the Himalayas, which Fa Xian called the 'Onion Mountains'. It was a brutal, cold crossing.

The snow rests on them both winter and summer. There are also among them venomous dragons, which, when provoked, spit forth poisonous winds, and cause showers of snow and storms of sand and gravel. Not one in ten thousand of those who encounter these dangers escapes with their life.[10]

Illustration 9 *Buddhist Monastic Caves, Cut into a Hillside along the Silk Road.* Courtesy of David Sa'dah.

When Xaunzang, another Chinese pilgrim, made the same crossing two centuries later, a friendly king gave his party 'face-covers, gloves, stockings, and boots'.[11] Fa Xian and his group of pilgrims apparently survived without this gear.

The logic of travelling in an armed caravan was obvious to all travellers. It might be slower to wait for a caravan to assemble, but the likelihood of actually arriving was substantially higher. The caravan benefited from the expertise of its leader. A large caravan also had emotional benefits. A traveller might find some people like himself, perhaps fellow Buddhist monks, or Indian traders, or Arabs. They might eat together, exchange information, and stave off the loneliness of long-distance travel.

On land, the walking pace and a distance of over 3,000 miles of desert and mountains made it impossible to complete the journey from China to India in a year. Fa Xian and his pilgrim friends took three years to reach India. The desirable travel seasons were the spring and fall, but these were brief. In the heat of the summer, travel was possible, but hardly pleasant, and travellers needed to reach a caravan city before the lethal cold of the winter arrived and before snow closed mountain passes.[12]

West and south of the Himalayas, the pilgrims passed into Hunza or Gilgit and, from there, into the Swat Valley in what is today northern Pakistan. Swat was a flourishing centre of Buddhism, like many other valleys along a thousand-mile front of the southern slopes of the Himalayas. Kings supported its monasteries and pilgrims who travelled there.

Fa Xian found that his mental expectations exactly matched actual practices in all of the monasteries he visited. Monasteries knew how to accommodate pilgrims and typically offered them three days' hospitality.

> When [the stranger] has enjoyed a very brief rest, they further ask the number of years that he has been a monk, after which he receives a sleeping apartment with its appurtenances, according to his regular order, and everything is done for him which the rules prescribe.[13]

The larger monasteries held sacred relics, the walking staff of the Buddha, his alms bowl, a piece of bone from his cremation, hair or nail clippings. The monks carried them in periodic processions. The pilgrims from China venerated the relics and were fully aware of their power. To have actually been in the presence of the body and essence of the Buddha was central to their pilgrimage.

These valleys of the Himalayas were the sites of the popular Jataka tales of earlier incarnations of the Buddha. Fa Xian knew these stories well and carried a full mental map of these sacred sites. For example, at Udyana, in current-day Pakistan, Fa Xian explored the place where the Buddha, in an earlier incarnation, was said to have seen a hawk about to attack a dove. Out of compassion, he gave a piece of his own flesh to satisfy the hawk, which spared the dove. The route from northern Afghanistan to the Indian plains had continuous Buddhist resonances for Fa Xian. The sacred imagined landscape he moved through co-existed with the actual mountains and valleys he encountered. He seems to have been fully immersed in what might be termed 'sacred time'. He experienced the sites of the Jataka stories in his present, but he also experienced them as if he lived in the time that they took place.

The journey had been hard on the group of Chinese pilgrims and 'painful reflections arose in their minds': '... Along with their like-minded friends, they had traveled through so many kingdoms: some of those friends had returned [to their own land], and some had [died], proving the impermanence and uncertainty of life.'[14]

The tally of the group with Fa Xian was grim. One pilgrim died of cold in the mountains and another died in a monastery along the way. Three lost heart and returned to China from western India. Several monks had scattered to monasteries in caravan cities. The remaining group that entered the heartland of original Buddhism was small, perhaps two or three pilgrims.

Fa Xian and his remaining comrades left the foothills of the Himalayas and turned south onto the plain of the Ganges River. Here, Buddhism also flourished. At Pataliputra (modern-day Patna), Fa Xian found two monasteries 'grand and beautiful' with a total of about 700 monks. 'The inhabitants are rich and prosperous and vie with one another in the practice of benevolence and righteousness.'[15] Fa Xian noticed that the trader caste (Vaisyas) supported Buddhist monasteries and also supported hospitals for the poor in the city. It was a natural match. The traders brought the medicines, the monasteries kept the knowledge of how to use them, and Buddhists had no caste restrictions on treating any who needed help.

and were well governed compared to the chaos and violence of China.

> In it the cold and heat are finely tempered, and there is neither hoarfrost
> nor snow. The people are numerous and happy: they have not to register
> their households, or attend to any magistrates and their rules; only those
> who cultivate royal land have to pay [a portion of] the gain from it. If they
> want to go, they go: if they want to stay, they stay. The king governs without
> decapitation or [other] corporeal punishments.[16]

Fa Xian's journey was striking to monks in India because he came to them
all the way from China. In that period, few monks, traders, philosophers,
or soldiers made the whole trip. The Silk Road was segmented. Everything
changed hands at the caravan cities—sacred objects, silk, cotton from India.
This segmentation lowered the risk for all involved. A caravan leader needed
detailed knowledge of only his segment of the route, such as the necessary
languages, the likely areas for attacks by bandits, the politics of the stopping
places, and the advisability of travelling late in the season. Traders likewise
specialized in a single segment of the route. Typically, agents informed them
of the profitability of selling their wares in one town or port or whether it
would be more profitable to push on to a further destination.

East of Patna, there were many sites associated with the life of the
Buddha, central to Fa Xian's pilgrimage. He knew them all by reputation
but here the reality did not match his mental expectations. All these sites
were deserted, crumbling ruins; the neglect evoked sadness in Fa Xian. For
all its emphasis on leaving the mundane life behind and joining a monastery, Buddhism could not survive without the active support of local
kings and wealthy traders who endowed the monasteries. If the population
migrated or the kingdom failed, the monasteries also disappeared. Fa Xian
implicitly acknowledged the importance of local patronage. At the site
where the Buddha attained enlightenment, there were three monasteries.
'The families of their people around supply the society of monks with an
abundant sufficiency of what they require, so that there is no lack or stint.'[17]

Fa Xian returned to Patna, the end of his pilgrimage, and joined a
monastery that held the text he sought. It was the 'most complete with the
fullest explanations'.[18] He and his one remaining companion settled into
a routine of meditation and ceremonies. Fa Xian learned written and oral

Sanskrit and spent three years copying texts and participating in the daily life of the monastery. By 410 CE, Fa Xian had acquired the texts and knowledge for which he had ventured to India, and was ready to return to China. His last remaining companion, Tao-ching, had grown accustomed to life in the monastery in Patna and opted to stay.

Fa Xian decided to return to China by ship, carrying his precious manuscripts through maritime Southeast Asia. He probably remembered all too well the cold and privations and the death of his companions on the Silk Road. The maritime route, in contrast, connected India through Sri Lanka and tropical Southeast Asia to the south coast of China. Ships that plied these seas handled both luxuries and bulk goods, heavy iron cooking pots, and pottery. The return cargo consisted of a variety of forest products, including aromatic woods and gums used in incense, medicines, spices, and ivory. Tin from the Malay Peninsula was an important item of southern trade, a component of a myriad of religious and secular objects of bronze, brass, and other metal alloys.[19]

Fa Xian booked passage south to Sri Lanka on a trading vessel from a port in Bengal, where he found two dozen monasteries. The coasts of India, Sri Lanka, mainland Southeast Asia, and coastal China are within the monsoon wind pattern: from June to October onshore winds predominate; by January, the pattern reverses, with offshore winds prevailing.[20] Fa Xian's ship left Bengal in the beginning of winter and exploited the favourable offshore winds for a swift and easy passage of 14 days to Sri Lanka. Travellers typically had to wait in Sri Lanka for the June or July onshore monsoon winds to carry them north and east through Southeast Asia to the coast of China. Entrepôt port cities were the answer to this problem of monsoon winds. Ships from China or India offloaded and warehoused their goods in a port in the Malacca Straits or on Sumatra. Smaller, locally built ships took a variety of warehoused goods to markets on the islands and the mainland when the winds favoured such a passage.

From Fa Xian's time to the present, Southeast Asian ports have competed with each other for this trans-shipping trade. The earliest recorded trans-shipping port was on the Malay Peninsula at the Gulf of Kra. In later centuries, such trans-shipping ports were located on Sumatra, Java, and the southern tip of the Malay Peninsula.[21] Singapore is the latest of these trans-shipping ports.

Fa Xian decided to stay in Sri Lanka for a while. For a Buddhist pilgrim, it had everything he needed: monasteries for basic needs, texts to study, relics to venerate, and fellow Buddhists with whom to perform rituals and meditate. The famous relics of the main temples were part of Fa Xian's sacred mental landscape. He already knew them by reputation. Fa Xian took up residence at a monastery and remained for two years, copying texts unknown in China.

China and the completion of his pilgrimage, however, still beckoned. Fa Xian was deeply touched by a chance encounter with a fellow countryman from China.

The men with whom he had been in intercourse had all been of regions strange to him; his eyes had not rested on an old and familiar hill or river, plant or tree: his fellow-travelers, moreover, had been separated from him, some by death, others flowing off in different directions; no face or shadow was now with him but his own, and a constant sadness was in his heart. Suddenly (one day), when by the side of this image of jade, he saw a [Chinese] merchant presenting a white fan of silk; and the tears of sorrow involuntarily filled his eyes and fell down.[22]

Across sixteen centuries, Fa Xian so clearly tells us the emotions of being on a route so far from home.

At last, Fa Xian knew that it was time to go home. He booked his passage on a large merchant vessel bound for Java that carried more than 200 men. The maritime route between India and China proved just as dangerous and difficult as the mountains and the cold of the land route. Three days east of Sri Lanka the ship sprang a serious leak and water began to fill the holds. Traders threw their cargo overboard to lighten the ship. Fa Xian dumped his few possessions, including his water pitcher and his basin. He vowed that he would die before letting anyone jettison his manuscripts.[23] The 'tempest continued day and night' for thirteen days, finally blowing the ship to an island where the crew beached the vessel and fixed the leak.

At the time of Fa Xian, ships did not have compasses. He well summarizes the terrors of such travel:

The great ocean spreads out, a boundless expanse. There is no knowing east from west: only by observing the sun, moon, and stars was it possible to go forward. If the weather were dark and rainy, [the ship] went as she was carried by the wind, without any definite course. In the darkness of the night, only the great waves were to be seen ... with huge turtles and other monsters of the deep. The merchants were full of terror, not knowing where they were going.[24]

Fa Xian was also aware of the dangers from pirates. 'On the sea there are many pirates, to meet whom is a speedy death.'[25]

It took the ship ninety days to get to Java, where Fa Xian disembarked and stayed for five months. Java, however, did not meet his needs or his expectations. He found 'Buddhism in it is not worth speaking of' and the place replete with various forms of philosophical 'error'. In April, Fa Xian boarded a merchantman bound for China with an expected passage of four to six weeks. The ship departed at the very beginning of reliable onshore winds, unfortunately accompanied by fierce monsoon storms, which swept the ship off course. Seventy days out of Java, the captain had little idea where they were and provisions had run out. During a clear patch, the captain observed the sun, and turned the ship north, hoping to make the China coast. The ship had been blown all the way around China's south coast and had landed on the Shandong Peninsula, almost as far north as current-day Beijing. Everyone was happy enough to make any landfall. The traders sent their goods to the port of Tsingtsao (current-day Qingdao). Fa Xian unloaded his manuscripts and accepted the hospitality of a fellow Buddhist who was the head of the province.[26]

Fa Xian's mental map of the way to India, with its centrality of Buddhist sacred sites and the richness of its repositories of sacred texts, was probably shared by Buddhist monks in China for half a millennium. In the 500 years following Fa Xian, the powerful, stable, and outward-looking Tang Dynasty ruled China. They extended their control with watchtowers all along the Silk Road. Travel, trade, and pilgrimage became much safer. Chinese records mention, during the Tang Dynasty, more than 200 embassies to India. They all included Buddhist monks, traders, and government officials. The embassies travelled both by land and by sea, with many originating in large Buddhist monasteries in China and travelling to a specific monastery in India. They brought ceremonial robes and sought paintings, texts, and relics.[27] Surviving inscriptions on the walls of monasteries record some of the religion, trade, and diplomacy in these missions.

Under the Tang Dynasty, new centres of Buddhism supplemented older monasteries along the Silk Road. Local families and traders patronized the new Buddhist paintings, sculpture and texts of Dunhuang, located in far western China at the junction of the northern and southern roads that skirted the Taklamakan Desert. Excavated two centuries after Fa Xian, Dunhuang eventually included nearly 500 cave temples and approximately half a million square feet of wall mural. It survived in active use for a thousand years. Its final use was as a repository for used, damaged, and worn texts. The thousands of scrolls unearthed there in the twentieth century have become one of the richest sources of texts on Buddhist thought and practice.[28]

After about 900 CE, Buddhism along the Silk Road route gradually lost out to the spread of Islam. Some Buddhist centres were simply conquered by Islamic armies. Missionaries and preachers converted other regions. Conversion to Islam was patchy and slow, beginning—like Buddhism—in the caravan cities. Over the next half a millennium Turks, Uyghurs, and Mongols became Muslim. Tibetans in the high valleys of the Himalayas remained Buddhist. The people of the Caucasus and the western steppe became Christian.

Ecological change eventually doomed the Silk Road. The route had always been dry. Caravans had to carry water from oasis to oasis. Over the centuries the whole broad region north of the Himalayas became much drier. Oases disappeared under sand. Rivers were less reliable. Lakes shrank. Some portions of the Silk Road, however, remained economically important. Well into the nineteenth century, for example, every year, tens of thousands of horses came down the route to India from the steppe grasslands north of Afghanistan. They were traded for spices, medicines, cloth, and sugar.[29] In the twentieth century, national boundaries cut the land route into awkward sections. National rivalries, such as between Russia and China or India and Pakistan, often closed the road at borders.

In contrast to the gradual decline of the Silk Road, the maritime route through Southeast Asia has played a long, storied, and important role right down to the present. Centuries after Fa Xian, Buddhism competed with Islam and various branches of Hinduism along these sea-lanes. For several centuries, from perhaps 800 CE to 1200 CE, the Buddhist 'world' included Bengal in eastern India, Myanmar, Sri Lanka, and Java. Monks frequently circulated between monasteries.[30] Mainland Southeast Asia—Cambodia, Laos, Vietnam, and Myanmar—became predominantly Buddhist. The people from the islands of current-day Indonesia had both Buddhist and Hindu influences and institutions, but eventually converted to Islam. By the early sixteenth century, along these same sea routes, European powers sought spices and established colonies. The Portuguese understood the importance of conquering Malacca, the predominant entrepôt port of the sixteenth and seventeenth centuries. These sea-lanes carried the exports of colonialism, such as rubber and rice, from British Burma and Malaya, and cotton, coffee, sugar, and spices from Dutch Indonesia. Because of the rich cargoes on the sea routes, piracy continued century after century. The Malacca Straits were the perfect spot to strike as ships manoeuvred slowly through the winding, shallow, narrow channel. Little has changed. Less than ten years ago, pirates seized a ship in the very same area.

And what of Fa Xian? The pilgrim eventually returned to Xian after an absence of more than fifteen years, bringing his precious texts to his monastery.

> From the sandy desert westwards to India, the beauty of the dignified demeanour of the monkhood and of the transforming influence on the [Buddhist] Law was beyond the power of language to describe; and reflecting how our masters had not heard any complete account of them, he therefore [went on] without regarding his own poor life....[31]

In the same simple, self-effacing prose of the whole of the memoir, Fa Xian pinpoints what the Silk Road meant for him. It had nothing to do with silk or any other commodity. In his mental map, the route was a pilgrimage that led from the periphery of Buddhism to its heartland, from texts plagued with errors to accurate ones, from harmful practices to correct procedures. The pilgrimage led through a sacred geography where the Buddha had preached and meditated. His memoir tells the story of this world of orderly monasteries and kings who supported them. For Fa Xian, his pilgrimage was worth all the cold and mountains, all the tropical storms and terrors of the sea.

Over the millennia, the boundaries of this Buddhist world have shifted, though Buddhism still has many followers. One can, even today, catch

distant glimmers of Fa Xian's world at Bodh Gaya, where the Buddha
attained enlightenment. In the flow of robes and languages are monks from
Japan, China, Tibet, Sri Lanka, Thailand, Cambodia, and the new Buddhist
centres in Europe and America. Fa Xian would perhaps understand their
mental map of Buddhist sites and the longing for spiritual truth that
guides their pilgrimages.

Notes

1. Fa-Hien, *A Record of Buddhistic Kingdoms: Being an Account by the Chinese Monk Fa-Hien of His Travels in Indian and Ceylon (A.D. 399–414) in Search of the Buddhist Books of Discipline*, translated and annotated by James Legge (New York: Paragon Book Reprint Corp., 1965 [1886]).

2. A pilgrim named Xuanzang followed the route of Fa Xian some two centuries later and left a much more detailed memoir of his trip. See Shaman Hwui Li, *The Life of Hiuen-Tsiang*, translated by Samuel Beal (London: Kegan Paul, Trench, Trübner & Co, 1911). Sally Hovey Wriggins, *Xuanzang: A Buddhist Pilgrim on the Silk Road* (Boulder, Colorado: Westview Press, 1996) stays quite close to the memoir, but adds useful maps and illustrations. There has been much recent research on the Silk Road, including both intellectual and material exchange. See, for example, Xinru Liu, *Silk and Religion: An Exploration of Material Life and the Thought of People, AD 600–1200* (Delhi: Oxford University Press, 1996). See also Xinru Liu, 'Silk, Robes, and Relations between Early Chinese Dynasties and Nomads beyond the Great Wall', in *Robes and Honor: The Medieval World of Investiture*, edited by Stewart Gordon (New York: Palgrave, 2001). On Silk Road cuisine and its history, see Najmieh Batmanglij, *Silk Road Cooking: A Vegetarian Journey* (Washington, DC: Mage Publishers, 2004).

3. The core idea and variety of practices in Buddhism can be found in Donald S. Lopez (ed.), *Buddhism in Practice* (Princeton: Princeton University Press, 1995).

4. See Kenneth K.H. Ch'en, *Buddhism in China: A Historical Survey* (Princeton: Princeton University Press, 1964), Chapters II and III. More detail is found in E. Zucher, *The Buddhist Conquest of China: The Spread and Adaptation of Buddhism in Early Medieval China* (Leiden: E.J. Brill, 1972), Chapter 2.

5. Fa Hien, *A Record of Buddhistic Kingdoms*, p. 10.

6. Fa Hien, *A Record of Buddhistic Kingdoms*, p. 11.

7. Over the centuries, Chinese Imperial power along the Silk Road waxed and waned. In Fa Xian's time it was non-existent. A few centuries later, the Tang

Dynasty established guardhouses for a thousand miles along it, which were, in turn, abandoned by the subsequent dynasty.

8. Fa Hien, *A Record of Buddhistic Kingdoms*, p. 12.

9. Fa Hien, *A Record of Buddhistic Kingdoms*, pp. 15–16.

10. Fa Hien, *A Record of Buddhistic Kingdoms*, p. 24.

11. Shaman Hwui Li, *The Life of Hiuen-Tsiang*, p. 30.

12. The pace of caravan travel did not change much in the millennium after Fa Xian's journey. In the thirteenth century, Marco Polo took three years to return from the Great Khan's capital in Mongolia across the Silk Road to the Black Sea.

13. Fa Hien, *A Record of Buddhistic Kingdoms*, p. 44.

14. Fa Hien, *A Record of Buddhistic Kingdoms*, p. 58.

15. Fa Hien, *A Record of Buddhistic Kingdoms*, p. 79.

16. Fa Hien, *A Record of Buddhistic Kingdoms*, pp. 42–3.

17. Fa Hien, *A Record of Buddhistic Kingdoms*, p. 89.

18. Fa Hien, *A Record of Buddhistic Kingdoms*, p. 99.

19. See Pierre-Yves Manguin, 'Trading Ships of the South China Sea: Shipping Techniques and Their Role in the History of the Development of Asian Trade Networks', *Journal of the Economic and Social History of the Orient*, 36(1993).

    Also, Bennett Bronson, 'Patterns in the Early Southeast Asian Metals Trade', *Early Metallurgy, Trade and Urban Centers in Thailand and Southeast Asia*, edited by Ian Glover, Pornchai Suchitta, and John Villiers (Bangkok, Thailand: White Lotus, 1992). In Arab accounts of the ninth century, copper was prominently mentioned as a desirable item to trade in China. S. Maqbul Ahmad (trans.), *Arab Classical Accounts of India and China* (Rddhi, India: Indian Institute of Advanced Study, 1979). See also Kenneth R. Hall, *Maritime Trade and State Development in Early Southeast Asia* (Honolulu, Hawaii: University of Hawaii Press, 1985), pp. 108–10. Also, Charles Higham, *The Archaeology of Mainland Southeast Asia From 10,000 BC to the Fall of Angkor* (Cambridge: Cambridge University Press 1989).

20. The basic pattern of the monsoon is laid out in P.K. Das, *The Monsoons* (New Delhi: National Book Trust, 1968). Also useful is David H.S. Chang, 'The Tibetan Plateau in Relation to the Vegetation of China', in *Annals of the Missouri Botanical Garden*, vol. 70, no. 3 (1983), pp. 564–70.

21. For an early entrepôt, see Alastair Lamb, 'Takupa: The Probable Site of a Pre-Malaccan Entrepot in the Malay Peninsula', in *Malayan and Indonesian Studies*, edited by John Bastin and Roelof Roolvink (Oxford: Oxford University Press, 1964), pp. 81–2.

22. Fa Hien, *A Record of Buddhistic Kingdoms*, p. 103.

23. Fa, *A Record of Buddhistic Kingdoms*, pp. 111–12.

24. Fa Hien, *A Record of Buddhistic Kingdoms*, p. 112.

25. Fa Hien, *A Record of Buddhistic Kingdoms*, p. 112.

26. Fa Hien, *A Record of Buddhistic Kingdoms*, pp. 114–15.

27. See Tansen Sen, *Buddhism, Diplomacy, and Trade: The Realignment of Sino-Indian Relations, 600–1400* (Honolulu: Association for Asian Studies and University of Hawaii Press, 2003).

28. See Roderick Whitfield and Susan Neville Whitfield, *Cave Temples of Mogao* (Los Angeles, Calif.: Getty Conservation Institute and the J. Paul Getty Museum, 2000). Also, Roderick Whitfield, *Dunhuang, Caves of the Singing Sands: Buddhist Art from the Silk Road* (London: Textile & Art Publishers, 1995).

29. This trade is nicely documented at the opening of the sixteenth century by Babur, founder of the Mughal Empire in India. See Babur, *Babur-Nama* [Memoirs of Babur], translated by Annette Sussanah Beveridge (New Delhi: Low Price Publications, 1989, reprint edition), p. 202.

30. See Tilman Frasch, 'A Buddhist Network in the Bay of Bengal: Relations between Bodhgaya, Burma, and Sri Lanka, c. 300–1300', *From the Mediterranean to the China Sea: Miscellaneous Notes*, edited by Claude Guilllot, Denys Lombard and Roderich Ptak (Wiesbaden, Germany: Harrassowitz Verlag, 1998), pp. 69–92.

31. Fa Hien, *A Record of Buddhistic Kingdoms*, p. 116.

Santiago de Compostela

Sometime around 1130 CE, a pilgrim wrote a memoir of his travel to the holy site of Santiago de Compostela in far western Spain. We do not know his name, but we know much of his travails and his temper. He railed against those who unjustly exploited pilgrims, such as the boatmen near the town of St Jean de Sorde (southwest of Paris, almost to the Spanish border):

> May their boatmen be utterly damned. For, although the rivers are quite narrow, nevertheless, they are in the habit of getting one *mummus* from every person, poor as well as rich, whom they ferry across, and for a beast four, which they undeservedly extort.[1]

He even more vigorously condemned toll-takers near the French-Spanish border: 'If someone passing through does not want to give them money in accordance with their demand, they both beat him with sticks and snatch away the assessed sum from him, upbraiding him and searching him down to his underwear.'[2] He called for excommunication for unjust collectors, their progeny, and nobles who received exorbitant tolls.

During the height of its popularity (1150–1600 CE), thousands of pilgrims set out for Compostela every year with hope, trepidation, faith, and doubt. Some travelled to expiate the guilt of sin. Others went as punishment by ecclesiastic courts. Many went in hopes of a cure for mental or physical ailments. Like Chaucer's pilgrims to Canterbury, some set out to

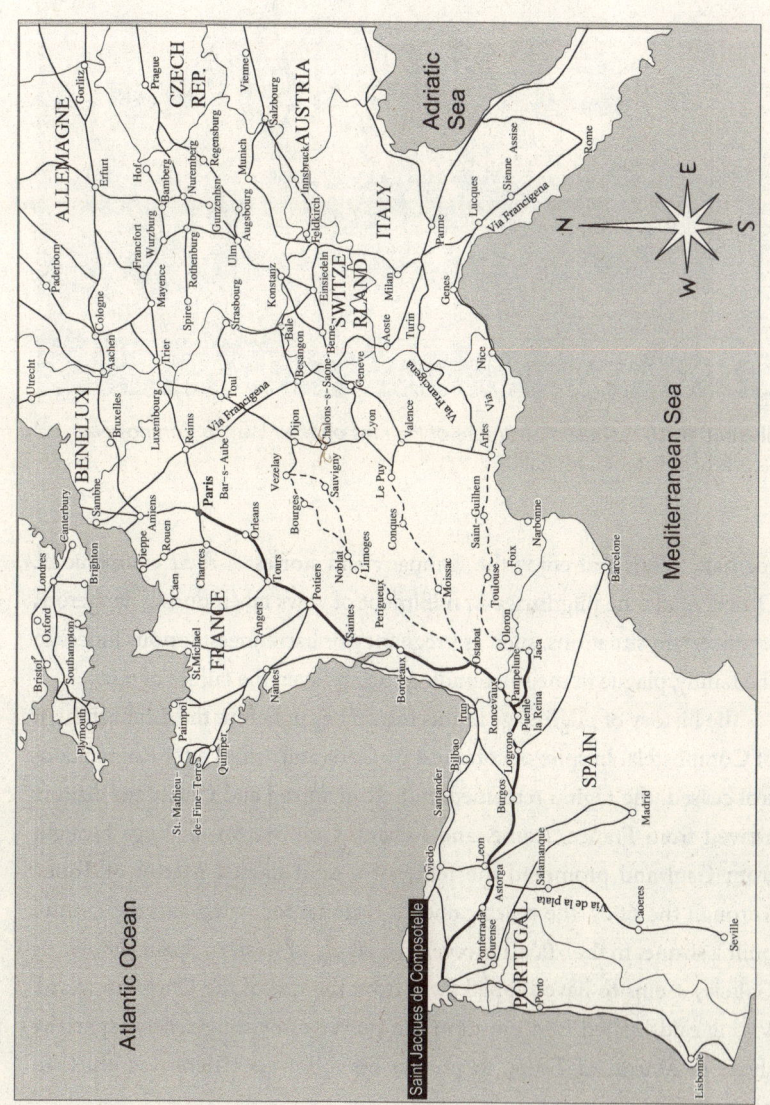

Santiago de Compostela

82

Illustration 10 *Ancient Sculpture of Pilgrims on their Way to Compostela.*
Courtesy of Peter Gottschalk.

see new things and enjoy the company and stories of their companions. Others made the pilgrimage in fulfilment of vows taken during dangerous or uncertain situations, such as pregnancy or barrenness, serious illness in the family, plague in the surrounding society, even the failure of rains.

The history of pilgrimage in this region began before the establishment of Compostela. In spite of conquest by Germanic tribes after Roman control ceased, the region remained quite Romanized and Christian. Visitors arrived from France, Rome, and Ireland. One Martin of Braga brought from Gaul and promoted the relics of a saint named Martin of Tours. Through the 600s, the relics gained a regional following and the faithful built a shrine. In the 700s, however, the whole of western Spain (known as Galicia) seems to have slipped away from the rest of the Christian world. Viking raids called into question the power of existing relics, especially those of Martin of Tours, to protect his followers. There was, thus, an opening for a new saint.

Shrines housed relics, that is, bones of a holy person and objects associated with him or her. Potential believers rated the power of relics first and foremost by their religious importance. The bones of Christ and Mary were unavailable because both had been transported bodily to heaven. The top tier of relics, therefore, consisted of the bones of the Apostles and objects closely and physically associated with Christ, swaddling clothes, robes, nails of the cross. A second tier of relics consisted of the body or bones of saintly local people, whether they had healed, taught, undertaken pilgrimages, or performed selfless service. Whether or not the bones in a local shrine were actually those of a local saint was, of course, relatively easy to establish. Relics brought from the Holy Land, however, were accepted or doubted based on the credibility of the chain of transmission by which they had arrived at its current site.

Compostela made an extraordinarily powerful claim for the power of its relics, namely that they were the bones of the Apostle St James, close associate of Christ and present at the Last Supper and the Crucifixion. How, then, did his bones end up in far western Spain? The story of St James' association with Spain began with a seventh century tract known as the *Breviarum Apostolorum*, probably produced in Western Europe. The tract asserted that St James took Christ's charge to his Apostles to spread his word 'to the ends of the earth' quite literally, and preached through what is now far western Spain. Scattered eighth-century texts reinforced this idea and, by the ninth century, St James' ministry in Spain gained broad acceptance.[3]

There was, nevertheless, the problem of St James' known martyrdom and presumed burial in the Holy Land. All of medieval European society assumed that true holy relics were quite alive. Relics chose where they wanted to reside and would, with unstoppable force, resist movement to a place where they did not want to go. Conversely, they would go with unstoppable force where they wished to reside.[4] The story associated with the Compostela shrine credits the bones of St James with such an unstoppable desire to return to the place of his teaching and ministry. The story and claim simply ignored the ways and means of transport of the bones from the Holy Land. A pious monk found the bones buried at the Compostela site sometime between 800 and 850 CE. The appeal of the bones was compelling. They were the only relics of any Apostle located in Europe and therefore accessible without the very long, dangerous pilgrimage to the Holy Land.[5]

The shrine at Compostela in the early centuries was a modest church. Nearby farmers supplied the needs of the clerics and such pilgrims as arrived. Documents of the time do not mention trade or traders, except for stray references to Jewish merchants who may have arrived from Portugal to the south. There is no evidence of coins minted in the region until the middle of the twelfth century.[6]

The reputation and pilgrim traffic of a shrine grew by the efficacy of its relics to perform miracles. People were looking for miraculous assistance in a dangerous, uncertain world. Everyone wanted the most powerful holy intervention possible. Pilgrims saw miracles and returned home to report the evidence: fetters broken, crutches and bandages left behind; barren women becoming pregnant; seemingly incurable illnesses getting cured; deformed limbs becoming functional; and sight being restored. Priests at shrines kept a log of miracles and the dates of occurrence. Written records suggest these stories, often quite similar for various shrines, circulated to illiterate believers in the sermons of priests across much of Europe.

Small local shrines tended to specialize in a limited range of miracles. Some were shrines that healed medical maladies, mental illness, or barrenness. Larger shrines like Compostela were 'broad-spectrum', efficacious for a variety of problems. Relative to a local shrine, the cost of travel to Compostela was high. To make the journey seem worth the cost, miracle stories recounted at Compostela tended towards the awe-inspiring. Not just the curing of illness, but the raising of the dead. Not just making limbs whole, but making them exceptionally strong.

Around 900 CE, Compostela was merely a regional shrine which drew some pilgrims from surrounding Spain and western France. Nobles local to the shrine were the main donors. All this was about to change. As the historian R.A. Fletcher aptly put it: 'In early medieval Europe saints' cults did not simply happen: they were made ... if influential people were persuaded that it was in their interests to show devotion to one, or several, saints' shrines.'[7] The patronage of Alfonso III (ruled 866–910 CE), king of Galicia, made Compostela wealthy and, in turn, the ambitious head priest at the shrine made Compostela known across the wider Christian world. Important ecclesiastical and secular pilgrims began to arrive at Compostela, such as the bishops of Le Puy and Rheims and the counts of Gascony and

Rouergue.[8] Well-placed clerics from distant lands spread the word of the shrine's efficacy and beauty when they returned home.

Rome made every attempt to judge and sanction which relics and miracles were authentic, but local shrines were too profuse for Rome to control. Larger shrines like Compostela, with claims to powerful and important relics, demanded the Pope's attention. The papacy was, however, always divided by factions and sometimes even split into competing Popes. So Rome could not simply dictate which miracles and relics were authentic. Powerful secular and religious allies backed their chosen site and lobbied for approval. Success required considerable money and religious and secular influence. Compostela was able to garner the necessary allies and patrons, and Rome approved the bones of St James and the associated stories of miracles.

After a century of patronage by kings—both in Spain and France— Compostela had grown into a shrine worth sacking and was, indeed, sacked by both Vikings and Muslims. Rebuilt after these attacks, Compostela boasted a much larger church designed by French architects, with new monks' quarters and recognition by Rome as a bishopric.[9] Nobles and kings endowed the shrine with lands located in a broad swathe across western Spain. By the 1120s, monks were fundraising for the new buildings as far away as Italy.[10] The bishop of Compostela engineered the theft of important holy relics from Braga, a large city 75 miles to the south in current-day Portugal. 'Holy theft' was justified by the strength and will of the relics. If the relics allowed the theft, then they were intended to go to a vigorous and developing site, such as Compostela, where more pilgrims would experience their power and acknowledge them. A new town arose around the Compostela cathedral, and contained six churches, two monasteries, several markets, and a number of houses, some with two stories.[11] Foreign merchants arrived with luxurious goods to sell to wealthy pilgrims.

During the twelfth and thirteenth centuries there was a surge in the general popularity of pilgrimage, fuelled by significant changes in Christian practice. From the earliest centuries, it had always been virtuous to be a traveller for Christ. One's life became a permanent, mobile personal ministry. What shifted in the twelfth century was that pilgrimage to a specific site was also viewed as service to Christ. Pilgrimage could also focus and enhance devotion and prayer.[12] At the same time, there was a change in the handling of sin and penance. Traditionally, priests had advised pilgrimage in repentance for sins. Absolution of the sin was granted, if at all, on return from the pilgrimage. In the twelfth century, priests across Europe began to grant absolution *at the time of confession*, thus prior to the actual penance. The sinner was given a written absolution of his sin and was, therefore, assured that his sin would be absolved by the assigned penitential pilgrimage.

This notion of the assured efficacy of pilgrimage developed into the system of indulgences, which gained great popularity. Broadly, there was a belief that the afterlife consisted of three regions: hell, purgatory, and heaven. On death, a person's soul was judged by God, who then consigned them to one of these three locations. People hoped they weren't going to hell, which consisted of eternal torment with no hope of cease. Few could be certain that their actions in life would get them into heaven. Most expected torments in purgatory but with a finite duration based on an assessment of their good and bad deeds. Indulgences guaranteed a shortened period in purgatory through the compassion and intercession of the saint. Pilgrims received such indulgences at the door of the shrine. These indulgences might be for a month or a year less in purgatory or even a decrease by half of the allotted time there.

Throughout the Middle Ages, each pilgrim needed permission to go: monks from their abbot, men from their liege lord, tradesmen from their guild, peasants from their master, nobles from their king, women from their husband or guardian. Society assumed that, in general, all members were better off remaining where they lived. Pilgrimage required a special reason, such as an illness or a vow.[13] In practice, these strictures meant that women could not generally go on long-distance pilgrimages while they had children and household duties. A written permission document usually specified the reason for the pilgrimage and the destination. Pilgrims sought these documents so they would not be mistaken for idle, suspicious, and dangerous vagrants.

The trip to Compostela began with local priests blessing the pilgrims, who wore a distinctive cloak, sandals, and hat, a look found in the sculptures and paintings of the time. They carried a distinctive hanging bag, known as a scrip, and an iron-tipped staff. Perhaps the easiest way to imagine the routes to Compostela is as a tall bush. The base would be Compostela, with the four main branches representing the four main routes to the site. All four connected to smaller branches, the feeder routes, and those to a myriad of twigs. Pilgrims started out from a twig, their hometown, and moved along the larger branches to one of the four trunks. This bush-like structure is common to many pilgrimage routes, whether famous, such as the Hajj, or obscure, such as a regional shrine in India or Italy.

Much is known about the inns, fords, churches, food, and dangers on the pilgrimage route to Compostela, because modern scholars have uncovered a unique sheepskin book titled the *Pilgrim's Guide*—the book mentioned at the start of this chapter. It's almost certain that a Frenchman wrote it. The knowledge of classical and devotional texts suggests a cleric who was wealthy, riding a horse on the pilgrimage rather than walking. Scholars know of a dozen later copies of the *Pilgrim's Guide*, none located outside of Spain.[14]

The *Pilgrim's Guide* provides a rich picture of life on the route to Compostela. The author travelled from Paris to the shrine but reported what he heard about the other routes, good and bad characteristics of peoples along the road, accommodations, dangers, spiritual opportunities, and what to expect at Santiago de Compostela. The *Guide* entirely ignored the important sea routes from England and Ireland directly to Compostela.[15]

Pilgrims on one of the land routes to Compostela began at St Denis (adjacent to Paris) passed Orleans (100 miles southwest of Paris), headed almost straight south to the Spanish border, joined the three more southerly routes near Pamplona, and proceeded west to the shrine. The first notable features of the pilgrimage were spiritual. In St Denis, pilgrims saw an impressive monastic complex, much of it developed only a century before the *Guide*.[16] In Paris, there was much to see, including, by the 1180s, a church and a hospital devoted to St James of Compostela. In Orleans, the *Guide* recommended that the pilgrim worship the True Cross relic, the knife used in the Last Supper, a chalice touched by the hand of God, and the shrine of 'the blessed Martin'.[17] The *Guide* recommended visiting the Church of St Martin at Tours, noting that it is similar in design to the church at Compostela. 'To it the sick come and are cured, the possessed are delivered, the blind are given sight, the lame are raised up, and all kinds of illnesses are cured.'[18]

The area south of Tours was easy travelling.

> ... after Tours, one enters the land of the Poitevins, fertile, excellent, and full
> of all sorts of good things. The Poitevins are valiant heroes and fighting men,
> very experienced in war with bows, arrows, and lances, daring in the front
> line of battle, very fast in running, elegant in their dress, distinguished in
> face, shrewd in speech, very generous in gifts, lavish in hospitality.[19]

At Poitiers, among a variety of convents, monasteries, and churches, pilgrims should not, the *Guide* suggested, miss the holy body of Hilaire, known for suffering during the Arian heresy and for raising a boy from the dead.[20] Of equal spiritual importance was the head of John the Baptist at Angeley, housed in an immense basilica. The miracles the head had performed en route from the Holy Land to France proved its authenticity.

Further south, pilgrims entered Bordeaux, having 'excellent wine and abundant fish but rustic language'.[21] The *Guide* recommended seeking the relics of Bishop Severinus and the horn of Roland. At Pons, there was a hospice, but scholars do not know whether it was only for treatment of locals or also for sick pilgrims. At Blaye was buried the body of Roland.

According to the *Guide*, south of Bordeaux, pilgrims would have a tougher time: 'This is a country devoid of all good things, lacking in bread, wine, meat, fish, water and springs, sparse in towns, flat, sandy but abundant, however, in honey, millet ... and pigs.'[22]

The Gascons, the *Guide* advised, 'talk much trivia, are verbose, mocking, libidinous, drunkards, prodigious eaters, badly dressed in rags and bereft of wealth'. All this was forgiven because they were 'remarkable for their hospitality to the poor'.[23] One important site in Gascony consisted of the tombs of the soldiers of Charlemagne's army who had fallen fighting the Saracens.

In theory, pilgrims travelled with safe passage and hospitality guaranteed by the Pope.[24] The reality was quite different. The long roads to the Holy Land, Rome, and Compostela were so dangerous that those with some wealth routinely made out wills before departing. In a common arrangement, the pilgrim signed over some of his land to a monastery, which loaned him the cash for the trip. If the pilgrim survived, he could reclaim the lands by paying off the loan. For pilgrims, death came from disease, bad water, bad food, or sheer exhaustion. Bandits and pirates knew the pilgrimage routes and the times of year that groups of pilgrims passed. The iron-tipped staves that pilgrims carried often served as weapons to fight off attackers. Along every pilgrimage route, confidence men selling religious relics, fake clerics, cutpurses, and scamps were all too ready to separate pilgrims from their money.

The *Guide* provided a spirited description of the mountains on the border between Spain and France, known as the Port de Cize (Gateway to Spain). 'The ascent is eight miles and the descent is similarly eight. For the height of the mountain is so great that it seems to reach to the sky. To him who ascends it, it seems that he can touch the sky.'[25] On the top of the mountain, a large cross commemorated Charlemagne's construction of the road and his prayer to St James for victory in Spain. The story was pure fiction, even in the twelfth century, but it inspired pilgrims to plant their own crosses. The *Guide* reported over a thousand pilgrim crosses surrounding the cross of Charlemagne. On the descent, pilgrims saw a hospice and a church 'which contains the rock that Roland, that most powerful hero, split through the middle from top to bottom with a triple blow of his sword'.[26] The planting of a cross and the touching of Roland's rock, like visiting shrines along the way, became part of the pilgrim's experience and, therefore, part of the mental map that made the road to Compostela into a route.

The author of the *Guide* disliked the dress, food, customs, sexual habits, and speech of the Navarrese, who lived west of the Gateway to Spain.

> For in fact all those who dwell in the household of a Navarrese, servant as well as master, maid as well as mistress, are accustomed to eat all their food mixed together in one pot, not with spoons but with their own hands, and they drink with one cup. If you saw them eat you would think them dogs or pigs.[27]

The author conceded, however, that the Navarrese were strong warriors, regular in giving tithes, and donating bread, wine, or wheat whenever they came to church.

West along the road to Compostela, pilgrims entered Castille and Compos, lands the *Guide's* author quite liked. 'This country is full of riches, gold and silver, blessed with fodder and very strong horses, well-provided with bread, wine, meat, fish, milk, and honey' but 'full of wicked and vicious people'[28]. There were a few important sites to visit, including a couple of martyr tombs and the body of the 'blessed Domingo', who built part of the pilgrim road. The city of León was dense with churches, monasteries, and hospices for pilgrims at the time, but the *Guide* only suggested worshipping at the 'venerable body of the blessed Isodore, bishop, confessor and doctor'.[29]

Pilgrims then passed over a set of high hills into Galicia. Unlike those in the central plains of Spain, Galician villages were not organized around a central plaza. Rather, they tended to straggle along the road. The way often had confusing twists and dead ends that accommodated farm layouts and land ownership.[30] There were no large towns. The larger farms had slaves, many of them Muslims captured in war who had since converted to Christianity. Owners worked the smaller farms. Above the gentry and free peasant group was a very small aristocracy of perhaps no more than 200 people.[31] The author of the *Guide* found Galicia pleasant travelling.

> This is wooded and has rivers and is well-provided with meadows and excellent orchards, with equally good fruits and very clear springs; there are few cities, towns or cornfields. It is short of wheaten bread and wine, bountiful in rye and cider, well-stocked with cattle and horses, milk and honey, ocean fish both gigantic and small and wealthy in gold, silver, fabrics, and furs of forest animals...[32]

At last the pilgrims arrived at Santiago de Compostela. On horseback, the trip might only have taken three weeks. Walking, it could have taken three months or more. The *Guide* mentioned Compostela's ten churches, but lavished attention on the main basilica, with detailed descriptions of the doorways, naves, fountains, lamps, and shrines.[33]

Let us leave the worn out but triumphant pilgrims and consider what made the roads to the shrine a route. It certainly did not have a uniform surface or dimensions. Some portions had been old Roman roads, but other portions were trade routes or even simple herding tracks. Through the course of the twelfth century, institutional support for the pilgrimage steadily improved. Various religious orders, such as the Dominicans and the Augustinians, built both hospitals and rest houses on the route to Compostela. The *Guide* called down special blessings upon those who built bridges and hospices and generally improved the roads to Compostela. A few of the sturdily built hospices survive today.

Part of what changed the road into a route was the regular flow of information, especially east to France and Italy. Soldiers and clerics carrying communiqués were common on the roads. The queen of the Galician region raced along the pilgrimage route in 1116 CE to put down a rebellion in Compostela.[34] By the 1120s, letters flowed steadily back and forth between the Bishop of Compostela and Rome. The bishop made a tenacious, drawn-out bid for the rank of archbishop, and sought Rome's assistance against Compostela's rival cities. The bishop offered the Pope gold, lots of it, and received recognition of his authority.[35] Virtually every year, papal legates visited the shrine and the Compostela bishop sent representatives to Rome. Regular news of papal politics flowed out to Compostela, just as did news of the first great Lateran Council of 1123 CE. A few years later, there was an ecclesiastical counsel at Compostela that brought representatives from kingdoms in Gaul, Spain, and Rome.

Central to a pilgrim's cognitive geography was the divine protection of St James. By the time the *Guide* was written, a body of miracle stories told of the intervention of the saint to save pilgrims in danger. Typical is the story of a group of knights who were on pilgrimage to Compostela. In southern France, one of the party became ill. The knights carried him for fifteen days, but finally decided to abandon him in the mountains on the Spanish border. One friend could not abide leaving him and stayed with his dying friend in the lonely, cold mountain pass. That night, the ill knight died, and his friend became afraid in that dark and lonely place. St James appeared to him on his horse, in the guise of a fellow knight, and carried the body and the knight through the air directly to Compostela. This miracle and others were recorded in a miracle book at the shrine. More importantly, the stories were told in sermons at Compostela. In the following centuries, these miracle stories of divine protection spread widely, appearing in sermons in France and Italy, but also in the further reaches of Christendom—England, Ireland, Scandinavia, Germany, and Eastern Europe. These stories, of the miracles on the route to Compostela, reinforced the sacred geography on the way to the shrine.

Another piece of the cognitive geography was the relic's efficacy at a distance. St James of Compostela freed prisoners, cured barren women, and restored sight at sites far from the main shrine. By the thirteenth century, this power was embodied in a network of churches dedicated to St James (or St Jacque in French) that reinforced the holiness of the saint and his miracles at a distance. Even in the time of the *Guide* (the mid-twelfth century), there was such a church outside Paris at St Denis. Churches dedicated to St James dotted what are now Germany, Italy, Scandinavia, and Poland.[36] Modern scholars disagree about how connected these churches were to Santiago de Compostela. Many seem to have been locally patronized and rather unconnected to the Compostela shrine. Others, especially in France, were 'extension' churches along the pilgrimage routes and reinforced the sacred geography.[37]

Compostela also exported music along the pilgrimage route. In several manuscripts bound with the *Guide* are notations for music sung at various services at the shrine. Though modern scholars dispute how innovative the forms of melody and harmony in this body of music were, the hymns and songs circulated far beyond Compostela.

One evocative symbol of the pilgrimage to Compostela was a particular kind of scalloped shell from the seashores of western Spain that every pilgrim took back as proof of reaching the shrine. Some wore it on the hat, others sewed it to the cloak. The shells were a sign of the road travelled, the dangers survived, and the blessings received. Hundreds of

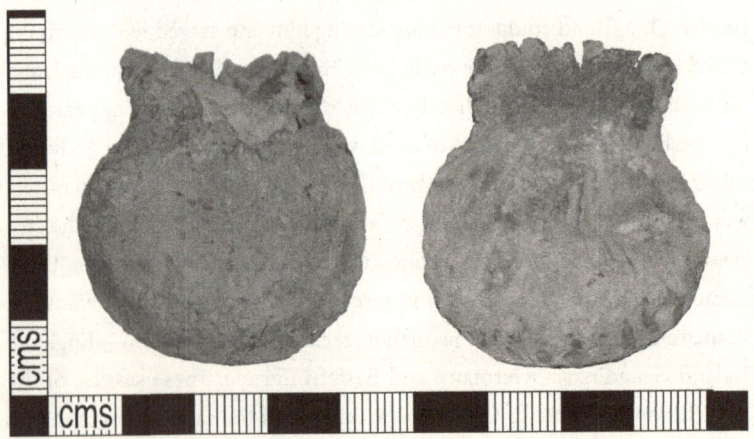

Illustration 11 *Medieval Lead Pilgrim's Medallions in the Shape of a Scallop Shell.* The Portable Antiquities Scheme/The Trustees of the British Museum. Creative Commons. Wikimedia.

such shells have been found in burial sites across Christendom, as far away as Scandinavia and Poland.[38]

In the centuries of the later Middle Ages (1300–1600 CE), a time of poor, dangerous roads and little government protection, Compostela remained the most heavily visited shrine in Europe, except for Rome. The town and its surroundings were especially full during the annual feast of St James in July. Donations flowed in and building continued. Probably the most significant redefinition of St James of Compostela was as a holy soldier, patron saint of the war to reconquer Spain from the Muslims and of the Crusades in general. The *Guide* does not mention St James in this role, so the recasting must have happened after 1130–1170 CE, when the manuscript was written. The revised mental map of the sacred landscape of St James put him on the frontlines as a warrior. The larger-than-life sculpture at Compostela of the saint on horseback lancing surrounding Muslims, his horse crushing Muslims underfoot, is one of the more gruesome images of holy war produced in the period. In this militant aspect, St James became the patron saint of all of Spain, first associated with the Crusades and, in the early sixteenth century, the conquest of the New World.

When the reformation swept Northern Europe in the 1600s, pilgrimage in general declined. Luther, Calvin, and other preachers of a new, more personal relationship with God railed against the Church as intermediary. It was precisely the practices associated with pilgrimage, such as penance and indulgence, which offended them the most. It was precisely the efficacy of relics that they most strongly disputed. For three centuries, from about 1650 CE to 1950 CE, pilgrim traffic to Compostela went into a long and slow decline. Hospices and monasteries closed. Churches along the way found only local support.

Some pilgrims continued to make their way to Compostela, though records at the shrine suggest that by the middle of the twentieth century the numbers were only a few hundred per year. The last three decades, however, have seen a striking increase in interest in the Compostela shrine. The routes to Compostela became the first to receive historical protection by the European Union. Hospices and churches along the way are being preserved. There have been more than a dozen published personal accounts of pilgrimage to Compostela and thousands of academic articles on all aspects of the shrine: art, history, sculpture, language, music, geography, and formation of identity. Today, the shrine is a popular historical tourist attraction. Mixed with the sightseers at the shrine are true pilgrims who have walked or biked hundreds of miles to Compostela and are profoundly moved by their spiritual experience. Pilgrims still receive the coveted scallop shell and a certificate as symbols of their spiritual journey.

Whether medieval or modern, pilgrims knew that they were not simply on a road but on a route to Compostela. They set off with the belief that St James would receive and succour them, whether they suffered physical illness, spiritual fears, or guilt from sins. They heard stories of St James' protection of pilgrims. The way was hard and some took ill and died. This, too, was part of the pilgrimage. Most pilgrims pushed onwards and eventually reached the sacred shrine of Compostela. They walked the streets, worshipped at the shrine, and returned home with a scallop shell as a symbol of their journey—their vows fulfilled, their penance paid. Their shared mental map of the sacred route was central to what they brought back to tell their family and friends.

Notes

1. Annie Shaver-Crandell and Paula Gerson, *The Pilgrim's Guide to Santiago de Compostela: A Gazeteer* (London: Harvey Miller Publishers, 1995), p. 69.

2. Crandell and Gerson, *The Pilgrim's Guide to Santiago de Compostela*, p. 72.

3. Richard A. Fletcher, *Saint James's Catapult: The Life and Times of Diego Gelmírez of Santiago de Compostela* (Oxford; New York: Clarendon Press, 1984), p. 57.

4. It is only in this context that the practice of 'holy theft' makes sense. Priests of one pilgrimage site stole the relics of another site and it was assumed that this practice was only possible if the relics wanted to be moved.

5. Note that claims to powerful bones were also rejected in this period. See the case of the debunked claims of a monk of Limoges in 'The Absence of St Martial of Limoges from the Pilgrim's Guide: A Note Based on Work in Progress', in John Williams and Alison Stones (eds), *The Codex Calixtinus and the Shrine of St James* (Tübingen: Gunter Narr Verlag, 1992), pp. 231–7.

6. Fletcher, *Saint James's Catapult*, p. 12.

7. Fletcher, *Saint James's Catapult*, p. 68.

8. Fletcher, *Saint James's Catapult*, p. 81.

9. The archaeological evidence suggests that the cathedral was completed in two phases: in the mid-1120s and around 1160 CE. See James D'Emilio,

'The Building and the Pilgrims' Guide', in John Williams and Alison Stones (eds), *The Codex Calixtinus and the Shrine of St. James* (Tübingen: Gunter Narr Verlag, 1992), pp. 185–98.

10. Fletcher, *Saint James's Catapult*, p. 171.

11. Fletcher, *Saint James's Catapult*, p. 181.

12. Klaus Herbers, 'Vis Peregrinalis ad Sanctum Jacobum', in the *Santiago de Compostela Pilgrim Routes*, Architectural Heritage Reports and Studies, no. 16 (Strasbourg: Council of Europe, 1989), p. 9.

13. Chaucer's pilgrims set off for Canterbury, as the Prologue tells us, to receive the blessing of the 'holy blessed martyr', whose relics were in the cathedral.

14. Crandell and Gerson, *The Pilgrim's Guide to Santiago de Compostela*, pp. 54–6.

15. *The Pilgrim's Guide to Santiago de Compostela* also ignores the roads that fed the French routes, particularly the Italian 'Via Francigena' and several routes east into what is now Germany. See, for example, Paolo Caucci von Saucken, 'The "Via Francigena" and the Italian routes to Santiago', in *The Santiago de Compostela Pilgrim Routes*, Architectural Heritage Reports and Studies, no. 16 (Strasbourg: Council of Europe, 1989), pp. 60–2.

16. The architectural features of towns along the pilgrim route to Compostela are taken from the relevant entry in Crandell and Gerson, *The Pilgrim's Guide to Santiago de Compostela*.

17. Crandell and Gerson, *The Pilgrim's Guide to Santiago de Compostela*, p. 49.

18. Crandell and Gerson, *The Pilgrim's Guide to Santiago de Compostela*, p. 51.

19. Crandell and Gerson, *The Pilgrim's Guide to Santiago de Compostela*, pp. 68–9.

20. Crandell and Gerson, *The Pilgrim's Guide to Santiago de Compostela*, p. 81.

21. Crandell and Gerson, *The Pilgrim's Guide to Santiago de Compostela*, p. 23.

22. Crandell and Gerson, *The Pilgrim's Guide to Santiago de Compostela*, p. 69.

23. Crandell and Gerson, *The Pilgrim's Guide to Santiago de Compostela*, p. 69.

24. The bishop of Compostela also declared that there should be no interference with pilgrims and traders in his lands. Fletcher, *Saint James's Catapult*, p. 248.

25. Crandell and Gerson, *The Pilgrim's Guide to Santiago de Compostela*, p. 72.

26. Crandell and Gerson, *The Pilgrim's Guide to Santiago de Compostela*, p. 73.

27. Crandell and Gerson, *The Pilgrim's Guide to Santiago de Compostela*, p. 73.

28. Crandell and Gerson, *The Pilgrim's Guide to Santiago de Compostela*, p. 74.

29. Crandell and Gerson, *The Pilgrim's Guide to Santiago de Compostela*, p. 87.

30. Fletcher, *Saint James's Catapult*, p. 9.

31. Fletcher, *Saint James's Catapult*, p. 16.

32. Crandell and Gerson, *The Pilgrim's Guide to Santiago de Compostela*, p. 74.

33. There is a large scholarly body of literature on the architecture of the Compostela site. Still essential reading is Kenneth John Conant, *The Early*

Architectural History of Santiago de Compostela (Cambridge, MA: Harvard University Press, 1926).

34. Fletcher, *Saint James's Catapult*, p. 140.

35. Fletcher, *Saint James's Catapult*, pp. 197–8.

36. Christian Krotzel, 'Pilgrims to Santiago and Their Routes in Scandinavia', in the *Santiago de Compostela Pilgrim Routes*, Architectural Heritage Reports and Studies, no. 16 (Strasbourg: Council of Europe, 1989), pp. 65–6.

37. There is, however, a great deal of scholarly controversy over how connected these smaller churches of St James were to Compostela. Were they a 'network' or merely copycat shrines? Art historians have, by and large, been unable to establish common elements of style or decoration at these churches.

38. Krotzel, 'Pilgrims to Santiago and Their Routes in Scandinavia', p. 66.

The Hajj

In the middle of June 1325 CE, Ibn Battuta set out on the Hajj to Makkah (Mecca). He was twenty-two and came from a family of Islamic judges. Two decades later, he would be the most travelled man of the Middle Ages, but all that was far in an undecided future. More immediate were his feelings on leaving home and family on a dangerous and uncertain pilgrimage. Most pilgrims set off with friends and neighbours, but Ibn Battuta began the trip from his home city of Tangier (at the Straits of Gibraltar) alone.

> I set out alone, having neither fellow-traveller in whose companionship I might find cheer, nor caravan whose party I might join, but swayed by an overmastering impulse within me and a long-cherished [desire] in my bosom to visit these illustrious sanctuaries. So I braced my resolution to quit all my dear ones, female and male, and forsook my home as birds forsake their nests.[1]

Two hundred fifty miles east, at the inland city of Tlemcen, a sympathetic young cleric explained just how dangerous it was to travel further alone. Ibn Battuta was heading into continuous warfare between the sultan of Tunis and various breakaway kingdoms on the North African coast. The young pilgrim joined the party of two judges heading east. Within a few days, he saw first-hand the dangers of the trip. One of the judges contracted a fever, sickened, and died.

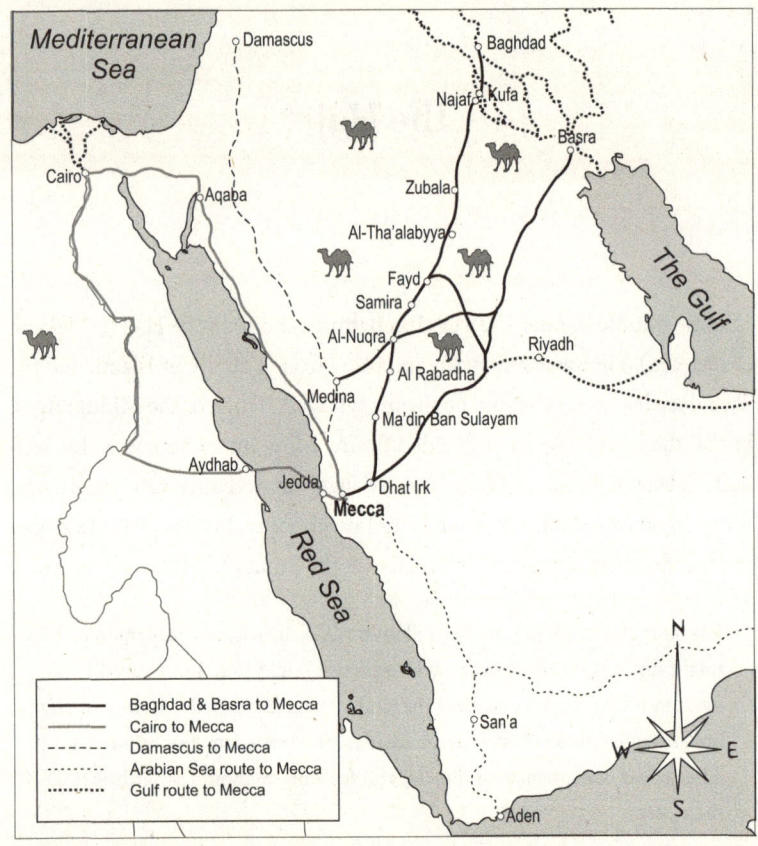

The Hajj

Ibn Battuta next joined a merchant caravan travelling east, and accompanied it more than 350 miles past Algiers along the coast road to Bejaia, in current-day central Algeria. In spite of a bout of fever, Ibn Battuta and the caravan made it to the city of Constantine, about 250 miles east of Algiers. The governor of the town noticed that Ibn Battuta's clothes were muddy and soaked with rain and 'gave orders that they should be washed at this house'.[2] He gave the young pilgrim a cloak to replace his ragged one and tied some silver coins in a corner. The caravan pushed rapidly on through the bandit-infested countryside. Ibn Battuta suffered recurrent bouts of fever and, at one point, tied himself to his saddle with his turban cloth.[3]

Let us leave Ibn Battuta—shivering, feverish, beset by bandits—and turn to the long history of Makkah, his goal. The holy site he sought was a forbidding place, deep in the desert of what is now western Saudi Arabia. When Makkah first became a sacred site is not known, but it was certainly many centuries before Prophet Muhammad and his followers fought for and seized it. The Quran, the word of god, as dictated to the Prophet Muhammad, credits the biblical Abraham with construction of the original enclosure at Makkah. God defined how the enclosure was to be used.

Remember that We made the House [Ka'ba]
A place of assembly for men
And a place of safety;
And take ye the Station
Of Abraham as a place
Of prayer; and We covenanted
With Abraham and Isma'il,
That they should sanctify
My House for those who
Compass it round, or use it.[4]

The Quran also recognized that the shrine had long been a place of pilgrimage and worship of multiple gods: Hubal, Manat, al-Uzza, and al-Lat. The Bedouins came to the area immediately outside Makkah perhaps twice a year to trade under a holy truce. Their rituals included sacrifice of animals, the picking up of stones, and worship at an enclosure in the centre of Makkah.[5]

Muhammad had a long and intimate association with Makkah. He was born in the city in 570 CE. His parents died when he was young, so he lived first with his grandfather, a respected leader of the city, and then moved to the household of an uncle. In his twenties, Muhammad was a caravan trading agent for a wealthy Makkan widow, whom he subsequently married. During these years Makkah was a prosperous trading city.

In 610 CE, at the age of forty, Muhammad undertook a series of long spiritual retreats in a cave near Makkah, and received revelations that led him to reject polytheism for a belief in one god, Allah. He took the message public three years later. The Quraysh, his own dominant kin-based group in Makkah, subjected Muhammad and his followers to a trade embargo and eventually attempted to assassinate him. Muhammad and a few hundred followers left Makkah for the trading city of Medina, 200 miles to the north, where they gradually built up a Muslim community. After three years of war (625–28 CE), power had shifted from Makkah to the Muslims of Medina and, in 630 CE, they entered Makkah without bloodshed.

Following the Muslim takeover of Makkah, Muhammad returned to Medina. He led only one pilgrimage to Makkah, the famous 'Farewell Pilgrimage' of 632 CE. On it, he preached and clarified the stations of the pilgrimage, their meaning, the correct dress of pilgrims, and where it should be donned. At this time, the new Muslim community decided that only those who had committed to Allah as the sole God could make the pilgrimage to Makkah.[6] Muhammad died only a few months after the 'Farewell Pilgrimage', but his close followers, known as the Companions, led several pilgrimages to Makkah in subsequent years.

The caravan road from Medina to Makkah became a holy route of pilgrimage. On the basis of this intimate involvement of the Prophet and his Companions, the pilgrimage to Makkah, known as the Hajj, became a once-in-a-lifetime obligation for every Muslim, but only, as the Quran says, for 'those who can make their way there'.[7] The credibility and efficacy of the pilgrimage were, thus, established from the very earliest years of the religion.

After the death of the Prophet, Makkah saw recurring bouts of warfare as factions fought for religious and political control. The Umayyads, who ruled from Damascus, besieged and conquered Makkah in 692 CE. Few records of the early years of the Hajj remain, but it is known that the holy structure at the heart of Makkah, known as the Ka'ba, was torn down and rebuilt twice as part of the factional fighting.

The Abbasids, who replaced the Umayyads in 749 CE and ruled from Baghdad, patronized the Hajj as part of their claim to legitimate rule. Harun al-Rashid (ruled 764–809 CE) led the Hajj, and his wife, Zubaya, accompanied him. The tenth-century historian Mas'udi quotes an earlier historian on their works:

> [Harun al-Rashid] undertook public works, the construction of wells, cisterns, and forts on the road to Mecca as well as inside that latter city and in Mina, Arafat, and Medina … [Zubaya] had numerous caravanserais built in Mecca and she filled this city and the pilgrim road, which bears her name with cisterns, wells, and buildings that still stand today.[8]

After Harun al-Rashid, it was rare for a Muslim king to undertake the Hajj. It was dangerous for a king to be away from his throne for months or years—because of slow communication, there was every chance of a coup. Instead of going themselves, kings generally sent emissaries with lavish presents that were duly received and noted by the keepers of the Makkah shrine. Kings competed for the largest donations and kept tabs on each other's largesse. Again, this was similar to the pattern at Compostela, which received kingly donations from much of Europe.

In addition to the Hajj, the premier pilgrimage in Islam, a complicated network of regional and local pilgrimage sites developed from about 900 CE to 1100 CE during the decline of the central authority of the Abbasids. These sites were centres of teaching, tombs of saints, or prominent mosques. Regional sites, such as the Shia holy sites of Najaf and Karbala (in present-day Iraq), continued to develop for centuries. As the philosopher and poet Ibn Arabi (1165–1240 CE) put it: 'At all places where the pious perished in this world, and in the places where their influence lingered, subtle hearts are affected.'[9] Just as in the Christian tradition, the spirit of the saint was assumed to be alive and active at the tomb site and quite capable of direct response to the prayers and needs of pilgrims.[10] Many local holy sites were associated with the granting of specific prayers, such as for children or the cure of a disease. As in Europe, the cost of a pilgrimage to a local shrine was low and consequently attracted less affluent believers and women.

Attendance at these local and regional shrines far outnumbered that of the costlier and more difficult pilgrimage to Makkah.[11]

Ibn Battuta still had a long and difficult time before he would reach the holy cities of Makkah and Medina. In the caravan on the North African coast, he was still socially alone and did not have the benefits of the camaraderie of shared food and stories. When he arrived in Tunis, the city folk greeted many of the pilgrims, but not Ibn Battuta.

> On all sides they came forward with greetings to one another, but not a soul said a word of greeting to me, since there was none of them that I knew. I felt so sad at heart on account of my loneliness that I could not restrain the tears that started in my eyes and wept bitterly. But one of the pilgrims, realizing the cause of my distress, came up to me with a greeting and friendly welcome and continued to comfort me with friendly talk until I entered the city...[12]

At Tunis, the pilgrims in Ibn Battuta's caravan ceased their forced marches through bandit country, found many others determined to make the Hajj, and departed in November in a proper caravan with an experienced leader. The reader might recall the overall shape of a pilgrimage route: a bush with many branches connected to a few trunks. Ibn Battuta had moved from a small branch to a much larger branch. Like the pilgrims going to Compostela, those going to Makkah gained strength and resolve as they met fellow companions and travelled in larger groups towards their goal. Since Ibn Battuta found travelling companions, he no longer wrote of bouts of loneliness. He had already been on the road for six months and was less than halfway to Cairo, much less Makkah. Travelling slowly had its compensations. He had time to stop at spiritually important places and meet luminaries. Near the town of Sfax, on the eastern coast of Tunisia, he visited the tomb and shrine of a famous jurist and author of a noted legal commentary.

Travel with the caravan was not, however, all fears and dangers. Ibn Battuta seemed to have a knack for leadership, and 'raised the banner' as leader of a group of pilgrims as the caravan proceeded east on the coast of Libya. He married a daughter of a jurist in the caravan and received her at Tripoli early in 1324 CE. A few towns to the east, however, Ibn Battuta became involved in a 'dispute with my father-in-law, which made it necessary for me to separate from his daughter'.[13] He promptly married the of feasting. This marriage also apparently did not last, as mention of the woman appears nowhere else in his memoirs. In early April, ten months after departing Tangier, the caravan arrived in Egypt.

Ibn Battuta spent a month in the Nile delta, meeting significant scholars, judges, and saints. For him, this was the set of mental expectations—architecture, learned men, and the miracles of saints—that gave his route to Makkah meaning and set it apart from mere caravan travel. Many on the Hajj at this time shared these mental expectations. As Ashraf Jahangir Simnani observed some decades after Ibn Battuta: 'Whenever one comes into a town, the first thing one ought to accomplish is to kiss the feet of the saints who are full of life, and after that, the honor of pilgrimage to the tombs of saints found there.'[14] Ibn Battuta moved in a world that expected miracles, and he experienced them himself. He visited a holy man who knew his dream of the previous night and predicted his journey to India.[15] Besides living saints and holy tombs, Ibn Battuta's mental expectations included significant architecture. At Alexandria, he toured the famous lighthouse.

Cairo astonished our pilgrim. He toured its gardens and tombs, met its learned men, and walked its streets. It was a month or two in Cairo before he settled down to the business of getting to Makkah.

The normal course of the Hajj from Cairo meant the assembling of a large caravan under a commander. Unlike the pilgrimage to Compostela, most pilgrims paid a one-time fee for provisions, accommodation, and travel. Clerics and jurists, however, who sought learning and spiritual development through contact with famous teachers, lived and studied in a network of donation-supported hostels and colleges, called 'madrasas', found in all Muslim cities of the time. The Muslim elite patronized these institutions as acts of piety and, besides teaching Islam, they offered hospitality to mendicant religious seekers. Ibn Battuta quickly added these accommodations to his cognitive geography of each town he visited. Each of perhaps thirty or forty madrasas in Cairo specialized in a particular branch of practice or belief. Ibn Battuta described one that he clearly knew from personal experience:

> The applicant comes to the gate of the convent and takes up his stand there, with his waist girt, a prayer mat on his shoulder, the staff in his right hand and the jug in his left. The gatekeeper informs the steward that he is there.

The steward then comes out to him and asks him from what country he has come, what convents he has stayed in on his way, and who was his shaikh [sheikh, leader]. When he ascertained the truth, he admits him into the convent, spreads his prayer-mat for him in a place befitting his station...[16]

There was also some assistance for the poor who undertook the Hajj. The Sultan of Egypt, for example, furnished 'camels loaded with provisions and water for those without means and the helpless, and for carrying those who cannot keep up with the caravan or are too weak to walk on foot, both on the Egyptian pilgrim-road and from Damascus'.[17]

Ibn Battuta's first attempt to reach Makkah failed. For two weeks he followed the usual trade and pilgrim route up the Nile (which he did on horseback, rather than by boat), then east across a desert and mountains to a port named Aidhab.[18] From there, he intended to sail across the Red Sea to Jeddah and find a caravan to Makkah. At Aidhab, however, Ibn Battuta discovered that warfare between the local tribe that controlled the city and Turkish ship owners had stopped all traffic on the Red Sea.

Conflict between larger empires like Baghdad or Cairo and whatever tribe controlled the Jiddah port was nothing new. When Ibn Jubayr arrived in 1183 CE he thoroughly cursed the same local authority.

> So it was when we arrived at Jiddah and were arrested by Amir Mukthir. That year he had ordered the pilgrims to guarantee each other's payment against the arrival of Saladin's allocation; only then might we enter the Sacred Mosque at Mecca. Should the bribes arrive in time, all would go smoothly; otherwise, he would demand his tax from the pilgrims. So ran his speech, as if God's Sacred City were an heirloom in his hand which he had a lawful right to lease to the hajjis. Glory to God, who has the power to alter laws.[19]

This anger at local obstruction and taxes on a holy route is strikingly similar to that found in the Compostela *Guide*.

Always practical, Ibn Battuta sold his provisions, re-hired the camels that had brought him to the port, and re-traced his route across the mountains and dessert to the Nile. A boat returned him, eight days later, to Cairo.

Battuta realized that he had to move on if he was, in fact, going to join the annual Hajj caravan assembling at Damascus. He set off from Cairo, staying

tions there is a hostelry, which they call a *khan*, where travelers alight with
their beasts, and outside each khan is a public watering-place and a shop
at which the traveler may buy what he requires for himself and his beast.[20]

The way from Cairo to Damascus was not primarily a pilgrimage route,
but rather a trade route with its full complement of government officials
who collected taxes. Military outposts guarded the road. Ibn Battuta, always
the pilgrim and never the merchant, found much to satisfy his spiritual
expectations. He visited important spiritual sites along the way, such as the
tombs of Abraham, Isaac and Jacob, and Joseph and Fatima. He lingered
in Jerusalem, explored the Dome of the Rock and several other mosques,
entered Bethlehem's Church of the Nativity, and listened to sermons from
a famous Sufi shaikh. The attraction of new sights, learned men, and new
cities was just so strong that he made a long loop through Lebanon and
northern Syria before finally returning south to Damascus.[21]

Ibn Battuta wrote in detail about his developing personal network along
the route he charted to Makkah, mainly imams of the mosques and teachers.
In Damascus he attended lectures on the *Sahih* (a book of the sayings of the
Prophet written around 850 CE), and proudly noted that he had been formally licensed to teach the book. Once again, Ibn Battuta was out of money:
'Meanwhile all the money I had for my expenses was exhausted. Nur al-Din
learning this, hired camels for me and gave me traveling provisions, etc.
and money in addition, saying to me, "It will come in useful for anything
of importance that you may be in need of"—may God reward him well!'[22]

Twenty-two days after he arrived, Ibn Battuta left Damascus with
more than a dozen licences to teach from prominent teachers of the city.
He had married for the third time and left behind a pregnant wife. On
1 September 1326, almost two years after Ibn Battuta left Tangier, the vast
Hajj caravan departed Damascus for Makkah. The Hajj traditionally took
placed place from 7 to 13 *Dhu al-Hihjjah*, the last month of the Islamic
calendar. Because the Islamic calendar is lunar, the dates of the Hajj varied
from year to year, precessing through the seasons.

Continuing with the image of a pilgrimage route as a bush joining a few
trunks, Ibn Battuta was now well and truly on a trunk. The entire caravan
had no other purpose than succeeding in the holy pilgrimage to Makkah.

The massed pilgrims reinforced their faith and hopes for the journey. Undoubtedly they traded stories of the trials and difficulties of even getting one of the two main caravans to Makkah.

Ibn Battuta travelled with a 'tribe of Bedouin called al-Ajarma'. Just two days south of Damascus, the caravan, by tradition, stopped for four days to allow stragglers to catch up. The local farmers brought fruit and vegetables to sell to the pilgrims. For the next week the caravan travelled south along the old Roman road that connected Damascus and Cairo.

The caravan halted for four days at a spring near Karnak to fill water containers, passed the last Syrian town, and entered the desert. After three days without finding a source of water, the pilgrims arrived at a spring known as Tabuk. Customary rituals were performed there. Muhammad had taken this spring by force and, as Ibn Battuta described it, Syrian pilgrims 'take their weapons and unsheath their swords, charge upon the camp and strike their palms with their swords, saying, "Thus did the Apostle of God (God bless and give him peace) enter it".[23] Just as on Fa Xien's pilgrimage and the pilgrimage to Compostela, mountains, springs, and other physical features gained shared meaning through the mental expectations of the pilgrims.

Beyond Tabuk, water sources were unreliable and whole caravans had perished on this part of the journey. On the fifth day beyond Tabuk, the caravan reached a well known as al-Hijr, but no one drank. More than seven centuries earlier, Muhammad had commanded his followers not to drink from this well but to push on to a village half a day farther.[24] The mental expectations of the faithful pilgrims trumped their need for water and Ibn Battuta's caravan pushed on to the same village that succoured Muhammad and his followers. The pilgrims stayed for four days, washing their clothes, filling water containers, and selling extra provisions they would not need. This village was 'the limit to which Christian merchants of Syria may come, and beyond which they may not pass.'[25] The next three days they travelled through a 'place of violent heat in which the fatal samoom-wind blows'. The only water available was brackish, drawn from holes dug in seasonal riverbeds. Three weeks from Damascus, the caravan reached the holy city of Medina with its reliable water supply.

In Medina, Ibn Battuta and his travelling companions entered the mosque by the traditional Gate of Peace, prayed in an area known as the Garden, saw the spot from which the Prophet preached, kissed a fragment of a palm trunk associated with him, and prayed for blessings on the Companions, his early and loyal converts traces of whose houses still remained.[26] Outside of town were important tombs of martyrs and saints.

Ibn Battuta struggled to describe his experiences of events that had happened centuries before but were also an immediate, tangible, experiential present. Pilgrimage created a special time, what might be called 'sacral time', which joined the present with a special past. Pilgrims knew that the Prophet and his Companions had walked these streets, prayed in this mosque, and done the same things they were doing. By doing those very activities, they recovered and shared that past within the present.[27] Unlike most time, which moves ever forward, sacral time is circular. Pilgrims recreate this sacred time every year, just as fresh and immediate as the year before—or even when the Prophet himself had been there. This strange 'then and now' time was experienced just as strongly by pilgrims to Compostela and by Fa Xian as he passed through the homeland of the Buddha in North India.

Ibn Battuta stayed only four days in Medina. It was long enough for him to realize just how networked and connected the Muslim world of learned

Illustration 12 *Pilgrims Camping East of Mecca, Near Arafah, 1889.*
Photograph by Abd al-Ghaffār, al-Sayyid, Physician of Mecca. Public Domain.
Courtesy of Library of Congress.

men was. The head of the mosque was from Cairo and the head of judicial administration was from Tunis. Scholars in residence were from Granada, Marrakech, and Fez. Ibn Battuta later met one of his companions from Damascus in Aleppo and then again in Bukhara.[28]

Outside of Medina, Ibn Battuta and his fellow travellers put on the garb of the Hajj. 'Here I divested myself of my tailored clothes, bathed, put on the garment of my consecration, and made a prayer of two bowings.'[29] The term for this sacred moment is *ihram*. Men gave up ordinary clothes for two pieces of unsewn white cloth. One covered him from the waist to the ankles. The second was draped over one shoulder. The head was uncovered. Women put on a simple white dress and covered the head but wore no veil. Men neither shaved nor cut nails until the pilgrimage was over. All pilgrims removed jewellery and vowed to refrain from quarrelling, committing violence to men or animals, and having sexual relations. The ihram ceremony had its suitable accompanying prayer, known as the *talbiyah*.

> Here I am, O God, at Thy command!
> Here I am at Thy command!
> Thou art without associate:
> Here I am at Thy command!
> Thine are praise and grace and dominion!
> Thou art without associate.[30]

On the second day of travel from Medina, the caravan passed Badr, site of an early important victory of Muhammad and his followers over a larger force of polytheists. The past and the present merged in a site called the Hill of Drums, which was reputed to resound with the drumbeats of battle on every Friday. Three more days of traversing the desert and the caravan came to Rabigh, where pilgrims from Egypt put on the garb of the Hajj. Every site and stopping place had significance, for example, the village of Khulais:

> The pilgrims make a point of supplying *sawiq* [a gruel of barley meal with water or butter] and bring it with them from Egypt and Syria for this purpose: ... It is related that when the Apostle of God (God bless him and give him peace) passed through this place his Companions had no food with them, so he taking some of its sand gave it to them, and they supped it and [found it to be] *sawiq*.[31]

On the 34th day of travel, Ibn Battuta's caravan reached Makkah 'with hearts full of gladness at reaching the goals of their hopes'.

The Hajj, beginning with the ihram, was a levelling experience. All Muslims were simply members of the *umma*, the community of Islam, regardless of their economic status. Ethnicity and language were not to matter. Even how far they had travelled to reach Makkah was not to matter. They shared a common purpose, to reach the holiest site in Islam and complete their sacred obligation.

Just as pilgrims arriving at Compostela or Fa Xien arriving at Bodh Gaya, there is no denying that Ibn Battuta's initial response to Makkah was an outpouring of religious fervour, as he experienced the prescribed things to do, see, touch, and experience. The pilgrims went immediately to the sanctuary, passed through the gate of Banu Shaiba, entered the Ka'ba, and kissed the holy stone. They then walked around the Ka'ba the traditional seven times, stopping to pray at the appropriate places. Pilgrims then clung to the cover of the Ka'ba and drank the water of the holy well of Zamzam.[32]

Illustration 13 *Pilgrims Head to the Mount of Mercy, 2009.* Photo by Omar Chatriwala. Creative Commons. Wikimedia.

The same day they performed the ritual 'running' between al-Safa and al-Marwa. Both within Makkah and immediately outside, there were sites to visit—the house of Fatima, the cemetery with tombs going back to the time of Muhammad, the hill where Muhammad alighted after his trip to Heaven, a platform where he rested. On the seventh day at Makkah, the noonday service included instructions for the ceremonies for the ascent to Mina on the eighth day, and the trek to Arafa on the ninth day. At Arafa, the Hill of Mercy, pilgrims prayed in the mosque, listened to a sermon, and waited for the sun to set before 'rushing' to a place known as Muzdalifa. Pilgrims gathered stones during the return to Mina and threw them at the 'Pillar of the Defile' there. They then shaved their heads, slaughtered animals, and returned to Makkah for the Day of Sacrifice, which included the installation of the new cover of the Ka'ba.

For a cleric there were also major professional benefits to going on the Hajj. Performing the pilgrimage enhanced a spiritual leader's credibility. Clerics heard sermons from famous teachers at Makkah, received a certificate of study with the teacher, and could later tell stories of their style and erudition. These certificates were weighty and useful credentials. This teaching, learning, and giving of certificates at Makkah was shared with other prominent Muslim centres, particularly Cairo and Baghdad. Perhaps most important for jurists and clerics were the networks and connections centred in Makkah. A travelling, literate population of clerics and judges called on friendships established in Makkah for introductions to employment in distant places across the far-flung Islamic world.

Ibn Battuta did not, as might be expected, perform the 'Farewell Circuit' at Makkah and return with the Damascus caravan. Instead, he joined the vast Baghdad caravan and so began his extraordinary adventures in Central Asia, India, Africa, and China.

Writing about it many years later in his memoirs, Ibn Battuta was eloquent on the spiritual power of the Hajj:

Of the wondrous doings of God Most High is this, that He has created the hearts of men with an instinctive desire to seek these sublime sanctuaries, and yearning to present themselves at their illustrious sites, and has given the love of them such power over men's hearts that none alights in them but they seize the whole heart ... Intensity of yearning brings them near while yet far off, presents them to the eye while yet unseen, and makes of little account ... the fatigues and the distress he endures ... May God Most High number us amongst those whose visitation is accepted ... and whose burdens of sin are effaced by the acceptance [of the pilgrimage], through His loving kindness and graciousness.[33]

Over the centuries, both before and after Ibn Battuta, what made the Hajj a route rather than merely a set of caravan tracks and sea lanes? The faith of Islam had a clearly stated obligation for each believer to make the pilgrimage once in his or her lifetime. A full set of mental expectations complemented this obligation. Makkah is a special place where prayers are answered and sin washed away. Each daily prayer for Muslims all over the world requires turning in the direction of Makkah. Mosques, of course, are oriented towards Makkah. The mental expectations of the pilgrim were— and are still—based on stories told by those who returned. The Hajj offers the chance to walk where the Prophet and his Companions had walked, touch what they had touched, and personally recreate some of the things they had done. Because pilgrims travelled in groups at the same time of year, special Hajj caravans and ships were filled with pilgrims, who all shared the same purpose. They donned special clothes and took vows to refrain from quarrelling and immoral behaviour. The return of this caravan was a day of special celebration in Cairo, Baghdad, and Damascus. For jurists and clerics, the networks created at Makkah could sustain a lifetime of employment and friendship. For many pilgrims, the sheer number of people sharing a profound religious experience embodied the community of the faithful, beyond language, gender, ethnicity, and factional splits.

It was faith, not government patronage, which sustained the Hajj. By the time of Ibn Jubayr (1183 CE), the rest houses built by Harun al-Rashid three centuries earlier were in ruins. Unlike the decline of Compostela during the Reformation or the virtual ending of Chinese pilgrimage to India around 1100 CE, the Hajj has continued and grown. One sixteenth-century observer estimated 50,000 pilgrims in the Baghdad caravan alone. There are no reliable statistics on the number of pilgrims before the late nineteenth century, but the numbers grew as travel became easier. Steamships plied from India and Alexandria to Jiddah. A railroad replaced the caravan from

Baghdad in 1900. By the 1930s, paved roads from Damascus and Baghdad made the trip a matter of days not weeks.[34]

Today, going on the Hajj requires passports and visas, birth certificates for children, and international vaccination books. As they did in the time of Ibn Battuta, most pilgrims buy an all-inclusive package that includes travel, lodging, food, and a guide to the spiritual and religious activities. About 3 million pilgrims make the Hajj every year. Of the 1.6 billion Muslims worldwide, only about 9 per cent complete the Hajj in their lifetime.[35] The Hajj is, however, among the largest recurring gatherings of humans in the world. It remains a profoundly moving pilgrimage, especially because of the shared experience of this vast body of Muslims, evidence of the umma who encompass believers across language, ethnicity, and origin, and their intense shared experience of a sacred cognitive geography.

Notes

1. Ibn Battuta, *The Travels of Ibn Battuta, A.D. 1325–1354*, translated by H.A.R. Gibb (New Delhi: Hakluyt Society, 1993), I, p. 8.

2. Battuta, *The Travels of Ibn Battuta*, p. 12.

3. The various feeder routes of the Hajj all had their pirates and bandits. There were well-organized bandits along the way, especially along the coast road in Morocco. Further along Ibn Battuta's route were other regions known for piracy, such as the mountains between the Nile and the Red Sea. The long caravan routes from Damascus to Makkah and Baghdad to Makkah were through the lands of desert nomads who often held travellers to ransom. For pilgrim ships coming from India, there was the threat of pirates all along the western coast, from Malabar in the south, north past the Konkan coast, to Gujarat. The island of Socotra, off the tip of the Horn of Africa, was a notorious pirate port. For the few pilgrims who came all the way from Southeast Asia, the pirates along the Malay coast were legend.

4. Al-Baqarah (The Cow): 124. See Abdullah Yusuf Ali, *The Meaning of the Holy Qur'an: New Edition with Revised Translation and Commentary* (Brentwood, Maryland: Amana Corporation, 1992), pp. 52–3.

5. My brief discussion of pre-Islamic and early Islamic Makkah follows F.E. Peters, *The Hajj: The Muslim Pilgrimage to Mecca and the Holy Places* (Princeton: Princeton University Press, 1994), pp. 3–97. See also Marshall G.S. Hodgson, *The Venture of Islam: Consciousness and History in World Civilizations*, vol. 1 (Chicago: University of Chicago Press, 1974).

6. In Islam there were doubts about recent converts. When an upper-class British woman convert wanted go on the Hajj in the 1920s, her right to do so was debated among the highest clerics at Makkah. Finally, it was conceded that she could do the pilgrimage but special arrangements were made for her.

7. See Michael N. Pearson, *Pious Passengers: The Hajj in Earlier Times* (London: Hurst & Co., 1994), pp. 51–8. Pearson makes a speculative attempt to access numbers of pilgrims on the Hajj in earlier periods. Through the eighteenth century, there appear to be somewhat over 100,000 pilgrims, though those numbers declined in the nineteenth century. The more interesting result is that only a few percent of Indian Muslims likely ever made the Hajj.

8. Quoted in Peters, *The Hajj*, p. 69.

9. Quoted in Carl Ernst, *The Shambala Guide to Sufism* (Boston: Shambala, 1997), p. 72.

10. The history of regional sites is quite complicated, especially their relations to kings and political power. See Richard M. Eaton, *Sufis of Bijapur, 1300–1700: Social Roles of Sufis in Medieval India* (Princeton: Princeton University Press, 1978). See also Carl Ernst, *Eternal Garden: Mysticism, History and Politics at a South Asian Sufi Center* (Albany: State University of New York Press, 1992).

11. Only three early Hajj memoirs exist: by Nasir-i Khusraw (1050 CE), Ibn Jubayr (1184 CE), and Ibn Battuta (1326 CE). Ibn Battuta's is the most heartfelt and detailed.

12. Battuta, *The Travels of Ibn Battuta*, I, p. 12.

13. Battuta, *The Travels of Ibn Battuta*, I, p. 18.

14. Quoted in Pearson, *Pious Passengers*, p. 74.

15. Ibn Battuta embodied both *individual* spiritual progress that required the seeking out of teachers, paths, and experiences, and also *group* practices, such as regular mosque-based prayer, taxation for the poor within the community, and rules as interpreted by Muslim jurists. The connection between travel and the search for knowledge is made explicit in a recent set of scholarly essays. See Ian Richard Netton, *Seek Knowledge: Thought and Travel in the House of Islam* (Richmond, Surrey: Curzon Press, 1996).

16. Battuta, *The Travels of Ibn Battuta*, I, p. 45.

17. Battuta, *The Travels of Ibn Battuta*, I, p. 53.

18. Even this early in Ibn Battuta's narrative, he relies on a standard schema for reporting about towns, which includes prominent architecture, especially mosques and madrasas, products, names and character of the chief administrators and learned men, and any local Muslim holy men, past or present.

19. Quoted in Michael Wolfe, *One Thousand Roads to Mecca: Ten Centuries of Travelers Writing About the Muslim Pilgrimage* (Grove Press: New York, 1997), p. 40.

20. Battuta, *The Travels of Ibn Battuta*, I, pp. 71–2.

21. Ibn Battuta wrote in great detail of the Damascus that was important to him—a long description of the main mosque, the names of the prominent judges, stories of clerics, past and present, and a good admixture of local gossip.

22. Battuta, *The Travels of Ibn Battuta*, I, p. 151.

23. Battuta, *The Travels of Ibn Battuta*, I, p. 161.

24. Battuta, *The Travels of Ibn Battuta*, I, p. 162.

25. Battuta, *The Travels of Ibn Battuta*, I, p. 163.

26. Battuta, *The Travels of Ibn Battuta*, I, p. 165.

27. For Sufis, the spiritual, metaphysical journey is generally more central than a physical pilgrimage. Progress on a spiritual path meant journeys to other realms. See Arthur F. Buehler, *Sufi Heirs of the Prophet: The Indian Naqshbandiyya and the Rise of the Mediating Sufi Shaykh* (Columbia, South Carolina: University of South Carolina Press, 1998), pp. 98–131.

28. Battuta, *The Travels of Ibn Battuta*, I, p. 182.

29. Battuta, *The Travels of Ibn Battuta*, I, p. 184.

30. Quoted in Ahmad Kamal, *The Sacred Journey, Being Pilgrimage to Makkah* (New York: Duell, Sloan and Pearce, 1961), p. 35.

31. Battuta, *The Travels of Ibn Battuta*, I, p. 186.

32. Readers unfamiliar with the central activities of the Hajj are referred to the following basic article: *Aramco World*, The Hajj: An Introduction (November/December 1974), www.saudiaramcoworld.com/issue/197406/the.hajj-an.introduction.htm. The Ka'ba is discussed in Paul Lund, 'The Ka'bah—House of God', *Aramco World* (November/December 1974), www.saudiaramcoworld.com/issue/197406/the.ka.bah.house.of.god.htm

33. Battuta, *The Travels of Ibn Battuta*, I, pp. 189–90.

34. It appears that there was less discrimination against Shias on the Hajj in the nineteenth century than there had been earlier. See *A Shi'ite Pilgrimage to Mecca, 1885–1886: The Safarnâmeh of Mirzâ Moḥammad Ḥosayn Farâhânî*, edited, translated, and annotated by Hafez F. Farmayan and Elton L. Daniel (Austin: University of Texas Press, 1990).

35. The figure of only 9 per cent of all Muslims going on the Hajj is from a 2013 Pew Research survey of Muslims worldwide. The results are available online at http://www.pewresearch.org/fact-tank/2013/10/11/5-facts-about-the-hajj/ Pilgrimage to local and regional shrines continues to be a strong movement in all Muslim countries, except in Arabia and Turkey where most of these shrines have been destroyed. The debate over the efficacy of pilgrimage to

tombs, especially tombs of Sufi saints, is at present particularly intense and contentious. See Carl Ernst, *The Shambhala Guide to* Sufism (Boston, Mass.: Shambhala, 1997), p. 54. Nevertheless, communication by the internet allows followers of a single teacher or a set of Sufi practices to easily communicate and support each other. Some Sufi institutions are now worldwide, with groups and institutions in dozens of cities. See Pnina Werbner, *Pilgrims of Love: The Anthropology of a Global Sufi Cult* (Bloomington: Indiana University Press, 2003), pp. 101–20.

PART III

TRIBUTE ROUTES

Introduction

Tribute routes served imperial needs. When the population of the capital had outgrown the food supply of its surrounding region, the empire needed a secure means to transport grain and other commodities from surplus areas to the capital, which otherwise faced periodic famine. These routes, therefore, had to be the most direct, most reliable, most predictable way to get the necessary commodities to the capital. All other uses of the route were, while important, secondary.[1]

The institutions of empire rather than trade or ecology determined these routes. Government impetus built the roads, whether the labour was slaves, impressed peasants, or the military. For this reason, the route usually had a distinctive look, mile markers, commemorative inscriptions, typical dimensions, construction techniques, or materials. The necessity of delivering the goods to the capital meant that these routes were rarely a single road or sea lane. They were, instead, a constellation of alternate routes to the capital, depending on the time of year and the state of security between the sources of commodities and the capital. Empires varied in how much they controlled the infrastructure of tribute routes, from total end-to-end bureaucratic control to limiting it to the origin and the destination. If a route was perceived by the empire as the only route between the production area and the capital, such as the Grand Canal of China, the empire went to extraordinary lengths to secure and control all aspects of it, even to the extent of building and staffing the boats that carried the grain.

Tribute routes generally had a name, fame, and a shared cognitive geography within the empire's military and civilian administration. They loomed large in written imperial history. They also figured in poems, stories, and artwork. As the most direct way to the capital, these routes were also sites of major battles for control of the empire. Entourages with tribute and defeated kings travelled on them. They were often central to the self-image of the empire. If a dynasty was to ensure peace, order, and some measure of prosperity, the successful moving and storage of food and other commodities was surely an important part of its duties. Successful control of tribute routes reinforced an empire's aura of power.

These critical tribute routes had way stations that served government travellers with fresh mounts, food, and a place to sleep. Only a person with an official pass or symbol of rank gained access to this system. Often, part of the burden of local taxes was to supply horses, pack animals, and food to these way stations. Tribute routes also carried, by a government system of runners or riders, taxes, imperial mail, and reports from and orders to outlying areas. Pirates and bandits were especially aware of the value and pattern of shipments along tribute routes. They came from mountains or isolated coves to plunder what they could. Fear of bandits and pirates often drove imperial policy. Empires built, maintained, and staffed garrisons along land-based tribute routes. The garrisons were often of a standard design and were not just military outposts, but outposts of imperial culture, including cuisine, fashion, language, and literature. On water-based tribute routes the government often organized large fleets and provided soldiers or warships to protect them.

The relation of tribute routes to private trade was complicated. There was no question that the necessary government food and commodity shipments took precedence, whether by land or sea. A few empires, such as the Inka, simply banned private trade. In most empires, however, private trade had important functions. It brought the fabrics, oils, spices, artist's colours, medicines, books, metals, animals, and high-end craft materials essential to the elite imperial lifestyle. Traders also brought news and gossip from faraway places. Private traders paid the tolls that helped maintain the route. The demand by the elite for luxury goods always far outstripped

The empire, therefore, had a serious balance of payments problem and generally shipped gold and silver coinage back along the tribute route to pay for its imports. This long-term balance-of-payments situation created a widespread zone where imperial currency was accepted.

Empires were never able to fully control the intangibles that moved along tribute routes. Perhaps the most well-known example is the movement of Christianity along the Roman tribute routes. Other examples include the spread of the Quechua language along the Inca routes and the movement of imperial culture from north China along the Grand Canal to South China.

The long-term history of a tribute route was intimately tied to the rise and fall of the empire it served. Just as the empires that built them, tribute routes, too, fell into decline. Who would maintain the roads, the way stations, the garrisons, or the postal system when the empire was bankrupt and failing? Who would bring luxury goods to a capital if no one could afford them? With the fall of an empire, a tribute route became an expensive and sophisticated luxury, and led to a place that no one wanted to go anymore.

While they still functioned as thriving tribute routes, let us travel along first with Horace the Roman satirist on one of Rome's most important roads; next, a destitute Korean official on the Grand Canal of China; and, finally, a Spanish scribe on the Inka route.

Note

1. Readers will note that the Nile could have been considered here with other tribute routes rather than in the section on river routes. I chose to discuss it with the Mississippi and the Rhine because of the common patterns imposed by the ecology of rivers. The Nile is clearly a case, as suggested in the introduction, of the different aspects of a route assuming prominence, depending on one's point of view.

The Appian Way

By the age of 30, the Roman poet Horace had had enough good and bad experiences on the Appian Way to the eastern Mediterranean to last him a lifetime. Born in the capital in 65 BCE to a freed slave turned auction broker, Horace was nineteen years old when he was sent to Athens to study philosophy, a typical education for sons of wealthy parents.

A few years later, he wrote an entertaining satire of his travels south from Rome on the Appian Way, the first leg of any journey to the east. Many of the inns he stayed in were rough:

> Mosquitoes keep away sleep, while the boatman, drowned
> In sour wine, sings of the girl left behind and a traveler
> Joins in. At last the traveler tires and falls asleep,
> And the lazy boatman turns out his mule to feed,
> Ties the rope to a stone, and snores away on his back.[1]

Classical literature confirms Horace's estimate of most Appian inns—dirty and noisy, bad food, the haunts of robbers and thieves. Prostitutes were readily available.

Horace's all too human experience is useful. It is easy to be overawed by the Appian Way, the most famous road in the classical world. Legions marched back and forth along it. A young Julius Caesar was its chief administrator. Mark Anthony set off to meet Cleopatra on it. Along it,

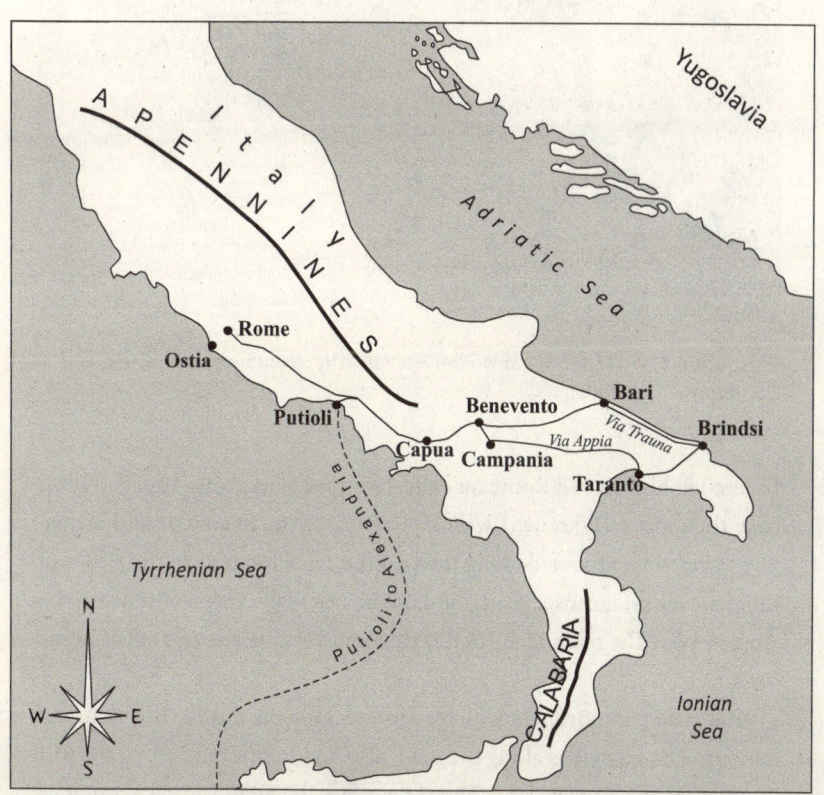

The Appian Way

Illustration 14 *Wheel Marks on the Appian Way.* Courtesy 'MM'. Creative Commons. Wikimedia.

Cicero left his beloved Rome for exile. Jews and Christians (Paul and Peter only the most well-known) walked it as prisoners. Spartacus and his fellow slaves were crucified along it when the rebellion failed. The riches of the east—silks, incense, pearls, and medicines—all came to Rome via the Appian Way. The rise and fall of this route mirrors the rise and fall of Rome itself.[2]

The road's importance was recognized even in death. The rich and famous, who had villas along the road, also had tombs built along the first 20 miles of the Appian Way. They knew that the architectural features of their tombs would be noticed by thousands of travellers. Hopefully some would read the eulogy carved on the tomb and remember its occupant. The oldest of these tombs had a simple message:

> I thank you for having stopped by my resting place: may thy business prosper, keep well, sleep peacefully.[3]

The earliest section of the Appian Way was built almost three centuries before Horace, at a time when Rome was simply a settlement of various tribes of farmers and herding folk fighting off invasions by similar tribes to the north. Rome's main enemy, however, was the Samnite kingdom to the south, which extended across the peninsula from the Adriatic to the Tyrrhenian Sea. It was by far the largest political entity in the region.

The Appian Way was a strategic by-product of a series of wars between Rome and the Samnites. The early battles had not gone well for Rome; they were defeated in 321 BCE. Appius Claudius, one of Rome's most powerful officials, decided that the city's future lay in the south. To defeat or at least neutralize the Samnites, Rome needed a good road to their country. Appius Claudius oversaw the expansion and upgrading of an existing track that connected Rome and Capua, 90 miles to the southeast. The road, like all later Roman military roads, was first and foremost to be straight wherever possible for ease of troop movement. Appius Claudius also specified the width, contour, radius of curves, depth of roadbed and stone for the base and type of blocks for the surface.[4] The road, higher in the centre for drainage, had regular mile markers and reached Capua in 310 BCE.

The Appian Way allowed swift movement of Roman troops into the lands of the Samnites. It and all other main Roman roads were termed *viae militariae* (military roads), as opposed to *viae vicinales* (byroads) or *viae agripae* (country roads).[5] If one traces the pattern of major Roman roads, they did not connect provincial capitals to each other, but relentlessly left from and returned to Rome.[6]

Part of the mental expectations for travellers on the Appian Way was the hope of acquiring the blessing of the God of Return for the journey. For instance, south of Rome, in the valley of Caffarella along the Appian Way, lie the remains of the Temple of the God of Return, where travellers stopped and prayed for a safe onward and return journey.[7]

What sort of people might Horace have met on the road from Rome? His journey seems to have been in warm weather, the time of year that the upper class moved from Rome to their villas, many of them built along the Appian Way. Horace surely would have made fun of the elaborate processions of the rich, with slaves and pack animals laden with fine banqueting equipment and household furnishings. Rome was considered a death trap in the summer months, and everyone who could afford to, left the city at this time.

At other times of the year, before and after big gladiatorial games or a major religious festival, tens of thousands of spectators crowded the Appian Way and overflowed the inns. Any Roman, such as Horace, would have known this yearly flux as part of his or her mental map of the route and probably heard stories of the accompanying riff-raff, such as pickpockets, medicine sellers, street entertainers, prostitutes, hucksters, and soothsayers.

Horace's description of boarding boats about 30 miles south of Rome is completely accurate. The Appian Way crossed a coastal bog known as the Pontine Marshes. Several attempts to drain the marshes had failed. The road, built on log pilings, was rough. Passengers and light freight generally boarded boats for a much smoother transit on a canal that paralleled the road.

A few days after his miserable inn experience, but still north of Capua and on the original Appian Way, Horace joined Maecenas, a close friend of the adopted son of Julius Caesar. Horace was well aware of the difference between the son of a freedman and a highborn noble. He respected Maecenas for bridging that gap with friendship.

> Denounced by everyone as 'the son of a freedman'
> … I didn't claim to be born of a famous father,
> Or rode a horse round a Tarentine estate,
> I said what I was … you recalled me, asking
> Me to be one of your friends. And I think it's fine
> To have pleased you, who separate true from false,
> Not by a man's father but by his pure life and heart.[8]

Maecenas' entourage travelled on what Horace termed a 'mission of state, men deft at settling the quarrels of sensitive allies'. They would have carried sealed and dated passes, entitling them to the use of government-staffed stations where they received food, fresh horses, and the services of blacksmiths and cartwrights. Overnight accommodations for those holding a pass were spaced every 18 to 30 miles, depending on the terrain.

Local towns and villages were required to provide a specified number of horses and pack animals at the changing stations for couriers (military or civilian), officials, embassies, and anyone carrying a government pass (*diplomata*). In similar fashion, Rome required certain farmers to provide food and hospitality for official travellers. The central Roman government paid for these animals and services.

Farmhouse accommodation for official travellers (*mansio*) was far better than the grubby inns. Travelling with Maecenas showed Horace the difference.

> A small villa by the Campanian Bridge offered us
> Shelter, and the officers, as required, salt and fuel.
> Then to Capua, where the mules shed their loads early.[9]

A few wealthy travellers, such as Cicero, avoided the inns altogether by building their own villas along the road. Others, such as Seneca, chose to travel light, pitching tents at the end of a day's travel.

At Capua the road split. The Appian Way turned east and south across the mountains to the Adriatic Sea. The short but equally important Via Campania went west to the port of Puteoli (known today as Pozzuoli), near modern-day Naples. It is to be emphasized that the Appian Way, the Via Campania, the port of Puteoli, and the connecting sea lanes to the eastern Mediterranean were all part of one complex tribute route that brought to Rome both grain from producing regions in the eastern Mediterranean and luxury commodities from even farther east. We will first follow Horace on the Appian Way to consider the land route to the east and then consider its maritime complement, the sea lanes from Puteoli.

At Beneventum, 35 miles east of Capua, in the hills, Horace separated from Maecenas' official entourage. He had to stay at public inns again. Here, the innkeeper nearly burned his establishment down.

> On, straight, to Beneventum: where our busy host
> Nearly burned the inn turning lean thrushes over the fire:
> As Vulcan's fumes dispersed through the ancient kitchen,
> Darting flames licked right up to the roof overhead.
> You saw scared servants and famished guests snatch food
> And everyone tried to extinguish the roaring blaze.[10]

From early in the Appian Way's history, the hills south of Beneventum had been a bandit hideout. Rome, therefore, had a strong garrison. Civil authority declined after the assassination of Julius Caesar (44 BCE), and banditry sharply increased. It was up to Augustus—who ruled from 43 BCE as part of the Second Triumvirate and, alone, from 31 BCE to 14 CE—to build and staff watchtowers and guardhouses along much of the Appian Way.[11] Even as late as 200 CE, there were well-organized bandit groups along the road. One bandit, known as Felix Bulla, had a band of 600 men, many of them slaves who had escaped from imperial servitude.

> [Felix Bulla] received intelligence of everyone who was traveling out of Rome, and everyone who disembarked at Brundisium; he knew who they were and how many were of the party and what and how much they had in their possession. Most people he would set free immediately, once he had taken a share of what they had; craftsmen, though, he detained for a while, and after he had employed them in work for him, he gave them something extra and let them go.[12]

The band survived for about two years before being hunted down by imperial troops.

Beneventum had the characteristic architectural features of Roman cities of Horace's time, an acropolis (a sacred precinct on top of a hill with a temple), public baths, and paved streets in a grid pattern. The city walls had gates in the four cardinal directions. Arched stone bridges crossed the river. An open 'theatre' (amphitheatre) and an open forum surrounded by columns were typical.

This common pattern made Beneventum familiar to travellers, part of their mental map, even if they had never visited the city before. As Roman power expanded in the first two centuries CE, these common features were built into every new colony and every development of an existing city. Archaeologists have found them from Spain to Turkey and from Britain to North Africa.[13] Expectations of these features and amenities of Roman cities formed a central part of the cognitive geography of travellers on the tribute route to the east.

All along the Appian Way, Horace would have found the non-official travellers, both on the road and in the inns. Poets and philosophers travelled in search of patronage. Mention of the road occasionally appeared in their poetry. Ovid, for example, when exiled by Augustus in 9 CE, compared his feelings to the use of the Appian Way.

> The plough is not more worn by constant use, nor the Via Appia ground by the curved wheels, than is my soul darkened by a series of misfortunes.[14]

Along it, itinerant craftsmen and tradesmen sought work. Farmers brought produce to market and petty traders travelled to weekly fairs. Pilgrims and those seeking cures for diseases also trod the Appian Way. Occasionally, emissaries and entourages from distant lands brought letters and presents to officials in Rome. Some men, such as Tacitus and Strabo, travelled simply to experience and write about the important places of the empire. Long distance traders carried silks, medicines, and gems from the East, about whom Horace commented.

> Too meager a fortune, some shameful lost election:
> Eager for trade you dash off to farthest India,
> Avoiding poverty with seas, shoals and flames.[15]

Most travelled by four-wheeled coach or wagon. The rich were carried in covered litters borne by slaves; the poor walked.

On the sixth day of his travels, Horace left the Appian Way, proceeded down the eastern side of the Napolitano hills, and eventually reached the Adriatic coast. There he followed an existing road south to the port of Brundisium (modern-day Brindisi). The emperor Trajan, a few decades later, improved this coastal road as an alternate road to the Appian Way. It is important to recall that no single road, not even one as famous as the Appian Way, was by itself a tribute route. Tribute routes carried such important food, information, and commodities that they were rarely confined to a single way, track, or road. The best road might depend on the time of year, for example, a road higher up on hillsides in the spring to avoid soggy river valleys. Some travellers might require speedier but steeper passes, but while others might need more gentle inclines for heavier loads. One road might be safer than another because of local conflict. Roads and towns, therefore, competed for traders and traffic.[16] Thirteen days after he left Rome, Horace arrived at the port of Brundisium on the heel of the 'boot' of Italy.

Even though he ended his satire at Brundisium, Horace, like other travellers to the east, boarded a ship for the approximately hundred-mile crossing of the Adriatic to Dyrrachium (modern Durres or Durazzo). The ships needed a sirocco or a southwest wind to make the passage. Later in the fall and all through the winter, ships might wait for weeks for a suitable wind for the passage.

Illustration 15   *The Egnatian Way*. Courtesy Marcus Cyron. Creative
Commons. Wikimedia.

The land-based tribute route to the east continued across the
Peloponnesian Peninsula. After Rome conquered and decided to administer Macedonia directly (146 BCE), there was a need for a road to move
troops in the restive region.[17] Roman teams surveyed three possible
routes across the Balkan Peninsula (present day Albania and Greece) to
Thessalonica and on to Byzantium.

Convicts, slaves, and the military built the 650 miles of roadway known
as the Egnatian Way sometime between 140 and 120 BCE. By any standard,
the road was an enormous effort. Workers first dug until they reached bed-
rock or clay. Next, a bed of sand 12–18 inches thick was laid down, followed
by large flat rocks held together by hard cement. A layer of coarse gravel
followed a thin layer of small pebbles. The top surface was large blocks, one
to three feet thick. For water runoff, the road was almost a foot higher in
the centre and varied from more than 12-feet wide in valleys to less than
six-feet wide in mountain passes. Most sections had a kerb at the edges of
the road and rocks piled beyond it.[18]

The Egnatian Way served multiple functions, but like the Appian
Way, its most important functions were as a direct imperial route to the

To thwart uprisings and hold Macedonia, three major garrisons were built along the road to reinforce numerous guardhouses. Besides a troop presence, Rome planted several colonies in Macedonia, the largest at Thessalonica. When an area along the Egnatian Way became safe, the government encouraged wealthy Roman families to establish villas and large farms.

Several important roads went north and south off the main Egnatian Way. These feeder routes were also crucial to holding and pacifying the region. For more than a century, Roman troops fought numerous invading tribes from Thrace, a frontier area north and east of Macedonia. On the whole, Roman campaigns succeeded in establishing a defensible northern boundary of Greece.

The army and the bureaucracy dominated the road. The most important thing moved was the tribute from the eastern Roman provinces, followed closely in importance by information and intelligence from there. Traders and travellers were required to give right of way to the military or entourages of government officials. Way stations, typically about five in a day's journey of 30–40 miles, served couriers and other officials with supplies and food. At the end of each day's stage, there were overnight accommodations. Major roads across the empire had a common institutional organization and the results of this standardization and organization were impressive. Couriers routinely delivered official letters between Rome and Byzantium, a distance of about a thousand miles, in less than a month, considerably less if the matter was urgent. It is not difficult to imagine the cognitive mapping of a high Roman official waiting for news from the Eastern provinces. He had likely travelled the Egnatian Way, and certainly the Appian Way, and could imagine the scroll moving from one imperial outpost to the next by swift courier.

In 45 BCE, Horace arrived in Athens to study philosophy, mathematics, and rhetoric. Only a year later he was swept into the maelstrom of imperial politics. Civil war followed the assassination of Julius Caesar. Brutus and Cassius, the assassins, fled east along the Appian and the Egnatian ways, and assembled an army. Mark Anthony and Octavian, loyal to the memory of Caesar, crushed opposition in the Senate and brought legions to Rome from outlying garrisons. Brutus actively recruited Roman youth studying in Athens, including Horace, who became a high-ranking field officer on Brutus's staff.

Mark Anthony, Octavian, and their forces sailed east across the Adriatic to the western end of the Egnatian Way. A scouting force marched east along the road and found the legions of Brutus and Cassius massed near Phillipi, about 200 miles east of Thessalonica. In two battles in October 43 BCE, the legions of Mark Anthony and Octavian defeated those of Cassius and Brutus, both of whom committed suicide.

Horace was, of course, on the losing side, and the government of Mark Anthony and Octavian seized his family lands. Horace's father died in these years, which were financially and emotionally difficult ones. His writings are silent on how he returned to Rome, though he was granted a pardon and regained some measure of favour. By the age of twenty-five or twenty-six, Horace used what family money remained to purchase a decently paid bureaucratic post in the treasury department, which would provide a basic income for the rest of his life. Two decades later Horace summarized this time in a letter to a friend.

> I happened to be raised in Rome, and to be taught
> How much the anger of Achilles harmed the Greeks.
> A little more learning was added by kindly Athens,
> And so I was keen to distinguish crooked from straight,
> And to search for truth in the groves of Academe.
> But turbulent times snatched me from that sweet spot,
> The tide of civil war swept me a novice into that army
> That proved no match for Augustus Caesar's strong grip.
> As soon as Philippi brought about my discharge,
> Wings clipped, humbled, stripped of my father's estate
> And farm, the courage of poverty drove me to making Verse:[19]

This is undoubtedly the reason that Horace was so appreciative of the friendship and patronage of Maecenas, highly placed and on the winning side, the powerful patrician whom he met through Virgil the poet in about 38 BCE.

Leaving Horace at Rome with his new circle of literary friends and the patronage of Maecenas, we have another journey to take. The road, known as the Via Campania, the reader might recall, split off from the oldest section of the Appian Way and led southwest about 20 miles to the of Italy.

Ostia, 150 miles further up the coast, should have been the natural port for Rome. It was at the mouth of the Tiber River, which led directly inland to Rome. Nevertheless, Ostia regularly silted up and provided little protection from storms. Later Roman emperors dug inner harbours to solve these problems, but ships were destroyed by storms even in the inner harbours. The solution to Ostia's problems was to dock the large long-distance ships at Puteoli and transfer cargo to small coasting ships. Such vessels could make it over the sandbars into Ostia and, hopefully, dodge the Mediterranean storms.

Puteoli in the fall would have been quiet. Just as there were better and worse seasons to travel on the Appian Way and the Egnatian Way, there were bad times to attempt a sea voyage on the Mediterranean. From the end of October until April, storms were fierce and came up quickly. The winter storms formed part of a widely shared mental map of the Mediterranean, and no one described these conditions better than the Apostle Paul, a prisoner on his way to Rome in the winter of 63 CE.

> Before very long, a wind of hurricane force, called the 'northeaster,' swept down from the island. The ship was caught by the storm and could not head into the wind; so we gave way to it and were driven along. ... Fearing that they would run aground on the sandbars of Syrtis, they lowered the sea anchor and let the ship be driven along. We took such a violent battering from the storm that the next day they began to throw the cargo overboard. On the third day, they threw the ship's tackle overboard with their own hands. When neither sun nor stars appeared for many days and the storm continued raging, we finally gave up all hope of being saved.[20]

In May and June, however, thousands of ships crowded the port of Puteoli, all carrying wheat. The largest were broad-beam vessels built especially for this trade with a 1,000-tonne capacity. Most ships were smaller, in the 300–400 tonne range, supplemented by many even smaller ships. Their crews and captains were drawn from many peoples of the eastern Mediterranean, such as Greeks, Egyptians, Jews, Syrians, some from as far away as the Black Sea.[21] Rome, with a population of perhaps a million in the first two centuries CE, could never feed itself from the surrounding country-side. The ships at Puteoli carried the wheat that fed Rome through the year.

At the time, only North Africa and the Nile valley were fertile and well-watered enough to produce a large grain surplus. The wheat production of the Nile had been the basis for Egyptian wealth and its dynasties for millennia. Everyone in Rome—those who could afford to buy it and the people on government dole—depended on the import of wheat from Africa. Wax scrolls preserved in the volcanic ash of Pompeii bear on the grain shipments from Egypt to Rome. The market for grain in Rome was so consistent that traders could borrow money, use it to buy and ship it from Egypt to Rome, sell it, pay off the loan and still make money.

Modern scholars have estimated that Egypt and other North African kingdoms returned more than ten grains of wheat for every grain planted. Other areas of the empire, such as Gaul and Greece, produced less than eight grains per planted grain. One writer of the time suggested that about two-thirds of Rome's grain came from North Africa (around Carthage) and the rest came from Egypt. Modern scholars have argued about the total tonnage, but 150,000–250,000 tonnes every year seems a reasonable guess.[22]

Eighteen centuries before railroads and steam power, large quantities of bulk goods like wheat could only move by water. Pack animals and caravans were prohibitively expensive. The frequency of bandits made Romans consider sea travel far less dangerous than caravan. The safety of sea travel versus road travel is a discussion that has taken place within and across countless cultures down through human history. The stories of ships lost at sea and brigand attacks on the roads were woven into oral traditions known by stay-at-homes and travellers alike. They formed part of the ethos of every route.

The sea lanes from Egypt to Puteoli formed an archetypical tribute route. For Rome, interruption of the wheat supply had particularly dire conse-quences. Rome either did not know about or did not develop any of the other available food grains, such as millet, rye, barley, rice, or sorghum. To make matters worse, the Senate had agreed to supply wheat as a daily dole to perhaps 200,000 poor Romans. The mental expectation of those affected by the success or failure of the grain shipments formed an important part of the tribute route to the east. Rumours of the interruption of the wheat dole brought panic and demonstrations in the streets. Actual interruption could mean an emperor lost his power—sometimes, even his life.[23]

Given the importance of wheat shipments, modern scholars have long debated the degree of government control exerted by Rome. A century ago most scholars believed that a strong state bureaucracy controlled grain shipments from their source to distribution in Rome. Recent research, however, rejects this viewpoint. There were, indeed, officials responsible for receiving wheat along the Nile in Egypt, other officials who oversaw its quantity and quality in warehouses in Alexandria, and an official broadly responsible for its distribution in Rome. The Roman government, however, neither financed nor built ships. It had no large state-run warehouses in Rome from which grain could be released. When grain shipments were interrupted, the emperor had limited policy options. He offered subsidies to ship owners to sail later into the winter season or sent groups away from Rome so that there were fewer mouths to feed. Emperors encouraged two grain fleet sailings a year from Egypt to Puteoli, but it rarely happened. Most years there was a single sailing in May and June, and Rome just had to make do with what it received.

Many ships carrying commodities besides wheat accompanied the grain fleet for safety: piracy had flourished for almost as long as the sea-going trade and seaport towns in the eastern Mediterranean. Rome's first campaign in Greece (229 BCE) was to destroy the bases of pirates who attacked ships on the Adriatic. Ridding an area of pirates was one of the justifications for Rome's conquest of states that bordered the Mediterranean. In Horace's time, the most active group of pirates was based in Cilicia, the west coast of modern-day Turkey.

It was an up-and-down battle to curb piracy until Pompey mounted a major naval campaign in 67 BCE to protect the grain fleet. He first attacked pirate strongholds in the western Mediterranean, then brought much of the fleet to Cilicia. Sources from the time suggest that the pirates surrendered without a fight because Pompey offered them clemency and resettlement. From that time, for more than a century, piracy was not a significant threat to the grain shipments or the accompanying vessels.[24]

And what, besides wheat, was in the holds of the ships that accompanied the grain fleet from Alexandria to Puteoli? There was Egyptian marble, linen produced from flax grown along the Nile, and Syrian glassware. The ships carried passengers and prisoners. The highest value items were, however, the 'riches of the east'. Alexandria was the western terminus of the maritime routes of the Indian Ocean, the Red Sea, and the Persian Gulf. We know much of these routes because a Greek ship captain of the time summarized the ports, the times of year to sail, and the opportunities for trade in a book titled *The Periplus of the Erythraean Sea*.[25] Eastern goods also arrived at Alexandria by land across Persia, Iraq, and Syria, and by sea from the Mediterranean port of Ephesus, the western end of the routes across what is now Turkey. The main commodities were silk and cotton, scented body oils, medicines, spices from India, and slaves and ivory from Africa.

Alexandria was also the northern terminus of the 'frankincense road' from southern Yemen. The trade in frankincense and myrrh, high-value scented gums, supported a string of towns and caravanserais east of the Red Sea, as well as the trading city of Palmyra (now a long-abandoned but scenic ruin).[26] In the context of the regular trade to Rome of frankincense and myrrh, it is perfectly understandable that these two scented gums would be two of the gifts of great value offered to the new-born Jesus.

While archaeologists have found amphorae and Roman glass on India's eastern and western coasts, overall, Rome had a serious balance of payments problem and found little to sell in the east. Horace complained about the drain of Roman gold to pay for the silks, pearls, spices, and medicines, and this concern was as much a part of the mental map of the roads to the east as the way stations and mile markers. Incidentally, Rome's balance of payments problem would continue for centuries. Nobody in found a raw material or fabricated a commodity that India much wanted or needed— not the Arab traders of the ninth century, the Jewish spice traders of the twelfth century, or even the British in the eighteenth century.

What of the subsequent history of the land and water tribute routes to the eastern Mediterranean? Their importance for tying the empire together, militarily and bureaucratically, cannot be overstated. Their strategic importance, however, rose and fell as borders and campaigns shifted to new locations. Within twenty years of Horace's trip, a new northern all-land route to the east through the Danube Valley superseded the Appian and Egnatian ways. Its location reflected the new military frontier that separated the Roman Empire from the northern tribes. The Appian-Egnatian route to the east again came into prominence three centuries later when the Empire lost the Danube and the northern portion of the Balkan Peninsula.

By 300 CE, Rome had ceased to be the centre of trade for much of the world. Trade and political patterns shifted to the east with the renaming of the old city of Byzantium as Constantinople. By 320 CE, the grain levy from Alexandria fed Constantinople, not Rome. Trade with India dropped off and there is no evidence of Roman trade goods on the coasts of India after about 300 CE. The spice trade would revive in another few centuries, but the destinations would be in the Islamic world. It would be more than a thousand years before any but a handful of families in Europe could again afford the riches of the east. Rome would shrink to one-quarter its imperial population.

Looking back from today, two thousand years after Horace, many of the changes brought about by the tribute route were subtle and barely documented. Plants and seeds moved along the route. Many were not bound for the exotic gardens of the rich. Rather, they were basic crops that obscure people traded and equally obscure farmers attempted to cultivate. The bitter orange, for example, moved into cultivation in Italy.

The military and bureaucracy were unable to control what peoples and commodities passed along the tribute route to the east. In the Balkan Peninsula, for example, there was much movement from what is today Turkey into Greece, as well as movement down the northern feeder roads from Bulgaria. Though there was moral opposition to silk in Rome— it was seen as too effeminate for men—as well as complaints about its cost draining Rome of treasure, no one could actually stop its import along the route from the east—or its fashionable uses. Eastern spices graced Roman tables and scents found their way into body oils and rituals.[27]

Perhaps intangibles were the most important commodities on the Roman route to the east. The Roman elite welcomed the Appian and Egnatian ways for the ease of sending their sons to Athens for education. It was through these roads that knowledge of some tropical medicines drifted into Rome. Roman town planning, urban culture, and books permeated Syria, Palestine, and what is now Turkey. The knowledge of Greek, Latin, and urban intellectual traditions were the background for Caliphate Baghdad, the extraordinary Islamic intellectual centre of the tenth and eleventh centuries. And moving along the same route was

Christianity, which spread along the Egnatian Way to Rome itself. Recall that several of the epistles of St Paul were addressed to a congregation at Ephesus, along the Egnatian Way. Thessalonica was one of Christianity's early strongholds.

Horace lived out his life at the Western terminus of the Appian Way. He went on to become one of Rome's most famous poets, his works published, recited, quoted, and passed down to us. He divided his time between Rome and a beloved villa near the Appian Way, about a day's journey south of Rome. Late in his life, as he looked towards his own death, the image of the Appian Way occurred to him again.

> Though Agrippa's
> Colonnade and the Appian Way note your face well,
> You still must go down where Numa and Ancus have gone.[28]

Notes

1. Horace, *Satires*, Book I, No. 5, 'Journey to Brindisium', translated by A.S. Kline, http://www.poetryintranslation.com/PITBR/Latin/HoraceSatiresBkISatI.htm, p. 24, accessed on 9 November 2017.
2. Roman roads have attracted much popular historical writing. A sampling of such books would include Raymond Chevallier, *Roman Roads* (Berkeley: University of California Press, 1976); Victor W. Hagen, *The Roads That Led to Rome* (Cleveland: The World Publishing Company, 1976); and N.H.H. Sitwell, *Roman Roads of Europe* (London: Cassell, 1981).
3. Umberto Leonini and Giovani Staderini, *On the Appian Way: A Walk from Rome to Athens*, translated by E. Fitzmaurice (Rome: R. Bemporad, 1907, p. 182. The poor and oppressed also wanted to be buried along the Appian Way. Because they could not afford large plots of land, they tunnelled and dug below the small plots they could afford, producing catacombs several stories deep. Seven major catacombs, six Christian, and one Jewish, dot the Appian Way, and are its most commonly visited feature today.
4. Appius refused to give up his powerful post when his term expired and was brought before a public trial. He escaped with a hung jury and carried on with his grand plans, including commissioning Rome's first aqueduct, which greatly augmented the city's water supply.
5. Firman O'Sullivan, *The Egnatian Way* (Newton Abbot: David & Charles: 1972), p. 27.

6. The centrality of the capital is hardly uniquely Roman. Recall that in England, for more than a century, it was virtually impossible to go by train from one provincial city to another without passing through London. The military impetus for some routes continues into our own time. The interstate highway system of the United States, built over the last four decades, was originally funded in a bill titled the National Interstate and Defense Highways Act. Its stated purpose was to move troops in case of continental invasion.

7. Many routes have similar traveller shrines, from the caves at Dunhuang in western China to the Sailor's Church in downtown Detroit.

8. Horace, *Satires*, Book I, No. 6, 'Maecenas' Discernment', p. 29.

9. Horace, *Satires*, 'Journey to Brindisium', p. 25. In the dry climate of Egypt, few documents survive that detail the supplies given to one or another official travelling entourage. See Colin Adams and Ray Laurence (eds), *Travel and Geography in the Roman Empire* (New York: Routledge, 2001), pp. 142–3.

10. Horace, *Satires*, 'Journey to Brindisium', p. 26.

11. For a broad consideration of banditry in the Roman Empire, see Brent D. Shaw 'Bandits in the Roman Empire', *Past & Present*, no. 105 (November 1984), 3–52.

12. Cassius Dio, *Roman History* (epitome), translated by Gillian Spraggs LXXVII, 10, accessed on 10 July 2010 at www.outlawsandhighwaymen.com/bulla. htm

13. See, for example, Arthur Segal, *Town Planning and Architecture in Provincia Arabia: The Cities along the Via Triana Nove in the 1st–3rd centuries C.E.*, B.A.R. International Series No. 419 (Oxford: Center Mead, Osney Mead, 1988). There is some evidence of public monuments or plaques in cities that were inscribed with distances to other cities along well-known routes. See Benet Salway, 'Travel, *Itineraria* and *Tabellaria*', in Colin Adams and Ray Laurence, *Travel and Geography in the Roman Empire* (New York: Routledge, 2001), pp. 22–66.

14. Horace, Epistles I, Book 1. Quoted in Dora Jane Hamlin and Mary Jane Grunsfeld, *Appian Way, A Journey* (New York: Random House, 1974), p. 131.

15. Horace, *Epistles*, Book I, 1 'Money or Virtue', translated by A.S. Kline, http://www.poetryintranslation.com/PITBR/Latin/HoraceSatiresBkISatI.htm, accessed on 10 November 2017.

16. The towns bypassed by Trajan's new route loudly protested and the result was new roads connecting the cities to the coast route. See Hamlin and Grunsfeld, *Appian Way, A Journey*, p. 143.

17. O'Sullivan, *The Egnatian Way*, p. 21.

18. Some small sections of the road exist today, though none of it is regularly used.

19. Horace, *Epistles*, Book II, Epistle 2, p. 123.

20. Paul, Acts 27. Available at www.usccb.org/nab/bible/acts/acts27.htm, accessed on 20 January 2011.

21. See, for example, Nicholas K. Rauh, *Merchants, Sailors and Pirates in the Roman World* (New York: Stroud, 2003). The grain barges on the Nile were operated by an equally diverse group. See D.J. Thompson (Crawford), 'Nile Grain Transport under the Ptolemies', in Peter Garnsey, Keith Hopkins, and C.R. Whittaker, *Trade in the Ancient Economy* (Berkeley: University of California Press, 1983), pp. 64–75.

22. To follow the debate over the size of the grain trade to Rome and its investors, see Peter Garnsey, 'Grain for Rome', in Peter Garnsey, Keith Hopkins, and C.R. Whittaker, *Trade in the Ancient Economy* (Berkeley: University of California Press, 1983), pp. 118–30. Also P. Termin, 'A Marketing Economy in the Early Roman Empire', *Journal of Roman Studies*, 91 (2001), pp. 169–81. The earlier argument is found in Lionel Casson, *Ancient Trade and Society* (Detroit: Wayne State University Press, 1984) and Geoffrey Rickman, *The Corn Supply of Ancient Rome* (Oxford: Clarendon Press, 1980). The most compelling evidence seems to come from the size of Roman grain ships. A few speciality grain carriers moved 1,000 tonnes, but the capacity of most grain carriers was 300–400 tonnes. Since there was only one crossing of the Mediterranean per year moving 150,000 tonnes required perhaps 40 large carriers and 250 smaller ones. A fleet of over 300 ships devoted to the grain trade just seems unlikely.

23. See Seutonius, *Claudius* 18–19, as quoted in Frik Meijer and Onno van Nifj, *Trade. Transport and Society in the Ancient World: A Sourcebook* (London: Routledge, 1992), p. 101.

24. See Phillip de Souza, *Piracy in the Graeco-Roman World* (Cambridge: Cambridge University Press, 1999), pp. 167–71.

25. Anon., *The Periplus of the Erythraean Sea*, translated and edited by G.W.B. Huntingford (London: Hakluyt Society, 1980).

26. See Gary K. Young, Rome's *Eastern Trade: International Commerce and Imperial Policy, 31 BC–AD 305* (London: Routledge, 2001), pp. 90–134.

27. Rome also discovered that tribute routes that led outward to conquest were of equal use to invaders. Hannibal used the Roman roads to reach the heart of Italy. Centuries later, so did the Goths and other tribes that invaded from the north.

28. Horace, *Epistles*, Book 1, Epistle 6: 'Of Virtue', p. 86.

The Grand Canal

Forty-three half-dead Korean men in an open boat washed up on the coast of China, about 200 miles south of current-day Shanghai in February 1488 CE. Aboard were Ch'oe Pu, a mid-level Korean bureaucrat, his staff and slaves, a military escort, and the ship's crew. Seven days of fierce storms had taken the masts and oars. They survived on dried rice, rainwater, and a few oranges. This was no trading ship. Pu came from a highly educated family and, at the age of thirty-five, served as commissioner of records for three towns on an island off the Korean coast. Pu was returning home to perform funerary rites for his father when high seas and contrary winds attacked this expedition of noble filial duty transforming him and his party to destitute castaways on the coast of China.[1]

The Koreans arrived in the relatively peaceful and stable middle period of the Ming Dynasty (1368–1644 CE), which undertook large construction projects, such as the improvement of the Grand Canal, the restoration of the Great Wall, and the construction of the Forbidden City in Beijing. More significant were a 'peace bonus' and government policies that resulted in vastly increased agricultural output. Though estimates by modern scholars on China's population vary from about 160 to 200 million people in this period, all agree that it rose steadily, producing rising demand for both staples—rice, wheat, and timber—and more elegant materials for the elite—furniture woods and incense from southeast Asia, black pepper and

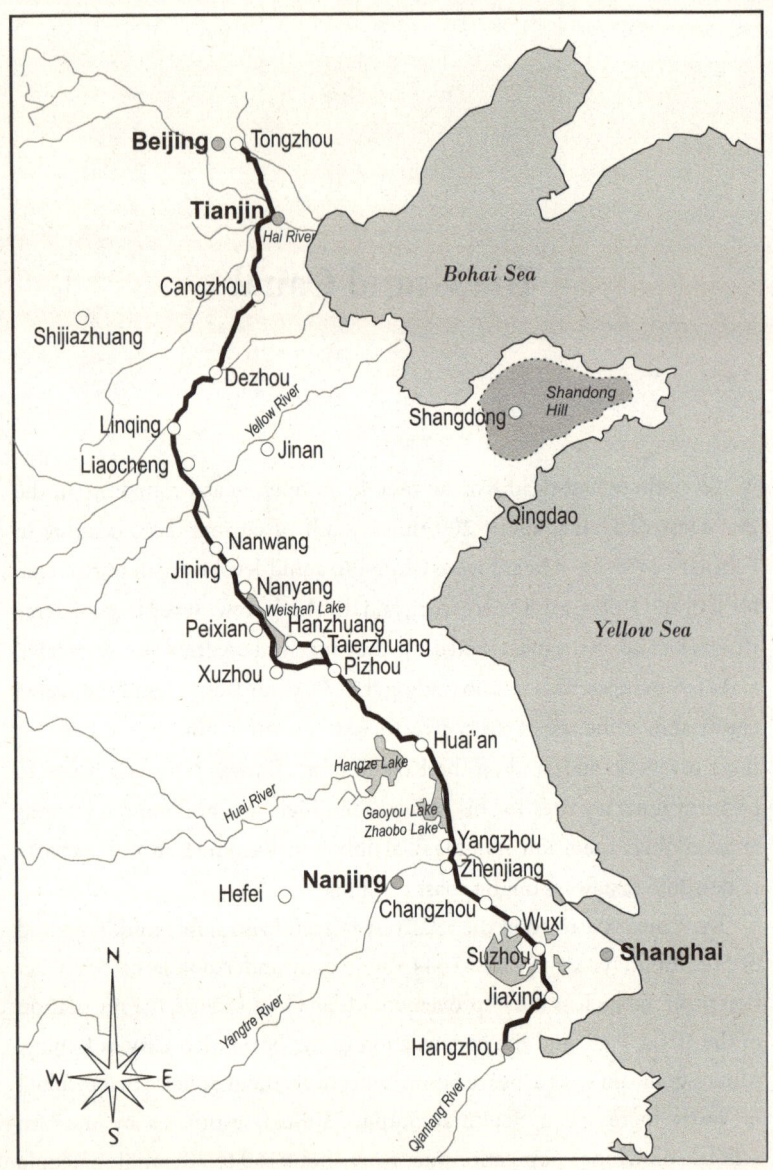

The Grand Canal

textiles from India, tropical medicines, and glassware from the Middle
East. The ports of Southern China hosted Hindu traders from India and
Muslim traders from the Middle East. Many families from southern
China moved to both mainland and island Southeast Asia to make their
fortune. The first third of the 1400s was the time of Chinese expeditions to
Southeast Asia and India, where fleets of huge ships established trading and
tributary ties with the existing kingdoms on their routes.

Internally, a vast literate bureaucracy administered China. The yearly
examination system staffed its upper levels with men who shared a
common culture, that of the 'Confucian gentleman', who knew the proper
protocols of dress and cuisine quite as well as they knew the proper forms
of government communications. These bureaucrats moved to new postings
every few years and, therefore, carried with them to places far from Beijing
shared norms, fashions, and ceremonies. They cultivated ties to the imperial
court, both to lobby for their next posting and to track shifts in factional
politics. The dynasty also fed, housed, and equipped an enormous stand-
ing army, perhaps a million men. It protected borders and roads, put down
rebellions, and undertook building roads and other infrastructure.

Though Ch'oe Pu and his men beached on a coast more than 1,500 miles
south of the capital, imperial policies immediately defined their situation. The imperial court had been unable to defeat Japanese pirates, who
periodically raided Chinese shipping and coastal villages.[2] The court,
therefore, decreed that coastal people must seize all foreigners and turn
them over to the authorities for punishment. Villagers beat the Koreans.
Pu and his men fled into the hills, but by dawn the local military commander located and arrested them. He marched them through the rain over
steep hills. Pu records that his feet became grossly swollen and bled. His
staff carried him the last few miles to a garrison.

The Korea from which Ch'oe Pu came, in many ways, paralleled China.
A vigorous dynasty, the Choson undertook building projects, such as
a new capital at Seoul, which housed government officials, and also had
markets for foreign goods and residences for delegations from Manchuria,
Japan, and China. An immense bureaucratic apparatus slowly developed
after 1400 CE, gradually permeating the countryside as never before: it
produced fine-grid land surveys; a detailed law code was promulgated and
the government required personal identity cards for all; government fleet

moved grain. Most importantly, the dynasty expanded the imperial army and disarmed many private armies. As in China, the elite, including the new bureaucracy, were trained as 'Confucian gentlemen'. They read the same books as their Chinese counterparts, provided by an expanding translating and printing industry in Korea. Exemplary biographies drawn from Chinese and Korean history highlighted proper moral behaviour.[3]

Ch'oe Pu spoke only Korean, but read and wrote classical Chinese. He explained in notes, long and short, to the garrison commander and other officials, that he and his party were Korean civil servants, not Japanese pirates. He brought out his sash, seal, and badge of office. The officials were sceptical; all these items could have been stolen. Pu emphasized that Korea paid regular tribute to the Chinese imperial court, followed Chinese ceremonies, and enjoyed Chinese music. What won the unconvinced officials over, according to Ch'oe Pu's account, was his Confucian learning. They asked about examinations, civil service ranks and accompanying dress, Chinese dynastic history, and what books he preferred. He gave satisfactory answers. The officials asked about mourning customs outlined in the *Chia Li*, a well-known Chinese text. Pu assured them that everyone in Korea observed just such mourning rules.[4]

The garrison commander assigned a twenty-man guard to the Koreans, ordered sedan chairs for Ch'oe Pu and some of his staff, and accompanied the Koreans through the next day. Pu proclaimed his appreciation of the kindness of the garrison chief.

> You, General ... filled me in the last stage of my hunger and thirst, and put life into me when I long before should have died. ... for seven or eight days you have helped and protected me. The extent of your kindness is immeasurable. Once we have parted, it is unlikely that we shall meet again, and I am sadder for that.[5]

Ch'oe Pu first saw Chinese canals as the Koreans were brought through the eastern districts of Zhejiang. Pu learned that every year the rivers rose dramatically during the same two-month period with the potential for disastrous floods. However, if the water was impounded, it could irrigate thousands upon thousands of acres of rice fields. Typically, local labour built up the banks of a river to keep it from flooding the fields. Gates along the embankment led water away from the river into a complex, highly

branching system of canals, which finally brought small rivulets to individual fields.[6] As Ch'oe Pu wrote: 'Throughout the region, the springs and
branch streams that arise and disappear and the dikes and dams that are
joined one to another are endless, like a labyrinth of veins and arteries.'[7]

These local irrigation canals did not form a coherent route and were
largely useless for imperial transportation.

Transportation canals were fundamentally different from these irrigation canals. For centuries, locally recruited labour had built two dykes,
perhaps thirty feet apart, parallel to a river, creating a canal that provided
better navigation than the twists, meanders, rocks, and shoals of the river.
These canals promoted regional transport of grain and other commodities but made for much interrupted travel. They often did not join locally
built canals, and boats had to be dragged over the banks to proceed on the
journey as Ch'oe Pu noted:

> An embankment was north of the station. ... We left the boats, passed the
> embankment, walked to the Ts'ao-e River, and went straight across it. On
> the opposite bank was another embankment ... Again we left the boats and
> walked past the embankment, coming to the Tung-kuan Station, two *li* to
> the west. We got into boats again ... [8]

Throughout this coastal plain, part land and part water, there were
named 'stops' for travellers, staffed by a government employee to provide
tea, food, and shelter. Several times each day, the entourage arrived at police
outposts, where officials interviewed them and duly recorded their passing.
These police posts were provisioned and equipped to house official travellers, even as large a group as the Koreans and their military escort.

Nineteen days after washing ashore, Ch'oe Pu and the forty-two other
Koreans arrived at the port city of Hangzhou, then the southern terminus
of the Grand Canal.[9]

Why did a Grand Canal exist at all? Like other tribute routes, the ratio-
nale was imperial, not local or regional. Like Rome, successive Chinese
capitals in the north (Chang'an, Loyang, and eventually Peking) were inca-
pable of producing enough grain to feed the court, the bureaucrats, and the
military on the northern frontiers. Only the productive coastal plain well
south of the capital region produced the necessary surplus. Dynasties even

before the Common Era, therefore, established that tribute from the productive Yellow River delta would be paid in grain, which was then moved north to cover the capital's shortfall. China's rivers were no help in moving grain to the north; they all ran from the western mountains east to the sea.[10] Moving the grain overland was prohibitively expensive. The answer was the Grand Canal, which eventually moved millions of tonnes of grain on an all-water route to the north. This huge undertaking proved technically feasible because the coastal plain was quite flat, rising only 100 feet from the southern end to the Yellow River, and excavation of the alluvial soil was relatively easy. Also, the Huai River was well situated to provide the additional water that every canal system requires.[11]

The first development of the Grand Canal began in the far distant past. Almost 3,000 years ago, dynasties realized the benefits of a water route that connected the south and the north, and began linking local canals and rivers into a south-north Grand Canal. The waterway first connected the northern capital to the Yellow River valley and the fertile valley of the lower Huai Ho River (between the Yellow and the Yangtze Rivers). The Sui Dynasty (580–618 CE) developed the Grand Canal greatly, extending it to the productive lower Yangtze valley.[12] Five million men and women are reported to have worked on the massive excavations.[13] The descendants of Chengis Khan, ruling as the Yuan Dynasty (1271–1368 CE), extended the canal even further north to Beijing and established frequent military garrisons along it. The Yuan Dynasty also shortened the route by means of dozens of locks to lift boats over a set of rocky hills rather than the earlier route, which wound east around the hills. They also extended the earlier canal well south of the Yangtze River. The Ming Dynasty (1378–1450 CE) strengthened the dykes and connected lakes to control the water level. At its longest, the canal stretched a distance equivalent to that from Miami to New York or from Stockholm to Central Greece.

At the time of Ch'oe Pu, an astonishing 10,000 boats traversed the Grand Canal with the annual tribute of grain. In a single line, nose-to-tail, the boats would have filled virtually the whole length of the Grand Canal. Instead, owing to weeks of delays at river crossings, severe crowding at locks, and limited manpower to pull the boats over hills, these boats often required nearly a year to make the round trip from the Yangtze Delta to Beijing and back. The fleet of grain boats, nevertheless, moved about 4,000,000

Illustration 16 *Boats on the Grand Canal,* by Xu Yang, 18th-century painter from Suzhou, China. Photograph by Szilas. Creative Commons. Wikimedia.

piculs—about 260,000 tonnes—of rice each year.[14] (Let us recall that, at its height, Rome moved perhaps 150,000 tonnes of grain each year across the Mediterranean to feed the capital.) More than 100,000 troops guarded the canal and the grain boats.[15]

A sea route up China's coast might seem a simpler solution than digging and maintaining the Grand Canal. Indeed, various dynasties did experiment with transport by sea up China's coast. A sea route, however, placed the critical food supply at risk from storms and pirate attacks. In 1488 CE, Ch'oe Pu talked with officials at Hangzhou and found them quite sceptical of ocean travel. Ku Pi, the stationmaster at Hangzhou, said of the traders and smugglers who left his port for Southeast Asia: 'for ten that leave, only five return'. He thought the Grand Canal much safer. As evidence, he said that the tribute from Malacca, Champa, and other places in Southeast Asia arrived at the south coast in Fujian province, then was transported 2,000 miles to the capital on the inland waterways and the Grand Canal. 'For going to the capital by water, only the river [canal] route is quite good'.[16] An unspoken reason for preferring the use of the Grand Canal to seaborne transport was also self-interest. The hundreds of Confucian bureaucrats who administered the Grand Canal vigorously opposed seaborne transport of the grain.

Besides transporting the annual grain tribute, there were several additional benefits to the state of using the Grand Canal for the state. It was an efficient means of moving troops and supplies for war, whether to attack beyond the borders or to suppress an internal rebellion.[17] The canal brought the grain to feed the troops on the restive northwest border. Some grain could be diverted to famine areas. The Grand Canal was also central to imperial military agricultural colonies by which the state extended control to new regions in the north and west. The new colonies needed grain to supplement what they could grow. The grain shipment from the south covered the shortfall. The Grand Canal also tied north and south together as a way to move bureaucrats to postings, send out auditors, bring examination candidates to the capital, and maintain the information flow of reports.[18]

At a deeper even spiritual level, a central obligation of any dynasty was full granaries and prosperity throughout the land.[19] The grain tribute, which moved on the Grand Canal, filled granaries, but in addition to this, water tapped from the Grand Canal provided irrigation that raised yields. The Grand Canal was also essential for flood control. At times of heightened river flow, it moved water into lakes and swamps, decreasing the likelihood of flooding. Peasants and nobles shared the belief that a dynasty that could not control floods had lost the Mandate of Heaven to rule. The massing of vast amounts of corveé labour for digging and maintaining the Grand Canal was a clear indication of the power and authority of a successful dynasty.

At Hangzhou, the southern terminus of the Grand Canal, Ch'oe Pu was subject to days of interrogation. Some officials asked about the history and geography of Korea and made it clear that they intended to compare Ch'oe Pu's answers to books available in the city. One of the chief officials of Hangzhou's schools wanted to know the books he studied in Korea and the examination system and the rewards for those who passed. He probed Pu's knowledge of Chinese classics. Other officials wanted to know about recent Chinese embassies to Korea. Pu was not only familiar with the embassies but also quoted a poem by one of the ambassadors. They demanded to know how Ch'oe Pu knew the geography of China and which Chinese

person had illegally given him this information. Pu, however, knew the
geography from Chinese books and maps printed in Korea.

The interrogation of Ch'oe Pu shows that the Grand Canal was more than just a set of connected waterways leading to the capital. Like other routes, it had a strong mental component. In addition to locks, dams, and connected rivers, the Grand Canal was a network of Confucian bureaucrats along its 1,100-mile length. They shared a sophisticated mental web of expectations that included rank and service, knowledge of Chinese classics and poetry, Confucian customs, hygiene, dress, forms of hospitality, courtesy, and honour. After days of interrogation, the officials of the Hangzhou region accepted Ch'oe Pu as one of them. His answers and manner established Ch'oe Pu as—to put it in the words of the education official—'truly a well-read gentleman'. Several officials openly sympathized with his anguish over not fulfilling filial obligations to his deceased father. They had vegetarian food prepared for him, respecting a son's Confucian obligation to refrain from meat for three years after his father's death. Two officials performed a ceremony with Ch'oe Pu that they both knew established formal ties between host and guest. One official took a companion of Pu's home for a meal to meet his wives, concubines, and children.

The Hangzhou officials used their intimate knowledge of the bureaucracy along the Grand Canal to present Ch'oe Pu as a welcome visitor unfortunately displaced from his own country rather than a hated Japanese pirate. They knew that all versions of Ch'oe Pu's depositions had to match in every detail or there would be questions by higher officials and, therefore, had him recopy his earlier deposition so that it matched a later one. The officials also had Ch'oe Pu edit out of his deposition that villagers beat his entourage. They explained that the emperor was newly on the throne and officials in the South did not want to give the impression that they lacked the authority to prevent attacks by villagers on foreigners.[20]

The Hangzhou officials knew that Ch'oe Pu must present his case at court in Peking in order to return to Korea, and they laid the groundwork for a swift, easy trip north on the Grand Canal. They sent word of the Koreans to Beijing, knowing that the courier service would take only forty days to get the message to the capital. They made sure that Ch'oe Pu had several essential documents, an official list of possessions, meagre though they were, personal identity cards for each of the Koreans, and a directive to all military and civilian officials along the canal to assist in their journey.[21] In part the directive read 'Let the stations and transfer stations under this office give the dispatched official food and boats and the escorting troops and Ch'oe Pu and his company rations, red boats, and laborers. It is fitting that all offices on the road should comply.'[22]

Ch'oe Pu's only actual observation of the city of Hangzhou's streets, bridges and shrines was made on his way out, a journey of more than 10 miles on a donkey across the city from south to north. Its markets extended more than 3 miles outside the walls. This thriving port was one of the largest cities in the world at the time.

> [Hangzhou] is a major urban center of the southeast. Houses stand in solid rows, and the gowns of the crowds seem like screens. The markets pile up gold and silver; the people amass beautiful clothes and ornaments. Foreign ships stand as thick as teeth of a comb, and in the streets wine shops and music halls front directly each on another. There are flowers that do not fade through the four seasons and scenery of everlasting spring all the year round. It truly seems a different world, as people say.[23]

A Chinese register of taxes collected on foreign goods in the province of Fukien about a century after Ch'oe Pu's trip on the Grand Canal suggests what might have been in the holds of the ships at Hangzhou. The largest category noted in the tax register was medicines and spices, including camphor, rhinoceros horn, opium, cardamom, cloves, nutmeg, birds' nests, liquid amber, dragons' blood, aloe, pepper, sandalwood, and various tree gums. Another category of taxed imports was incense, such as benzoin and sandalwood. Yet another category of taxed imports was animal products used in high-end crafts, such as bird feathers, ivory, tortoise shell, mother of pearl, animal horns, and skins, as well as sandalwood and black wood. The mineral products included copper, gold, tin, and lead.[24] Besides foreign imports, the imperial court requisitioned as tribute large amounts of goods from the south; these travelled by private toll-paying boats on the Grand Canal. The commodities included salt pork, wax, honey, brooms, silk fabric, porcelain, arrow shafts, paper, cowhides, glazed bricks, lumber, bamboo, tea, and even live animals.[25] This trade was an important part of the Grand Canal as a route, not just for the substantial taxes paid on imported items, but also the centrality and importance of many of the items to the maintenance of an elite lifestyle both at the capital and in outlying areas that bureaucrats served.

Just north of Hangzhou, the Korean entourage and the escorting Chinese officials boarded three official boats and started north on the Te-she-pa River, the first stage of the Grand Canal. The banks of the canal were often high dykes that blocked the view of the surrounding countryside and villages. On the third day, the canal opened out into Lake T'ai. Ch'oe Pu was impressed by a 14-storey pagoda and generally liked what he saw. 'The houses were beautiful, with stone plinths and well walls laid below and stone columns erected above. The lake water wound in and about them, and masts and sails stood grouped in the villages.'[26]

Ch'oe Pu could not have known what a complex problem of hydraulics he was passing through. Excess water in the Grand Canal had to be drained off into the lakes, but at other seasons of the year the lakes threatened to inundate the canal. The only solution was an enormous dyke that separated the lakes from the canal, maintained and raised by each successive dynasty.[27] After Ch'oe Pu's, time drainage tunnels were added. The complexity and labour of maintaining the Grand Canal was staggering. Most sections required yearly maintenance, especially dredging the silt to keep the canal open. The dykes needed constant repair and, often, additional height. Openings in the canal, which were often wood doors, needed periodic replacement. The myriad of bridges had to be kept in repair.

Days passed. Pu and his entourage proceeded at about 2 miles per hour, the speed that rowed and sailed boats could maintain on the Grand Canal, which always allowed time for polite exchange with the heads of the stations along the route. Ch'oe Pu noticed a difference in attitude as he moved north. Koreans were not considered 'barbarians' as they had been in the south. One stationmaster knew the names and titles of two ambassadors who had gone from the Chinese court to Korea about a decade earlier. He even knew the name of a Korean poet who had written a verse praising them. A week later, he met an administrator who knew the details of Korean castaways who had arrived on the coast of China only six years earlier.[28]

Nine days north of Hangzhou, the boats came to the Yangtze River, one of the two main east-west arteries of China. Scholars and administrators have studied the river for millennia; poets have described it and artists have painted it. The Yangtze has always been a complex force in its vast basin, nurturing in its irrigation, but vicious in its floods. In its upper reaches, the Yangtze cut through fine clay loess soil, converting it to massive amounts of silt, which held phosphates and other trace chemicals beneficial to agriculture. Farmers wanted and needed the river to flood their fields. The sheer quantity of silt, more per gallon than any other major river on earth, was the problem. As the silt settled out of the river, the riverbed rose. Dykes meant to control and slow the flow only exacerbated the settling, resulting in a river tens of feet higher than the surrounding farmland. In flood the river was so powerful that it inexorably changed its course like a snake flexing its body. Floods and human catastrophes were inevitable. Controlling the Yangtze has always been beyond human capability, no matter how much labour is invested in dykes, channels, and weirs.[29]

The Yangtze has always been a seasonal river, rising twice a year and then falling to expose rocks and shoals. Much of the year, the Yangtze was so low that Grand Canal traffic could not cross it. Hundreds of boats lined up to cross the river, which was more than 3 miles wide at that point. Ch'oe Pu's group was fortunate to be travelling in the late summer, a rainy monsoon season. They waited one day for a tidal bore, which made the river deep enough for boats to cross. Official boats, such as Pu's, passed out of locks onto the river, but most traffic was hauled over dykes and down stone sluices. With a following wind, Pu's crew put up the sail, and the boat swiftly crossed the Yangtze.

North of the Yangtze, dykes rose far above the boat and Ch'oe Pu was unable to see the surrounding countryside. His experience of the Grand Canal shifted to the mental, his memoir filled with literary and historical details of the places on the route: poetry he had read about a city the boat passed ('The spring breezes caress the city, and music fills the ears'), the names and histories of Buddhist monasteries on nearby mountains, a myth about a place where a king slept and dreamed, and the site where Confucius asked questions about government.[30]

After travelling for two weeks north from Hangzhou on the Grand Canal, the Koreans came to the Huai River. This was the site of one of the major shipyards along the Grand Canal. 'Garrisons for the regions south of the Huai and north and south of the Yangtze were gathered here to build boats, and they all had shipyards.'[31]At that time the Yellow River, the second major east-west artery across China, had actually been diverted south, and fed the Huai River about 100 miles inland from the coast.

Ch'oe Pu did not describe either the shipyards or the boats. Fortunately, other sources did. The shipyards consisted of long narrow strips of land separating narrow canals. Supplies were brought along the strip of land, on which shipwrights built the boats and launched them into the adjoining canal.[32] The grain boats were of a standard size, about 10 feet wide and 50 feet long. They just fit through the narrowest locks on the Grand Canal.[33] Construction to replace worn-out boats in a fleet of 10,000 was continuous. A century after Ch'oe Pu, the government shipyards were producing more than 600 riverboats per year.[34]

The area north of the Huai River was flat coastal plain with only dykes to hold the river in its course, especially difficult because of the vast quantities of water added from channelling the Yellow River into the Huai. For example, a century after Ch'oe Pu's journey, this section of the Grand Canal changed course and completely dried up. Hundreds of official and private boats, plus 930 boats carrying grain tribute, all ran aground.[35]

Over eons, the enormous load of the Yellow River silt pushed the coastline eastwards into the sea and gradually engulfed a rocky island, which became the Shandong Peninsula. Earlier versions of the Grand Canal had gone west around Shandong. The Mongols, when they ruled China in the fourteenth century, had decided to build a shorter route, utilizing locks, over the peninsula:

> ...it took over one hundred laborers, following the towpaths on both banks, to pull the boats upstream with bamboo ropes that had been fastened to them. I, Fu Jang, and others climbed onto the bank and walked along the tow-path. I saw that the paving stones were firm and in good repair...[36]

The boats took five days to get over the hill, whose summit stood 178 feet above the surrounding plain.[37] This 50-mile section of the Grand Canal contained so many locks that it was known as the 'Canal of Gates'. North of the Shandong was the old bed of the Yellow River, which the canal crossed. The boat stopped at a few towns. Signs of famine were everywhere and the military guards kept careful watch for desperate bandits.[38]

On this section of the Grand Canal, along the Wei River, Ch'oe Pu noticed a human-powered wheel for raising water that he had never seen before. At first, the accompanying Chinese officials dismissed it as unimportant, but the Korean persisted in his questions. He saw that it was much more efficient than designs for wheels in Korea. At last the officials described the design in detail and Ch'oe Pu took careful notes. He is credited with bringing this wheel design to Korea.[39]

Late on his 45th day on the Grand Canal, Ch'oe Pu reached Peking. He had experienced the ecology and the hydraulics of the Grand Canal, the shared customs and sensibilities of the Confucian officials who oversaw it, the power of the military that guarded it, and the myriad of traders who plied it. The next day, Ch'oe Pu underwent interrogation at the Ministry of War, which consisted of pointing out his travels on a large wall map. This incident shows just how close the mentality of elite Chinese and Korean officials were. They shared conventions of mapmaking. Earlier in the memoir, Ch'oe Pu hinted at his map knowledge. When asked how he knew where he was on the Grand Canal, he replied that he had studied Chinese maps in Korea.[40]

The Koreans settled into their guest quarters and received an allotment of rice. Each day brought revelations to Ch'oe Pu. He learnt that there had been an embassy from Korea to Peking only a few months earlier. He met his first competent bi-lingual speaker of Chinese and Korean. He found that the Chinese court had already sent word of his safety to his family.[41] Even though he was not allowed to move about the capital, he had a steady stream of visitors—officials, students, a translator who had been on numerous official trips to Korea, even neighbours.

Within a week, both the War Ministry and the Ministry of Rites approved the return of Ch'oe Pu and his 42 men to Korea. (It is perhaps worth noting that the Ministry of Rites had other functions besides overseeing court and religious ritual. It also oversaw the examination system and all relations with foreign powers.) In another week the court arranged a ceremony in which the Koreans were honoured with clothes and boots, quite fine and functional. In their new outfits the Koreans followed the university students in a procession into and out of the imperial palace. The scene was impressive.

I put on [a] festive dress and entered the Palace [and passed through several gates]. Troops were drawn up smartly, lights burned brightly ...

Soon, drums were beaten at the left end of Wu Gate and bells struck at the right end. Three arched gates opened, and at each gate two big elephants stood on guard, their forms spectacular.[42]

Two days later, Ch'oe Pu's entourage and their Ministry of War escort mounted horses and rode out on the straight road to the Korean border. An emissary from China, whom they met on the road, related that the Korean emperor had taken a personal interest in Ch'oe Pu's disappearance and had ordered searches along the Korean coast. When Pu finally returned to the Korean court, the emperor commanded that he write his memoirs. After completing that task, he retired from public life for three years to mourn the death of his father and comfort his mother, acts of filial piety he had been unable to perform during his sojourn in China.

* * *

The Grand Canal was typical of a fully controlled tribute route, considerably more, for example, than the Appian Way. Only the Chinese imperial government could have afforded the cost of building the canal. The thousands of grain boats were built in government shipyards with government-requisitioned timber. The grain fleet pre-empted all private boats when it passed along the canal.[43] The military guarded the fleet and the canal with garrisons and thousands of troops. The government bureaucracy that ran the canal shared a Confucian-educated ethos. The canal administration marshalled a vast amount of corveé labour for maintenance each year. As a tribute route, the Grand Canal had a long period of fame, during which paintings and maps of it were produced;[44] stories and poems featured it; while foreigners and Chinese travelled up and down it and wrote memoirs.[45]

The Grand Canal continued largely unaltered in structure and function for three centuries after Ch'oe Pu's trip, always with unsolved problems. It froze in the winter and low water made it unusable for several months every year. The grain tribute seems to have actually done little to alleviate famine, but the canal did produce tolls from private boats and food for the capital and the military garrisons on the western frontier. The ecological effects of the canal were profound. A whole region became saline and unproductive. Large forests were cut for construction of the boats.

Illustration 17 'Portions of the Grand Canal are Still in Use for Transport of Heavy Materials'. Photograph by Ican. Creative Commons. Wikimedia.

The unalterable imperatives of China's rivers ultimately doomed the Grand Canal. The silt build-up from the loess soil inexorably raised the level of the riverbeds. The dykes had to be raised higher and higher and the water runoff and catchment areas more carefully controlled. Periodic serious floods were inevitable. The Yangtze River finally destroyed the Grand Canal in 1851, bursting through the dam that had, for centuries, rerouted it on a southern course through the Huai River. Because the dynasty was in financial crisis and colonial powers were pushing up from the south, the canal was never rebuilt. As with the Mississippi as a route, in the later decades of the nineteenth century, trains largely replaced the Grand Canal. Today, like the Rhine and the Mississippi, barge traffic moves heavy goods on the remaining sections of the canal, though much of it has silted up and been abandoned.

Notes

1. Ch'oe Pu, *Ch'oe Pu's Diary: A Record of Drifting across the Sea*, translated by John Meskill (Tucson: University of Arizona Press, The Association for Asian Studies: Monographs and Papers, No. XVII, 1965), pp. 24–45.

2. See So Kwan-wai, *Japanese Piracy in Ming China during the 16th Century* (East Lansing, Michigan: Michigan State University Press, 1975).

3. See William E. Henthorn, *A History of Korea* (New York: The Free Press, 1971), pp. 138–53. The Korean and Chinese courts had their mutual suspicions, including relations with the Jurchen, a nomadic tribe who held eastern and southern Manchuria.

4. Ch'oe Pu was dissembling in his statement to the Chinese officials that everyone in Korea at the time followed Confucian customs. In fact, most people did not and Ch'oe Pu belonged to a minority of intellectuals who clung to and promoted Confucian learning and customs.

5. Pu, *Ch'oe Pu's Diary*, p. 66.

6. Ray Huang, 'The Grand Canal during the Ming Dynasty: 1368–1644', Dissertation, Department of History, University of Michigan, 1964, pp. 16–20.

7. Pu, *Ch'oe Pu's Diary*, p. 76.

8. Pu, *Ch'oe Pu's Diary*, p. 69.

9. Local officials confined Ch'oe Pu's entourage to accommodations at a police station. Ch'oe Pu's actual description of Hangzhou is sparse and consists of history and views of nearby mountains.

10. Huang, 'The Grand Canal during the Ming Dynasty', pp. 5–7.

11. Lyman P. Van Slyke, *Yangtze: Nature, History and the River* (Reading, Massachusetts: Addison-Wesley Publishing Co., 1988), pp. 68–9.

12. See Victor Cunrui Xiong, *The Emperor Yang of the Sui Dynasty* (Albany, New York: State University of New York Press, 2006).

13. Joseph Needham, *Science and Civilization in China*, vol. 4, Part III (Cambridge: Cambridge University Press, 1971), p. 308.

14. The *picul* was generally defined as the weight a man could carry. At different ports of Southeast Asia, the *picul* seems to have varied in the range of 125 to 133 lbs. The Chinese bureaucracy certainly knew how accurately to measure the weight of a *picul* of rice. Standardized imperial Chinese weights pre-date Ch'oe Pu by centuries, if not millennia.

15. Huang, 'The Grand Canal during the Ming Dynasty', p. 81.

16. Pu, *Ch'oe Pu's Diary*, p. 82.

17. Huang, 'The Grand Canal during the Ming Dynasty', pp. 98–102.

18. There was centuries-long continuing tension between grain collection as government revenue and the obligation to distribute it for the good of the people. See Pierre-Étienne Will and R. Bin Wong, *Nourish the People: The State Granary System in China, 1650–1850* (Ann Arbor, Michigan: Center for Chinese Studies, 1991), pp. 6–7.

19. Will and Wong, *Nourish the People*, pp. 1–4.

20. Pu, *Ch'oe Pu's Diary*, pp. 69–88. Much of what travelled up and down the Grand Canal on the bureaucratic information network was the ebb and flow of power and faction at court, whose star was in the ascendant and who was in disgrace.

21. Ch'oe Pu's memoir makes clear that the bureaucracy of the time consisted of three departments with separate offices covering the same geographic unit, respectively termed 'Administrative', 'Surveillance', and 'Military'. On matters of importance, such as the Korean castaways, the heads of the three offices met and reviewed both reports of their departments from the field and a preliminary judgment from their provincial superiors. There appears to be considerable overlap and redundancy in what officials actually did. The three heads of the departments at Hangzhou jointly interrogated Ch'oe Pu and decided that his story was sound. All three signed off on the official account of the incident and directed their respective counterparts along the Grand Canal to provide the necessary transportation and support for the Koreans' trip to the capital. The opportunities for personal enrichment in handling the grain levy in this Byzantine bureaucracy were understood and commented upon at the time.

22. Pu, *Ch'oe Pu's Diary*, p. 85.

23. Pu, *Ch'oe Pu's Diary*, p. 88.

24. See Stephen Tseng-Hsin Chang, 'Commodities Imported into the Chang-chou Region of Fukien during the Late Ming Period. A Preliminary Analysis of Tax Lists Found in the Tung-his-yang k'ao', in Roderich Ptak and Dietmar Rothermund (eds), *Emporia, Commodities and Entrepreneurs in Asian Maritime Trade, c. 1400–1740* (Stuttgart: Franz Steiner Verlag, 1991), pp. 166–86. In the same volume, articles discuss the tortoise shell trade and the use of cowry shells from the Maldives in the southern provinces of China. The first Portuguese trade mission to China carried a few of the items listed in the tax list, such as tortoise shells, cloth, and pepper. See Tomé Pires, *The Suma Oriental of Tomé Pires*, translated by Armando Cotesao (London: Hakluyt society, 1944), pp. xl–xli. Also, Roderich Ptak and Dietmar Rothermund (eds), *Emporia, Commodities and Entrepreneurs in Asian Maritime Trade, c. 1400–1750* (Stuttgart: Franz Steiner Verlag, 1991). The whole issue of trade and tribute is well considered in David C. Kang, *East Asia Before the West: Five Centuries of Trade and Tribute* (New York: Columbia University Press, 2010).

25. Huang, 'The Grand Canal during the Ming Dynasty', pp. 150–69.

26. Pu, *Ch'oe Pu's Diary*, p. 91.

27. Huang, 'The Grand Canal during the Ming Dynasty', p. 25.

28. Pu, *Ch'oe Pu's Diary*, pp. 90, 93, 98.

29. Van Slyke, *Yangtze*, pp. 10–14. The current attempt to control the Yangtze is, of course, the controversial Three Gorges Dam.

30. Pu, *Ch'oe Pu's Diary*, pp. 98–102.

31. Pu, *Ch'oe Pu's Diary*, p. 100.

32. Huang, 'The Grand Canal during the Ming Dynasty', p. 57.

33. Huang, 'The Grand Canal during the Ming Dynasty', p. 71.

34. Huang, 'The Grand Canal during the Ming Dynasty', p. 93.

35. Huang, 'The Grand Canal during the Ming Dynasty', p. 29.

36. Pu, *Ch'oe Pu's Diary*, p. 103.

37. Needham, *Science and Civilization in China*, p. 319. After 1415 CE, with the completion of these locks, transport of the grain levy was entirely by the Grand Canal, rather than partially by sea.

38. Ch'oe Pu's memoir shifts to recording conversations with the officials who accompanied him north. They talked of tea ceremonies, the character of southerners versus northerners, raids by nomads, the latest colours for officials' umbrellas, administrators dismissed from court, and how to keep princes from usurping thrones.

39. Often, historians have no idea exactly when or how technology transfer occurred. This is a documented case.

40. Pu, *Ch'oe Pu's Diary*, p. 120.

41. Pu, *Ch'oe Pu's Diary*, pp. 121–2.

42. Pu, *Ch'oe Pu's Diary*, p. 130.

43. The fame of the Grand Canal spread to the West from Marco Polo's memoir and early Jesuit accounts. A number of accounts of travel on the Grand Canal are available in translation, including a ninth-century Japanese Buddhist pilgrim named Ennin and a twelfth-century Chinese poet named Lu You. See Ennin, *Ennin's Diary: The Record of a Pilgrimage to China in Search of the Law*, translated by Edwin O. Reischauer (New York: The Ronald Press Company, 1955) and *Grand Canal, Great River: The Travel Diary of a Twelfth-Century Chinese Poet* (London: Frances Lincoln Limited Publishers, 2007).

44. The author was able to examine two eighteenth-century Chinese maps of the Grand Canal located in collections in the United States. One is at the Metropolitan Museum in New York, the other at the Freer Gallery in Washington, DC. The Metropolitan Museum also owns a series of landscape paintings of an Imperial barge on the Grand Canal. There are additional images of the Grand Canal located on the internet, generally without attribution.

45. Huang located 42 Chinese poems about the Grand Canal. Huang, 'The Grand Canal during the Ming Dynasty', p. 230.

The Inka Route

Members of Pizarro's inland expedition of 1532 CE wrote the first descriptions of the great Inka (Inca) road system. The troops marched up from the coastal plain into the Andes Mountains on a well-developed track, but were amazed when they arrived at the great north-south trunk road.

> A broad road, made by hands ... traverses all that land from Cuzco to Quito, a distance of more than three hundred leagues. The road is level, and the part of it which traverses the mountains, is very well made, being broad enough for six men on horseback to ride abreast. By the side of the road flow channels of water brought from a distance, at which the travellers can drink.[1]

Modern archaeology confirms this observation. The Cuzco-Quito trunk road was 18–24 feet wide, even in difficult terrain, and spread out to more than 45 feet in less steep portions.[2]

The last thirty years of excavations of the Inka roads have produced astonishing results. Archaeologists have mapped more than 14,000 miles of highways and feeder roads. The Inka roads were the expression and back-bone of the empire. In no sense were these roads 'natural' routes. Labourers cut steps, built bridges, and constructed terraces through some of the most forbidding terrain on earth. The upland trunk road stretched more than

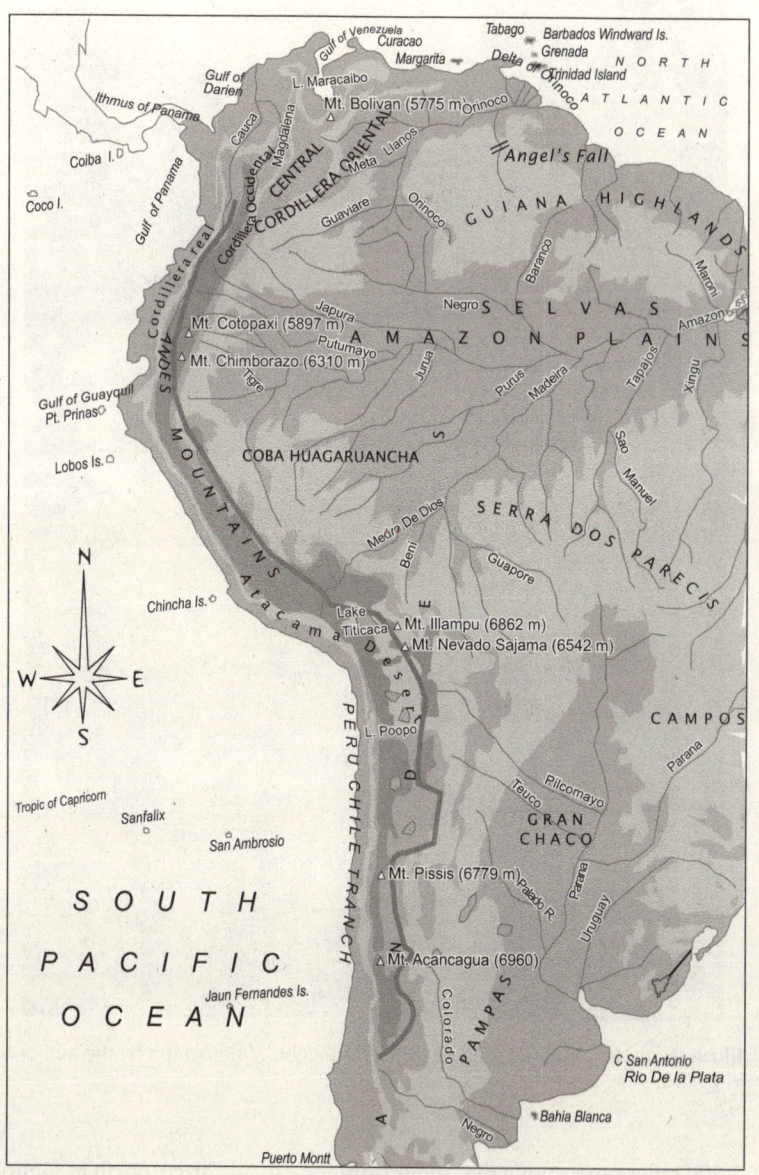

The Inka Route

Illustration 18 'An Inka road near Machu Picchu'. Photograph by the author.

2,500 miles north along the Andes from the capital Cuzco, north to Quito in Ecuador, and south to Santiago in Chile, and was certainly the longest maintained road in the Americas before the paved twentieth century roads of the United States.

A second trunk road, parallel to the mountain road, traversed more than 2,000 miles of coastal plains and deserts. Numerous east-west feeder roads, some not yet mapped, joined the upland and coastal trunk roads. The Inka built these roads in a remarkably short time—less than fifty years— without the wheel, any form of currency, or a written language.

Who were the builders of this extraordinary route, a monumental triumph of ingenuity and architecture? The lack of written records renders the early history of the Inka murky. Some years after the Spanish conquered the kingdom in the 1540s, they recorded the recitations of professional bards to the Inka. Unfortunately, each of the bards was in the employ of a noble Inka family, and tailored his story to flatter his patrons. The same historical figure was, depending on the teller, a hero or a scoundrel, but the stories contain several points of agreement. The Inka clan began as a group of interrelated families. During centuries without any strong central government, the clan left Lake Titicaca on the border of current-day Peru and Bolivia, and moved north in search of good land. Sometime in the early 1400s, they arrived in the highland valley around Cuzco and, in small fierce battles, seized land from other clans in the area. Internal conflict seems to have been as frequent as external warfare. Sons killed fathers and brothers and families annihilated rivals in the struggle for the throne.

Around 1450 CE, the Inka defeated the Chancas, the largest kingdom in the Cuzco region. This event triggered the Inkas' meteoric rise from a clan involved in local rivalry and internal conflict to the creators of a kingdom. The Inkas seized from the Chancas vast quantities of corn, potatoes, beer, textiles, coca leaves, and gold jewellery, and used this loot to expand their influence over other local powers.[3] The kingdom expanded through con- quest and negotiation. Road building was necessary to connect populous, productive river valleys across unproductive mountains. Troops needed to move rapidly to conquer new areas and put down rebellions. Information, loot, tribute, and impressed labour were needed at the capital. And yet it was not only the logistics of an expanding kingdom that defined the Inka roads. The main north-south trunk road had a distinctive, indeed unique, mix of ecology, information flow, bureaucracy, economics, politics, and spiritual beliefs that made it a route rather than just a road.

As the Spaniard forces of 106 infantry and 26 cavalry marched into the mountains, they would have noticed that the Inka generally paved it only in short sections.[4] Flat stones raised the roadbed where inundation by snow-melt or rainfall was likely. Runoff channels sometimes led water under or away from the road. When the route encountered a steep slope, the Inkas either zigzagged the road or built steps of fieldstone set in earth, scaled for a walking human. On a lateral slope, Inka construction crews excavated the high side and used the dirt for a retaining wall on the low side, creating a terrace for the road. All materials for road building came from the immediate surroundings.[5]

One Pedro Sancho, who was on this Spanish expedition, was impressed by Inka bridges that crossed steep gorges.

> If the two banks of the river are stoney, they raise upon them large walls of stone, and then they place [ropes of] pliable reeds two palms or a little less in thickness, and between them ... they weave green osiers [long flexible branches] two fingers thick and well intertwined ... and all well tied. And upon these they place branches crosswise in such a way that the water is not seen, and in this way they make the floor or the bridge. And in the same manner they weave a balustrade of these same osiers along the sides of the bridge so that no one may fall into the water ... the bridge bends as one goes over it, so that one goes continually downward until the middle is reached, and from there he keeps going up until he has finished crossing to the other bank, it trembles very much, so that it goes to the head of one not accustomed to it ... And those who guard these bridges have their houses nearby, and they always have in their hands osiers and wattles and cords in order to mend the bridges if they are injured or even rebuild them if need were.[6]

After a two-month march, the Spaniards arrived at Cajamarca, high in the Andes (in today's northern Peru), one of the planned Inka cities. Each such city repeated a signature urban pattern, a mix of the ritual, political, and practical.[7] The capital, Cuzco, was the template. The Inka conception of space divided cities into 'upper' and 'lower' semicircles, the division line running through the central temple of the sun. Ley lines radiated from the sun temple to urban areas named for and presumably inhabited by various noble families. In Cuzco, the ley lines led primarily to residences outside the central city owned by the descendants of prior Inka kings. Each residential area had its own source of water.[8] A large open plaza was the centre

Illustration 19 'Inca Bridge'. Photograph by David Broad. Creative Commons. Wikimedia.

of each city, often paved and surrounded with walls of mortar-less, closely fitted stone. Cuzco's plaza included a thick layer of sand brought more than 300 miles from the Pacific coast.[9] The focal point of the Cuzco plaza was a boulder with a hewn seat. Priests moved an image of the sun god back and forth from the seat to its home in the great temple. Smaller but similar temples were at the centre of all Inka cities. Just as at Cuzco, local noble families often occupied named areas outside the city's centre.

The Inka feasted in the plaza, distributed gifts to nobles, and received tribute of valuable commodities, such as feathers and cloth. Each new Inka city had a raised platform in the plaza on which the administrator sat. This platform was the focus of religious ceremonies and feasts. Long rectangular halls with doors facing the plaza were typical of Cuzco and other Inka cities. Early Spanish records recount that some halls were used for banqueting in inclement weather. Others may have housed soldiers or transient workers. One of the halls typically housed women who served the temple of the sun. Near the plaza were great warehouses for commodities for tribute, including grain, textiles, weapons, feathers, and corn beer. The plaza of Cajamarca was the site of the battle in which Pizarro captured the Inka ruler and, a few months later, executed him.

In 1533 CE, the Pizarro expedition started south to Cuzco, hoping to complete the conquest of the Inka Empire. Pedro Sancho noticed storage buildings along the route, especially concentrated close to the cities:

> ...storehouses full of mantles, wool, arms, metals, and clothes and all things which are grown or made in this land. There are houses where the tribute is kept ... and there is a house where are kept more than a hundred dried birds, because they make garments of their feathers, which are of many colors ... There are bucklers, oval shields made of leather, beams for roofing the houses, knives and other tools, sandals and breast-plates for the warriors in such quantity that the mind does not cease to wonder how so great a tribute of so many kinds of things have been given.[10]

In the Inka kingdom as a whole, there were a staggering number of storehouses. Archaeologists have identified remains of nearly 10,000 storage buildings and estimate their volume at more than 1 million cubic metres.[11] Many sites consist of rows of simple rectangular fieldstone buildings with a single door. All had thatch roofs. Microscopic remains from the floors of some of these buildings show that many were used to store hulled corn (maize).[12] Storage of potatoes and other tubers was more difficult. Potatoes rot or sprout and spoil unless stored at 40–42 degrees Fahrenheit. They also require constant airflow through the stored potatoes and do best with 89–90 per cent humidity. The Inka solved the problems of potato storage by carefully selecting how high into the mountains to put the buildings and constructing them with raised ventilated floors.[13] Potato storage buildings must have been staffed continuously to maintain proper conditions. The high concentration of storehouses along the Cuzco-Quito trunk road is one of the defining features of the route.

The trunk route also had periodic way stations, known as *tampu*, generally a day's walk apart. The staff provided individuals and groups on state business with food, fodder for animals, and wood for fires. Larger way stations also probably stored tribute: textiles, crafts, and weapons.[14] In much of the empire, larger or smaller tampu were the principle Inka administrative presence.[15] Archaeologists have found hundreds, and speculated that the system probably had thousands of such way stations. All had water, generally brought by a channel from a spring or river. A walled compound enclosed several small, single-room buildings, which archaeologists believe provided shelter for travellers, especially in rainy areas.[16] Stucco and paint covered these buildings. Some way stations included a corral for llamas and a long undivided rectangular one-story stone structure, possibly a tribute warehouse. Bernabé Cobo, a Jesuit missionary and writer who observed tampu about a century after the Spanish arrival, thus described them:

> With respect to their design and form, they were large houses ... with only one room, one hundred to three hundred feet long and at least thirty to a maximum of fifty feet wide, all cleared and unadorned without being divided into chambers or apartments, and with two or three doors, all in one side at equal intervals.[17]

The Spanish expedition next encountered the Inka planned city of Huánuco Pampa (current-day Huánuco in central upland Peru), today the best preserved of these Inka cities, consisting of about four thousand remaining structures. Built in the middle of the fifteenth century on a flat plain at an altitude of 3,800 metres, it was abandoned a few decades after Spanish conquest.[18] Overall, Huánuco Pampa was divided into two sections by the Cuzco-Quito route, which entered the city at the southeast corner and exited at the northwest corner, in the same urban pattern as the road divides at Cuzco.[19] The layout of buildings at Huánuco Pampa is virtually identical to the Cuzco template. At the centre was a huge plaza with a raised platform. Large halls with typical trapezoidal doorways surround the plaza.[20] Beyond the halls were residential compounds, including one for 'virtuous women', who lived celibate lives, served the main deity, and wove textiles. Up the hillside to the south in tidy rows were thousands of tribute storage buildings.[21] Tons of broken pottery shards from the city represent Cuzco styles, not local forms.[22]

Huánuco Pampa formed part of the trunk route and was a permanent Inka presence. Away from the trunk route, the Inka built no plazas, temples, or feasting halls in any of the smaller towns in the hinterland of the Huánuco Pampa. A small percentage of the broken pottery in many village sites was Inka-style, suggesting some Inka presence in these villages, perhaps seasonally or at periodic festivals.

At a steady walking rate of 20 miles per day, in a little over a month, the mission reached Hatun Jauja (termed Xauxa by the Spanish), about 750 miles north of Cuzco. One of the early Spanish observers described the typical features of the city:

> In all these parts there were great lodgings of the Inkas: although the principal ones were at the beginning of the valley in the part they call Xauxa: because there was a large enclosure, where there were strong and very excellent stone lodgings: and a house of women of the sun: and a very rich temple: and many storage structures full of all the things that could be had. Besides that, there was a large number of smiths, who worked large and small vessels of silver and gold for the service of the Inkas and [for] temple ornaments. There were more than eight thousand Indians for service of the temple, and of the palaces of the lords.[23]

At the Inka city of the Vilcas Huaman, the road turned east towards Cuzco, and eventually entered a lush highland river valley, which was divided into estates owned by the noble Inka families. On most flatter sections of the route, workers had merely pulled stones out of the way and piled them on either side, but along this productive valley, high walls separated the road from the estates. One of the members of Pizarro's mission counted 5,000 storage buildings in this valley.

Just north of Cuzco was Saqsawaman, the largest complex built by the Inka, consisting of an enormous re-configuring of a rocky hill with the addition of fortress-like walls, niches, terraces, and storage units. Even those who saw it at the time of the Spanish conquest did not know its exact function, though recent aerial pictures have established its ritual relationship with Cuzco. The complex represents the head of an enormous puma with Cuzco as its body. Pedro Sancho, on the expedition of 1533, assumed that Saqsawaman was a fortress.

> Upon the hill, toward the city, rounded and very steep, there is a very beautiful fortress of earth and stone. Its large windows which look over the city make it appear still more beautiful. Within there are many dwellings, and a chief tower in the centre, built square, and having four or five terraces one above another. The rooms inside are small and the stones of which it is built are very well worked and so well adjusted to one another that it does not appear that they have any mortar ... there are so many rooms and towers that a person could not see them in a day.[24]

When the Spanish expedition entered Cuzco they found it architecturally much the same as the cities they had encountered along the Inka trunk route. Four roads led out of the plaza in Cuzco, each connecting to portions of the empire. The Spanish had just covered much of the northern route. A western road led to the coastal lowlands. The southern portion of the trunk route proceeded through upland sites, where llamas were raised for more than 1,500 miles, terminating in what is today Argentina. Leading to the east was a relatively high and difficult road that led over the Andes to the tropical peoples and products of the upper reaches of the Amazon basin. The early Spanish observers had no idea of the cultures at the far ends of these roads. Pedro Sancho, for example, reported what he heard:

> Those who dwell on the other side of the mountains, are like savages ... they have very great forests and maintain themselves almost entirely on the fruit of the trees; they have no domicile, nor fixed settlements that are known ... the land is so useless that it paid all of its tribute to the lords in parrot feathers.[25]

Sancho could not have been more wrong about the societies and cultures in the western Amazon basin. In the past decade, archaeologists have located remains of sophisticated cultures and agriculture in this area, including huge mounded earthworks, terraced fields, irrigation, and complex permanent fish weirs.[26]

Let us turn from the physical features of the route to what Spanish records and current archaeology suggest was the role of the north-south route in the workings of the Inka kingdom. Perhaps most striking is the lack of any evidence along the road of trade or traders. For example, there were no markets, wholesale or retail, and no evidence of an independent craft area in the entire ruins of the best-preserved Inka city, Huánuco Pampa. Archaeologists know that before the Inka kingdom there had been trade between the Andes uplands, the river valleys, and coastal plains. Such trade seems logical, since each zone produced different and complementary products, such as textiles, maize, coca, potatoes, dried fish, and seashells.[27] The Inka apparently suppressed this interregional trade, enforcing a system of tribute paid to the empire both in commodities and labour.

Rather than trade, temporary impressed labour was at the core of the Inka Empire. The social hierarchy consisted, at the bottom, of subsistence herders, craftspeople, labourers, and farmers from a variety of ethnic groups. Above them were local nobles with small armies, who were also not Inka. Above both groups were the representatives of the Inka—administrators, soldiers, and priests who lived in the Inka-designed cities along the trunk road. And above all these in the hierarchy were Inka families from Cuzco.

The Inka were the last and largest of many indigenous empires, some based in the mountains, but most based on the plains. They adopted two pre-existing methods of amassing labour from the bottom of the social hierarchy. The first method centred on lavish feasting and gift giving. The Inka feasted local nobles, often over several days.[28] Corn beer, food, and coca were liberally consumed. Local nobles received gifts of textiles, crafted metal, and feathers for high-prestige clothes. The local nobles, in return, agreed to provide a certain number of men and women from their areas for a certain number of days of unpaid labour. These feasts, as the empire expanded, were held on an enormous scale, which is a plausible explanation for the massive open plaza at the centre of every Inka city. Covered halls that surround each plaza made feasting possible in inclement weather.[29]

Almost a century ago, a brilliant French sociologist named Marcel Mauss laid out the general characteristics of feasting and gifting, regardless of where in the world it occurred.[30] Gifts in this context were neither religious nor ceremonial. They established real and practical obligations from those groups or clans feasted and gifted. As Mauss put it, '... what they exchange is not exclusively goods and wealth ... they exchange rather courtesies, entertainments, ritual, military assistance, women, children, dances, and feasts';[31]

The central idea is that every gift must be repaid in a known manner. The Inka gave the feasts and gifts and, in return, local nobles committed to provide a certain number of men and women for a certain number of days of labour. Their labour built the cities and the roads, worked the mines, and filled the storage buildings with the food, crafts, and beer they produced, the coca they grew, and the feathers they gathered. Some impressed labour crews worked the great Inka estates that grew the grain and tubers that fed the city dwellers. Other labour obligations were highly specialized and were provided by certain ethnic groups, such as providing message runners on the roads or weaving a particular type of textile as tribute.[32]

When labour crews worked away from home, the kingdom provided basic food and shelter. In Huánuco Pampa, the best preserved of the Inka cities on the Cuzco-Quito trunk route, archaeologists found Inka-style pottery rather than local pottery in the housing for the labour crews, suggesting a dormitory for various labouring groups, stocked from Inka warehouses.[33] Pedro Sancho, on the Pizarro expedition, knew that much of the food for the Inka cities came from the lowlands, carried by temporary impressed labour.[34]

> None of the lords who have governed these [mountain] provinces have ever been able to make any use of these coast-people ... they are fit to be used for nothing else than to carry fish and fruits [up into the highlands] for as soon as they come into the mountainous regions, their own land being very hot, they sicken for the most part...[35]

If anyone doubts what this impressed labour could do, consider the city of Saraguro in Ecuador. Recent chemical analysis has established the long-distance transport from a mine near Cuzco to Saraguro of huge building stones for mortar-less architecture. These stones were transported on rollers through the Andes for nearly a thousand miles. This astonishing feat is the longest known transport of massive stones in the pre-European Americas.[36]

A careful historical study of an agricultural area near Huánuco Pampa shows that the Inka kingdom combined ethnic groups into units over which they appointed nobles. Unlike pre-existing local nobles, it was not the local community that controlled succession. Rather, at the death of an Inka-appointed noble, the heir had to seek permission to take up the office. In fact, the hopeful young noble had to go personally to Cuzco along the trunk route and show everyone on the route his obedience to the Inka.[37]

The second method by which the Inka amassed impressed labour also pre-dated the kingdom. It consisted of wholesale moving of entire peasant groups and captured populations. Evidence of this practice has been found for the earliest known Andean empire, the Wari Empire (c. 600 CE). Under Inka rule, uprooted labourers retained their distinctive headgear and tools when they were required to move along the trunk road to Inka estates and cities. Known as *mitmaqs*, the transported populations became labourers, soldiers, service personnel, and weavers. Some mitmaqs, for example, maintained way stations.[38] Others served religious sites. Many were re-settled on new Inka estates, not only around Cuzco, but also in any agricultural areas serving various Inka cities.[39] Mitmaq settlements formed the core of Inka agricultural development zones, produced important goods like corn and coca, and served as local soldiers to control recalcitrant populations, either on the frontier or among restive ethnic groups. Mitmaqs were not, however, simply transported and enslaved populations. The reality was more complex. Some peoples became mitmaq as a reward, others for punishment.[40] Many were valued for their loyalty and were probably better off than the surrounding population. A few mitmaqs rose to high administrative positions in the Inka state.[41]

The great north-south route was at the very heart of the Inca Empire, connecting all its provincial cities.[42] The trunk roads allowed rapid movement of judges and other administrators, armies, priests, and information between the capital and new regional cities. Local nobles passed along the trunk route on their way to Cuzco. Their fears, hopes, and expectations must have formed part of the mental aspect of the route, though there is no remaining evidence. The Inka cities along the route reflected the ethos of the empire and were centres of Inka sun worship. Trunk roads conveyed runners carrying *khipu* (also phonetically spelled as '*quipu*'), bundles of coloured, knotted string that contained information from distant parts of the empire.[43] Impressed labour carried produce from the fertile river valleys and coastal regions up the Andes to thousands of storage buildings that archaeologists have located on the main trunk route. The Inka moved artisans from the coast to the capital to work metals and produce fabrics. Men and women from the lowest tier of society were removed from their homes and travelled on the trunk route to settle and develop new agricultural areas. Temporary impressed labour supplied by local nobles walked on the route to the capital or far-flung building projects. On the route, an army might march to quell dissent by local nobles.[44] The Quechua language spread along the route throughout the highlands.

While Inka roads were a feature of the empire's strength, they could not compensate for other more serious weaknesses. First, Inka cities and outposts depended on food and other materials brought from lower and

more productive areas. The relatively unproductive highlands could not
feed the cities, which were fatally vulnerable if the food supply from the
lowlands was disrupted. Second, the Inka administration was quite weak
in many areas. There might be a concentration of administrators and officials at a new city, but very little administrative or military presence in the
countryside. Third, there were peoples both within the Inka kingdom and
on several frontiers who were not subdued, but rather required considerable resources to keep in check.[45] Fourth, Inka armies consisted of largely
untrained peasants fulfilling labour requirements. The armies had impressive numbers but little training in fighting, and none in large-scale strategy
or tactics. Fifth, the Inka were singularly unsuccessful in convincing local
groups of the value of their style of sun worship, which does not seem to
have flourished anywhere outside their own cities. Finally, probably the
empire's single most important weakness was factional warfare, not only
at times of succession, but also during reigns. The bard stories are replete
with interrelated families waging all-out war. Such warfare was inevitable
when a reigning king died, as there were no fixed rules of succession. This
factional warfare routinely involved conquered but restless and militarized
local nobility. Local nobles became allies and rivals rather than subordi-
nates to the Inka. At the time of the Spanish arrival in 1533 CE, the Inka
were involved in just such a protracted bloody civil war, over who would
be the next ruler.

Just as Roman roads expedited conquest of the empire, the Inka route
greatly facilitated Pizarro's audacious conquest. His troops moved up a
feeder road from the coast to the Inka regional city of Cajamarca. The band
was given accommodations along the way. After the capture and execution
of the Inka ruler, Pizarro led his soldiers several hundred miles south on the
trunk road to Cuzco for the next phase of the conquest. He went back to
the coast on yet another feeder road.

The Spanish had radically different economic, political, and social pri-
orities from those of the empire they replaced. They developed a lowland
empire, oriented towards the river valleys, the coastal plain, and the sea.
The Spanish, as a matter of policy, forcibly moved populations out of the
highlands to more-easily controlled lowlands. Land became owned. The
productive lowland river valleys were granted to various Spanish nobles
and soldiers as enormous haciendas.[46] They introduced money and turned

all produce into commodities, replacing the earlier system of feasting, labour obligations, and large-scale tribute. At a deeper level, the Spanish repudiated the sun worship that was at the centre of the Inka claim to establish order in the world. Churches were often built in the central plazas directly on Inka foundations. Along with priests came vigorous attempts, of course not successful, to stamp out all pre-existing beliefs, especially upland oracles and religious sites.

And what of the Inka route roads after Spanish conquest? What had once been the highland heartland of the Inka Empire now became a backwater as coastal Lima replaced Cuzco, La Paz replaced Cajamarca, and Santiago flourished. The highland Inka cities sharply declined in population and power. Huánuco Pampa, for example, was abandoned within a decade of conquest. Some of the east-west feeder roads became important connections between coastal centres and remaining populations in the highlands. In many places, however, the decline of the Inca route was remarkably rapid. Way stations were vacant; maintenance ended.

Overall, the north-south Inka trunk route languished. Local populations maintained some bridges for local traffic, but some sections of the route were simply abandoned. For the surviving highland populations, ethnic networks and the local economy were more important for survival than the grand Inka route. Today, the Inka route and its feeder roads still serve local highland populations, but the overall route is mainly the stuff of archaeological research.

Undoubtedly the most heavily used Inka road is the hiking trail from the river valley north of Cuzco up to Machu Picchu. About 25,000 tourists and guides every year traverse this high, steep trail through lush rainforest and over rocky passes. The 25-mile trek takes four days. In the last decade, the government of Peru has proposed restoring the whole of the Inka trunk road from Lake Titicaca in the south to the Ecuador border in the north. None of the work has actually been started, but it is a grand vision that the Inka would well have understood.

Notes

1. Francisco De Xerxes, 'A True Account of the Province of Cuzco', translated by Clement R. Markham in *Reports of the Discovery of Peru* (London: Hakluyt Society, 1872), p. 29.

2. John Hyslop, *The Inka Road System* (Orlando, Florida: Academic Press, Inc., 1984), p. 257. Even side roads were generous. The Cuzco-Machu Picchu road was 10–12 feet, as observed by the author. The reader will note that this chapter has relatively less on 'mental maps' and the cognitive geography of the route. In the absence of any written sources, I remain cautious about what can be inferred about mental states from archaeological remains and later colonial accounts.

3. The Inka were the last in a very long series of kingdoms both in the Andes and on the coastal plain of Peru. Archaeologists have found evidence of sophisticated urban civilizations that date back well before the Common Era. Many kingdoms were regional, but some were quite large. The genius of the Inka was to stitch together an empire composed of many smaller regional powers by force and negotiation. In this process, the road system and new Inka cities were particularly important.

4. Machu Picchu, the popular tourist site, now seems remote and somehow mysterious. It was far less so in Inka times. The site is located on the headwaters of the Vilcanota River, whose valley below Machu Picchu was heavily farmed as Inca estates. The current-day Machu Picchu hiking trail was a side road off the main north-south trunk road between Cuzco and Quito.

5. Hyslop, *The Inka Road System* , pp. 225–44, 246. The author has observed all of these Inka road building solutions.

6. Pedro Sancho, *An Account of the Conquest of Peru*, translated by Phillip Ainsworth Means (New York: The Cortes Society, 1917), pp. 61–2. While there is archaeological evidence of habitations at some of the bridge sites, many had none. Perhaps local communities maintained these bridges, as some did until the last century. See Hyslop, *The Inka Road System*, p. 332.

7. For a 'holistic' attempt to understand Inka monumental architecture, see Jerry D. Moore, *Cultural Landscapes in the Ancient Andes: Archaeologies of Place* (Gainesville, Florida: University Press of Florida, 2005).

8. See Jeanette Sherbondy, 'The Canal System of Hanan Cuzco'. Doctoral Dissertation, Department of Anthropology, University of Illinois at Champaign-Urbana, 1982. Also, I.S. Farrington, 'Ritual Geography, Settlement Patterns and the Characterization of the Provinces of the Inka Heartland', *World Archaeology*, vol. 23, no. 3, Archaeology of Empires (February 1992), pp. 368–85. The Inka used clay models to locate buildings in the terrain of new cites. Water sources were prominent parts of these models.

9. John Hyslop, *Inka Settlement Planning* (Austin: University of Texas Press, 1990), pp. 37–8.

10. Sancho, *An Account of the Conquest of Peru*, pp. 158–9.

11. Craig Morris, 'Storage in Tawantinsuyu', Ph.D. Dissertation, Department of Anthropology, University of Chicago, 1967, p. 155.

12. John R. Topic and Therese Lang Topic, 'A Summary of the Inca Occupation of Huamanchuco', in Michael A. Malpass, *Provincial Inca* (Iowa City: University of Iowa Press, 1993), p. 27.

13. See Craig Morris, 'The Technology of Highland Inka Food Storage', in Terry LeVine, *Inka Storage Systems* (Norman, Oklahoma: University of Oklahoma Press, 1992), pp. 238–58. Also, Craig Morris and Donald E. Thompson, *Huánuco Pampa: An Inca City and Its Hinterland* (London: Thames and Hudson Ltd., 1985), pp. 102–7. The general use of storage to maintain an elite commodity probably predates the Inka. Morris attributes the invention of the system to the Wari Empire of c. 600 CE. See Craig Morris and Adrianna van Hagen, *The Inka Empire and Its Andean Origins* (New York: Abbeville, 1993).

14. Hyslop, *The Inka Road System*, p. 275. As observed by the author, some of these tampu developed into substantial Inka towns, such as Ollantaytambo, north of Cuzco.

15. Some features of the roads seem more human and universal than distinctly Inka. At the summit of high passes, there are piles of stones, thrown there by centuries of travellers. The piles continue to accumulate today. Also, travellers marked certain stones or outcroppings or simple shrines with donations or colour. The author has observed both practices in the Himalayas.

16. Hyslop, *The Inka Road System*, pp. 282–3.

17. Cobo, translated in Hyslop, *The Inka Road System*, p. 281. Contrary to Cobo, archaeologists have found considerable variety among Inka way stations, for example, round buildings that reflected local style.

18. The site has been studied for several decades. The initial results are summarized in Craig Morris and Donald E. Thompson, *Huánuco Pampa: An Inca City and Its Hinterland* (London: Thames and Hudson Ltd., 1985).

19. Morris and Thompson, *Huánuco Pampa*, p. 72. Some of the *tampu*.

20. Morris and Thompson, *Huánuco Pampa*, p. 15.

21. See plan in Morris and Thompson, *Huánuco Pampa*, pp. 54–5. Also Morris, 'Huánuco Pampa and Tunsukancha: Major and Minor Nodes in the Inka Storage Network', in Terry LeVine, *Inka Storage Systems* (Norman, Oklahoma: University of Oklahoma Press, 1992), pp. 152–75.

22. Morris and Thompson, *Huánuco Pampa*, pp. 73–80.

23. Translated in D'Altroy, Provincial, 103. See also Xerxes, 'A True Account of the Province of Cuzco', pp. 45–7.

24. Sancho, *An Account of the Conquest of Peru*, p. 155.

25. Sancho, *An Account of the Conquest of Peru*, p. 147.

26. See Charles H. Mann, 'Ancient Earthmovers of the Amazon', *Science*, vol. 28 (August 2008), pp. 1148–52.

27. On the seashell/copper trade of the northern coast, see María Rostworowski de Diiez Canseco, *History of the Inca Realm*, translated by Harry B. Iceland (Cambridge: Cambridge University Press, 1999), pp. 159–63, 208–11. An east-west transit from the Pacific coast over the Andes and into the Amazon rainforest represents more types of climate in less distance than perhaps anywhere else on earth. The possibilities for interchange between these microclimates seem myriad. See I. Shimada, 'Introduction', in *Andean Ecology and Civilization: An Interdisciplinary Perspective On Andean Ecological Complementarity*, edited by S. Masuda, I. Shimada, and C. Morris (Tokyo: University of Tokyo Press: 1985), pp. xi–xxxii.

28. It is only in the last decade or so that scholars have explored the central role of negotiations and accommodations between the Inka and local elites. The arrangements varied from region to region. See, for example, Steven A. Wernke, 'The Politics of Community and Inka Statecraft in the Colca Valley, Peru', *Latin American Antiquity*, vol. 17, no. 2 (June 2006), pp. 177–208.

29. Archaeobotany has established the urban storehouses that contained materials used in feasting were quite different from foods eaten in ordinary houses. See 'Stores and Homes: A Botanical Comparison of Inka Storehouses and Contemporary Ethnic Houses', in Terry LeVine, *Inka Storage Systems* (Norman, Oklahoma: University of Oklahoma Press, 1992), pp. 287–310.

30. Marcell Mauss was a nephew of Emile Durkheim and one of the few French sociologists to survive World War I. Much of his professional life in the interwar years was spent editing and recovering the writings of his fellow French sociologists.

31. Marcel Mauss, *The Gift: The Form and Reason for Exchange in Archaic Societies*, translated by Ian Cunnison (London: Cohen & West Ltd., 1966) p. 3. See also Aldona Jonaitis, *Chiefly Feasts: The Enduring Kwakiutl Potlatch* (Washington State: University of Washington Press, 1991).

32. The Inca did not stop craft production. They gathered it as tribute. Craft villages must have also produced food. Otherwise, the craft workers would have starved.

33. Morris and Thompson, *Huánuco Pampa*, p. 94. The authors suggest that labour crews might have been fed out of large common kitchens.

34. See Morris, 'From Principles of Ecological Complementarity to the Organization and Administration of Tawantinsuyu Andean Ecology and

Civilization', in Izumi Shimada, Yoshio Masuda, and Craig Morris, *Andean Ecology and Civilization: An Interdisciplinary Perspective on Andean Ecological Complementarity: Papers From the Wrenner-Gren Foundation for Anthropological Research Symposioum No. 91* (Cedar Grove Conference Center, 1983).

35. Sancho, *An Account of the Conquest of Peru*, p. 146.

36. Dennis E. Ogburn, 'Evidence for Long-Distance Transportation of Building Stones in the Inka Empire, From Cuzco, Peru to Saguro, Ecuador,' *Latin American Antiquity*, vol. 15, no. 4 (December 2004), pp. 419–39.

37. Sue Grosbill, '... and he said in the time of the Ynga, they paid tribute and served the Ynga', in Michael A. Malpass, *Provincial Inca* (Iowa City: University of Iowa Press, 1993), pp. 49–53. Such an assertion of control of succession of local elites has been a common feature of empires. The British monarchy asserted such a right quite early. When the British conquered India in the early nineteenth century, the control of succession of the remaining semi-independent Indian princes was hotly disputed and was one of the leading causes of the uprising of 1857.

38. Terence N. D'Altroy, *Provincial Power in the Inka Empire* (Washington: Smithsonian Institution Press, 1992), p. 101.

39. Grosbill, '... and he said in the time of the Ynga, they paid tribute and served the Ynga', pp. 69–71.

40. See Diiez Canseco, *History of the Inca Realm*, pp. 172–4.

41. For the mobilization of mitmaq labour in one region of the empire, see Mary B. La Lone and Darrell E. La Lon, 'The Inka State in the Southern Highlands: State Administrative and Production Enclaves', *Ethnohistory*, vol. 34, no. 1, Inka Ethnohistory (Winter 1987), pp. 47–62. In many parts of the world, there were examples of slaves rising to high position. The Mamlukes in Egypt, the Janissaries in the Ottoman Empire, military slaves in western India, and eunuchs in China come readily to mind.

42. Inka trunk roads, however, bypassed pre-existing regional capitals.

43. Though several hundred authentic Inka khipu (which must have had numeric information on quantities in storage areas or troop strengths) exist today, scholars have been unable to decode them. It has been suggested that they were memory aids for the runners as they passed messages along.

44. A recent study used network analysis to quantify the efficiency of the network in moving both information and goods to these new cities and the capital. On the whole, it found the placement of both storage centres and cities highly efficient in meeting the needs of supplying good and information to the capital and the new cities. See David Jenkins, 'A Network Analysis of Inka Roads,

Administrative Centers and Storage Facilities', *Ethnohistory*, vol. 48, no. 4 (Fall 2001), pp. 655–87.

45. For the Quito area, see Frank L. Salomon, 'Ethnic Lords of Quito in the Age of the Incas: The Political Economy of North-Andean Chiefdoms'. Doctoral Thesis, Cornell University, 1978.

46. Much of the Spanish discussion of how the Inka Empire should be ruled and changed was couched in comparisons to the Roman Empire. See Sabine MacCormack, *On the Wings of Time: Rome, the Incas, Spain, and Peru* (Princeton: Princeton University Press, 2007).

PART IV

TRADE ROUTES

Introduction

Trade routes were created by the availability of goods that could be sold somewhere other than where they were cultivated or created, with transport costs low enough to allow for a profit. Trade routes often connected two different ecologies, such as tropical to temperate or highland to lowland. In the pre-modern world, overland transportation costs were high, and successful trade routes had to transport a variety of high-value commodities, such as slaves, salt, medicines, ivory, gem stones, refined metals, high-end cloth, weapons, and glassware. Transportation costs were far lower on water routes than on land routes, making water routes profitable for heavier, bulkier commodities, such as grain, functional pottery, bulk metals, timber, and building materials.

Trade routes have traditionally been visualized as a kind of two-ended, fuzzy bottlebrush—with one end as supply and the other end demand—joined by a long wire handle. The supply end often reached deep into hinterland areas, far from the route. Medicines, for example, came from forests and mountains, often collected by hunters and gatherers. Cotton for fabrics was grown hundreds of miles inland from the looms on the coast. Slaves were brought to urban slave markets from far inland. Commodities were accumulated, stored, and transported from cities or ports. The handle of the brush represents a road or waterway from the point of collection to another city, the distribution centre, from which the goods went out to many destinations for sale.

This traditional metaphor misses several important features of a trade route. First, trade routes were not a single road or waterway. They consisted of a variety of roads or waterways, chosen on the basis of factors such as local war, weather, and perceived haunts of bandits or pirates. Second, trade routes were seasonal. Storms, freezing cold, or severe heat closed most routes much of the year. Some trade routes permitted only one round trip per year. Much of the trade, therefore, was segmented and moved between cities. Third, the central handle of the bottlebrush was far more complex than the image suggests. Many towns and cities along trade routes did not simply provide travellers with water, fuel, fodder, and a place to sleep. Instead, these towns were also processing centres for goods moving along the route. Some towns processed food from the hinterland of the city into preserved forms that could be transported. More common was the transformation of commodities into new value-added products, such as cotton or wool into rugs, semi-precious stones and wood into inlaid boxes, or illiterate slaves into increased-value educated slaves.

Towns along trade routes were places of meeting and mixing. The architecture reflected both the designs of large empires of the time and local influences. Religions and sects jostled and competed for patronage. These towns were places of a variety of languages; men often spoke several languages. Trade routes promoted many kinds of transfers—plants, cuisine, medical knowledge, fashion, books, kingly symbols and ceremony, and board games.

Traders competed but none were alone. Their most important competitive edge was information, which they received from a network of kinsmen, co-religionists, or other members of their trade group. Their mental map, therefore, included not only their own experience, but also the experience of older members of the network and what might be thought of as 'common knowledge' accumulated by generations of traders working the same route. Reputation was established by astute trading, hospitality to travelling members of their trading group, and extensive correspondence with other members of their group. Letters included assessments of politics and security, in addition to family gossip and specific trade recommendations. Fashion changed rapidly and what sold the previous year might not sell the next. Trade letters, therefore, often specified a particular type of cloth in a certain weight, colour, and pattern. Traders watched for the rise in popularity of a commodity, such as feathers or ivory. They also watched for the rise of new kingdoms, which might become a demand area for their products. The reverse flow of information sent by traders directly affected production centres along the route. A trader generally tried to make money not only by shipping goods for sale, but by specifying what the member of his group who received the goods was to buy in return for the trader. Traders' constant exchange of goods and information promoted the acceptance of common currencies over the full length of the route.

Besides traders, different mental expectations were held by professional ship captains and heads of caravans who knew each other, exchanged information, and trained the younger generation. Processors of goods in towns along the way expected that their value-added products would find a market.

The long-term history of trade routes is complicated. Large empires regularly attempted to conquer, control, tax, and provide security along trade routes. Technology could doom a trade route, as when trains and steamships supplanted the trans-Saharan caravan route. Over time many routes have shifted functions or specialties and are almost untraceable in the modern world.

Let us, then, travel along trade routes with an African slave bound for greatness in India, an Islamic traveller crossing the Sahara, and a retired British naval commander on the Erie Canal.

The Indian Ocean

In 1610 CE, a slave from Africa named Malik Ambar led an army of 10,000 fellow African slaves into the extraordinary fortress of Deogiri. Located 150 miles inland from the west coast of India, and high on the Deccan Plateau, Deogiri dominated its surrounding region. For a thousand years, from 700 to 1700 CE, every dynasty had to hold this fort to rule the region.

Even today, it is an arduous two-hour climb to reach the royal apartments on the top of the citadel. The road begins at the first outer wall that once protected the city below the fort. An attacker climbing the broad stairs would have had no cover from lethal arrows, stones, and hot oil from above. The steps twist and turn to prevent the attacker's war elephant from gaining momentum to crash the single massive gate in the inner wall. A moat protected the citadel. Sluices and gates channelled water stored at the top to submerge the bridge over the moat. The final ascent to the top of the citadel consisted of a tunnel and an interior staircase cut from the living rock. A brazier could fill the tunnel with smoke to choke attackers.

In spite of these defences, the Mughal garrison that held the fortress was so awed by Malik Ambar's might, that the soldiers marched out and surrendered without a fight. Ambar was a great lord and, under his crucial leadership, the fragile sultanate of Ahmednagar not only survived repeated invasions by the much more powerful Mughal Empire from North India,

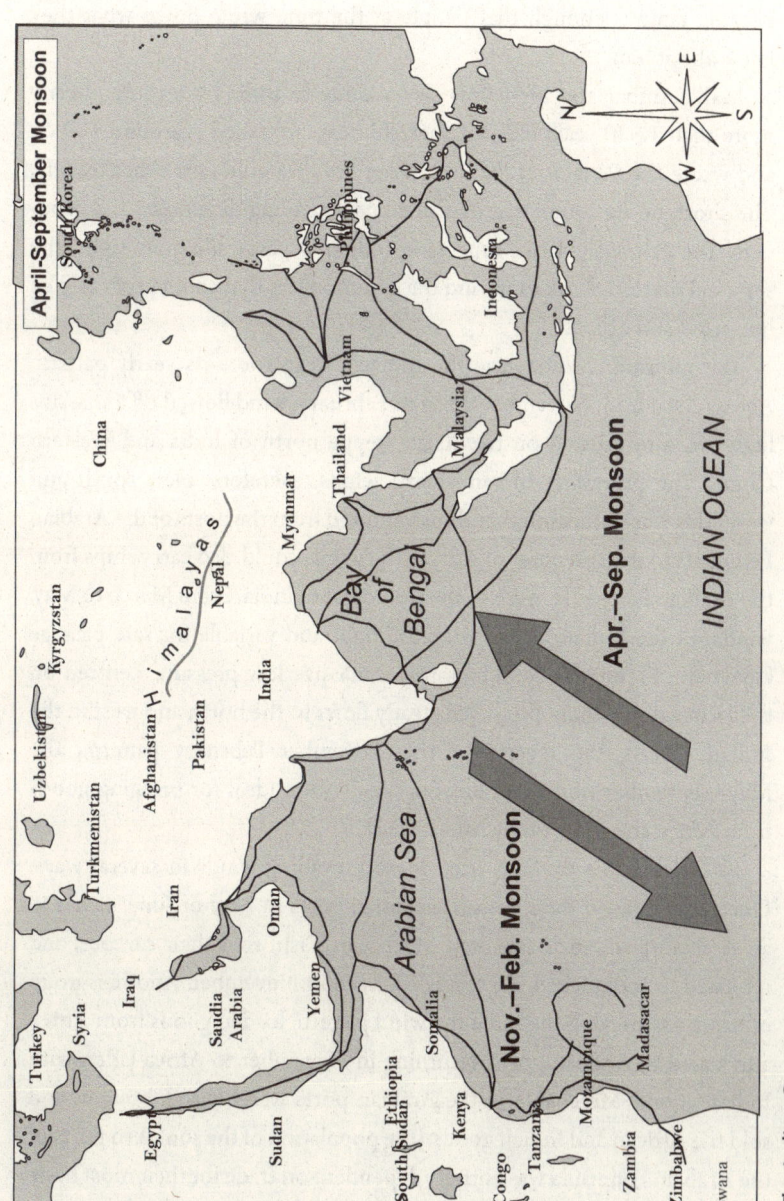

The Indian Ocean

but successfully counterattacked. Ambar had come far from the shackles and chains of his early life. He left no memoir but, unlike most slaves, became famous enough that people at the time wrote down what they knew about him.

Malik Ambar and his fellow slaves came to India by a route already more than 1,500 years old. A Greek ship captain sailed it around 100 CE and wrote the *Periplus of the Erythraean Sea* as a guide for other traders. The short, no-nonsense text described ports, sailing directions, and products. The *Periplus* got two aspects of Indian Ocean trade quite right: the seasonal rhythm of the route and the commodities that could profitably be imported and exported.

The monsoon winds gave the Indian Ocean route its yearly pattern. Across Asia, from November through February, wind flowed off a massive high pressure centred on the Asian steppe north of India and Western China. The prevailing Indian Ocean winds, therefore, blew south and west. This was the season that ships ventured from the ports of the Arabian Peninsula to the east coast of Africa. The winds could also carry ships from the Arabian Peninsula south to the west coast of India. From March to May, winds on the Indian Ocean were too light and variable for safe passage anywhere. From May to September, a massive low pressure, centred on the Himalayan region, produced steady flows to the north and west in the Indian Ocean, the reverse of the November–February pattern. The May–September northwest flowing winds were ideal for bringing goods from Africa and India to the Middle East.

Knowledgeable captains used these prevailing winds in several ways. One group loaded their vessels in Indian ports in May or June, sailed to an Arabian port, such as Aden, Mocha, or Kish, sold their cargoes, and returned to India when the winds reversed in November. Another group of captains, utilizing the same the wind pattern, loaded goods from Africa and sailed to Arabian ports, returning in November to Africa laden with Indian goods. Merchants in the Arabian ports warehoused, bought, and sold the African and Indian goods. The population of the southern ports of the Arabian Peninsula was entirely dependent on trade for their most basic needs—food, fuel, and building materials. The land behind these ports was barren of agriculture and home to raiding Bedouin. The Arabian Peninsula ports, thus, were as fortified on the landward side as they were facing the sea. No port had a decisive advantage over others, and they all competed for the trans-shipping trade. The wealthiest merchants of these ports fitted out ships to venture for spices from India and beyond.

The boldest of ship captains braved the open-ocean crossing from the Indian coast on the May–November monsoon winds directly to the coast of Africa, returning on the reversed May–September winds.[1] The author of the *Periplus* claims to be the first to describe this direct crossing to his Greek readers. Whichever route a captain chose, only one round trip per year was possible, and ships could sail only as far south as Zanzibar on the African coast, with enough time to load and catch the reversing winds north.[2] This short favourable sailing season on the far south of the African coast is the probable reason that Indian Ocean captains did not venture below Madagascar and never rounded the Cape of Good Hope.

The *Periplus* also got the commodities of the Indian Ocean trade quite right. It recommended that fellow Greek traders bring a variety of fabrics and other manufactured goods to the coast of Africa—cloth made in Egypt, coloured cloaks, linen, fringed mantles, pottery, several sorts of glassware, copper for cooking pots and ornaments, iron for spears, axes, adzes, and swords. For sale in Arabian ports, the book recommended African slaves, ivory, tortoiseshell, and rhinoceros horn. The *Periplus* was well aware of the availability of spices and fabrics on the west coast of India.

The writer of the *Periplus* knew that Greek traders and ship captains sailed on an Indian Ocean dominated by Arabs and Indians. To compete successfully, Greek traders needed the particular varieties of Indian cloth that Africans expected, such as mallow-cloth, belts, and a cloth known as 'monakhe'. Traders could buy these items at the ports of the Arabian Peninsula, such as Mauza and later Mocha, at the mouth of the Red Sea, before proceeding to Africa.

Let us summarize the considerable information that formed the cognitive geography of ship captains even as early as 100 CE. The basic knowledge began with the yearly rhythm of the monsoon winds, from what direction they came and in which month they reversed. Ship captains also knew the specifics of what sorts of goods could be profitably traded in which ports, down to the details of what colours of cloth sold best where. The compass was unknown in the Indian Ocean at this time. A ship captain's more detailed mental map had to know the correct stars by which to navigate during the sailing season. Some of this knowledge was in the form of memorized songs. From a much later version here, in translation, is a verse about the African coast below Mogadishu. 'Aqrab' here refers to a known star that matched up with the correct compass heading:

Aqrab now is your star. Follow it.
Where it goes we accompany it.
It covers all the Banadir coast
As far as Barawah – after that lies safety.[3]

For centuries after the *Periplus*, slaves in relatively small numbers were transported north from Africa into the eastern Roman world; they were predominantly women and girls for domestic service and harems, young boys for court eunuchs, and men mainly for manual labour in fields and courts. Mostly, the slaves went unnoticed in the records of the time.

An incident in 850 CE known as the Zanj Rebellion, however, was serious enough to warrant attention. It began when the financially strapped caliph of Baghdad gave large areas of marshland upstream from the mouth of the Euphrates (near current-day Basra in Iraq) to his nobles for plantation development. Male slaves from East Africa were brought to drain the fields, which was difficult work under brutal conditions. The revolt began with a small number of slaves, but grew to include nearly 100,000, both from the marshland and nearby cities. After a decade of fighting, the casualties numbered more than 10,000 men. The memory of the Zanj Rebellion remained in the Middle East for centuries, during which African slaves were never used for plantation agricultural work.

The most profitable commodity of the Indian Ocean route was certainly spices from the hills overlooking the southwest coast of India, today's Kerala. The coast receives heavy monsoon rain from June to October, much of it returning as rivers that flow down the western hills to the sea. The coastline is, thus, interrupted by many rivers, each one a port. Many such ports supported independent and competing states, all of which exported much the same items. Black pepper was native to Kerala. Cumin, ginger, and coriander were domesticated early or harvested from the forest. Several of these tropical spices are mentioned in Roman culinary books and pharmacopoeias. As we saw in the chapter on the Appian Way, Rome's exports to India were olive oil in amphorae and primarily coinage, both

Rome, Kerala's spices flavoured the cuisine and filled the pharmacopoeias
of the Islamic world, and were traded through Cairo and Baghdad as far as
North Africa, Spain, the Caucasus, and Russia.

Plants also moved in this early Indian Ocean exchange. The banana,
for example, moved from India to Africa and spread through much of
the continent. Unfortunately, we have no records of this process and no
one knows who first brought it or when. It is also likely that attempts were
made to grow valuable black pepper outside its native range in Kerala.
From the fact that Kerala remained the world's single source of black
pepper until the colonial period, we know that these attempts failed.
The pepper vine, then and now, needs a particular upland monsoon
microclimate.

Between the *Periplus* (c. 100 CE) and Malik Ambar's occupation of
Deogiri (1630 CE) appeared in the Middle East a new sort of slave, the
military slave. Ethiopian slave soldiers fought for Muhammad in Makkah.[4]
By 800 CE, the core of the caliph of Baghdad's army consisted of military
slaves, many of them arriving from Africa at the Arabian Peninsula ports.[5]
Thereafter, the system of military slavery reappeared in Islamic kingdoms
many times—in Delhi in the thirteenth century; Egypt in the fifteenth
century; the Ottoman Empire for many centuries; and, in the sixteenth
century, Malik Ambar's employer, the Nizam Shahi Sultan, one of several
sultanates of southern India.

Islamic rulers bought slave soldiers for a common reason. They all knew
that their strongest rivals were members of their own family and clan and
sought a fighting force of utter and complete loyalty, unsullied by crosscut-
ting attachments of family, religion, ethnicity, faction, or language. If the
king instructed slaves to fight, they fought. They insured the king against
violent coups.[6] Military slavery was, however, never a perfect solution for
a king's quest for loyal soldiers. Slaves were always expensive and military
slaves sometimes became a powerful faction in their own right. By 850 CE,
for example, in Baghdad, the slave army literally controlled the selection of
the caliph, and required large payments at accession.

The proliferating and endemic wars in southern India produced a
mental map of the Arabian Sea shared by all rulers of the region. The
African coast was the source of reliable military slaves. The seaborne trade

also, however, brought horses. Rulers in southern India knew that mounted soldiers were a far more effective fighting force at the time than infantry. They encountered two problems in equipping such an army. Large horses, powerful enough to carry a soldier in armour, did not breed well in India. Also, the ample supply of such horses from the steppe was cut off because the southern kingdoms of India were rivals and enemies of the northern kingdoms, which controlled the horse importation routes from the steppe. The only source of suitable horses, therefore, was by sea from the Middle East. Captains and traders knew that many of the horses would die at sea, but the profits were so high for those that did survive the journey, that this trade flourished for half a millennium, from about 1300 CE to 1800 CE.

With this background, let us return to what is known of Malik Ambar. He was born in 1548 CE in the city of Harar on the Ethiopian coastal plain and, according to one manuscript, sold into slavery by his parents around 1565 CE.[7] Large caravans moved slaves like Malik Ambar on feeder routes from inland Ethiopian towns to the Red Sea port of Massawa. Women and children made up the majority of these sad caravans of slaves.

Tomé Pires, an apothecary who sailed from Portugal to India in 1510, recounted common knowledge that Ethiopian slaves were 'considered in these parts to be loyal, true, and faithful knights, and often from being slaves they rise to be kings, chiefly in Bengal'. Expectations about Ethiopian slaves, thus, formed part of the mental aspects of the Indian Ocean route.

Father Alvarez noticed that Ethiopia in the sixteenth century was a full slave society. Male slaves provided all the labour for tilling the fields and harvesting the grain on estates owned by the king, his nobles, and the many churches.[8] Slave women did the washing, cleaning, and cooking in noble houses. The king of Ethiopia regularly sent out shipments of slaves for sale. It had perhaps been so for several centuries, as Ethiopia's earliest written legal code, c. 1240 CE, had defined the acquisition and holding of slaves as the natural order of things.

> ...war and the strength of horses bring some to the service of others, because the law of war and victory makes the vanquished the slaves of the victors. Mosaic Law shows that unbelievers and their children must be held as slaves since it is written there: 'Those whom you take from the people who dwell around you and the aliens who dwell among you, let them, men

and women, be your slaves. You shall buy [slaves] from among them and from among their offspring born in your land and they shall be for you and your children after you as an inheritance.'⁹

The effects of large-scale slaving passed far beyond the borders of Ethiopia. Hunting and gathering tribes in the hills south and west of the Ethiopian highlands regularly fought and raided one another and, just as regularly, sold the captives—the majority of which were women and children—in trade for iron utensils, cloth, and weapons. Except in the rainy season, when roads were impassable, Muslim slavers regularly sallied forth from the lowlands east of the Ethiopian highlands and captured slaves. During the frequent wars between the people of the Muslim lowlands and the Christian highlands, both sides made deep incursions into enemy territory, raiding crops and cattle and taking large numbers of slaves. Several outlying provinces on the western fringes of the Ethiopian highlands also paid tribute to Ethiopia in slaves. Thus, as seen in the case of the Nile, the Inka route, and the Compostela pilgrimage, here too, the effects of demand for a commodity spread far from the route itself.

At the time of Malik Ambar, slaves were also captured south of Ethiopia. A bustling port named Zeila was located in the coastal desert of Somalia, but received regular slave caravans from populous inland Somalia. Most slaves were sent to Baghdad, but some were shipped directly east to India. Pieter van den Broecke, a Dutch trader, was on the coast of Yemen in 1616 when he observed two boats arrive from Zeila containing 240 male and female slaves. Indian merchants readily bought the lot for export to the west coast of India.¹⁰

Further south, the stretch from Somalia to Zanzibar was known as the Swahili Coast, dry at the northern end with gradually increasing rain and population the further south one goes. The northern portion of the Swahili Coast had only two ports: Mogadishu and Mombasa. The southern portion eventually developed several competing ports including the Pembe Islands, Zanzibar, and Kilwa. Its known history goes back to 100 CE, with a brief mention of its products in the *Periplus of the Erythraean Sea*—exotic feathers, ivory, and slaves.

Beginning in the eighth century, we get a few clues to a changing cognitive geography of the peoples of the Swahili Coast Many ex-fisherman who had become traders converted to Islam, bought Indian cloth, and changed their dress to look like the Arabs with whom they traded. Their mental maps connected them outward from the African coast along the sea lanes.

Successful local merchants built large houses in the new coastal towns. They bought domestic slaves to keep these houses. A polyglot language, known as Kiswahili, developed from the local Bantu language and became the language of trade even in areas far inland from the coast. Traders developed genealogies (perhaps partly true), which made them descendants of Arab or Irani traders, and emphasized their urbanity and gentility.[11] Islam, as it arrived on the Swahili Coast, was not one unified movement, but consisted of various sects which competed and jostled for local influence.

Along the Swahili Coast, the slave trade actually worked against the inland spread of Islam. Muslims were forbidden to enslave other Muslims. If the interior peoples converted, they could no longer be enslaved. The coastal Muslims, therefore, made no effort to convert inland peoples whom they regularly enslaved.[12]

By the fourteenth century, the great medieval traveller, Ibn Battuta observed that the people of the coast were fully Muslim and court ritual was much like that of the Middle East. At Mogadishu, the sultan presented Ibn Battuta with a truly international set of clothes.

> On the fourth day, which was a Friday, the Qadi [Qazi, that is, a teacher] and students and one of the Shaikh's viziers came to me, bringing a set of robes; these [official] robes of theirs consist of a silk wrapper which one ties round the waist in place of drawers (for they have no acquaintance with these), a tunic of Egyptian linen with an embroidered border, a furred mantle of Jerusalem stuff, and an Egyptian turban with an embroidered edge.[13]

Let us summarize the subtle intertwining of the physical and the mental in the development of this route. Dress and fashion changed to match the overseas Islamic traders. A new language developed, used both on the coast and far inland. House styles changed. The new elite bought imported luxury goods, such as Chinese porcelain, which were internationally known signs of wealth and taste.[14] A new religion connected the coast with its overseas trading partners. Recall a very similar pattern in the movement of Islam and kingly ritual into sub-Saharan Africa.

Malik Ambar walked, probably chained, the 400 miles from Harar, on the Ethiopian coastal plain, north to the Red Sea Shore. From there slaves went by boat to Massawa, a set of small islands just off the western coast of the Red Sea, which provided shelter against storms. The islands formed the only port in 500 miles of coastline. The Portuguese, at about the time Malik Ambar passed through, found that the islands had 49 large cisterns that stored rainwater. The island's entire food supply came from the mainland. The population of Massawa was perhaps 3,000; observers noted that it doubled with the arrival of a big slave caravan.[15]

Father Francisco Alvarez, a Portuguese ambassador to the Christian court of Ethiopia in 1520 CE, described the caravans from the interior highlands of Ethiopia to Massawa.

> No one passes here by road except in a cafila [caravan] which they call a *negada*. This assemblage passes twice a week, once in coming and another time in going, or to express it better, one goes and the other comes; and there always pass [more than] a thousand persons and upwards, with a captain of the *negadas*, who awaits them in certain places.[16]

If Father Alvarez's observation on the size of slave caravans is even close to correct, it suggests an enormous amount of slave trade at the time. A caravan of a thousand slaves every week works out to 50,000 per year, or half a million slaves every decade. To these slaves directly brought by land from Ethiopia must be added slaves transported by sea from further south. Even though the sailing season along the Swahili Coast was relatively brief and the ships relatively small, it is entirely possible that another 10,000–20,000 slaves per year were transported by sea to Massawa. The Ethiopian caravan road and the East African sea lane combined shipped perhaps three-quarters of a million slaves every decade.

The next stop after Massawa for slaves on the route to Baghdad was a large port, such as Mocha or Aden, near the mouth of the Red Sea. A Dutch memoir from the period recounts that Malik Ambar was sold in Mocha for 20 ducats.[17] A few decades later a Frenchman observed that '... young slaves sell at Moka, one with another ... at five-and-twenty or thirty crowns per head.'[18]

Three routes connected Aden or Mocha and Baghdad. The first was sea transport to the slaving port of Jiddah, halfway up the eastern side of the Red Sea, followed by a brutal overland march to Baghdad. The second route brought slaves Ambarinland to the city of Zabid on the coastal plain of Yemen. Ibn Battuta described in 1330 CE:

> There is no [place] in al-Yaman that is larger nor whose population is wealthier. It lies amid luxuriant gardens with many streams and fruits, such as bananas and others ... It is great and populous, and contains groves of palms, orchards, and running streams—the pleasantest town in al-Yaman. Its inhabitants are courteous in manners, upright in conduct, and handsome in figure, and its women are of exceeding and preeminent beauty.[19]

Then, as two centuries later in the time of Malik Ambar, the slave trade was the basis of the town's prosperity. Slaves walked from Zabid northeast across the desert to Bahrain on the Persian Gulf and were shipped up the Euphrates River to Baghdad.

A third route took the slaves by sea east from Aden or Mocha to the island of Socotra off the tip of the Horn of Africa. From there, they went by boat to Kish at the mouth of the Persian Gulf, up the Gulf and the Euphrates River to Baghdad.[20]

Illustration 20 'View of Aden at the time Malik Ambar passed through the port'. From *Tractado de las drogas y medidinas de las Indias orientalis* by Christobal Acosta. Venetia; F. Ziletti, 1585. Courtesy of Rare Book Collection of the Museum's Collection. University of Michigan.

In Baghdad, Malik Ambar was again sold, this time to a prominent merchant who recognized Ambar's intellect, trained him in Persian, and generally treated him well.[21] A slave was a commodity; teaching him to read and write added value.

Let us consider a few other examples of value-adding activities around the Indian Ocean. Shipbuilding itself was such an activity, which assembled wood for the hull and masts, mastic to seal the hull, ropes from fibre, and cotton for sails. Iron was processed in many locations in East Africa and shipped from Swahili ports to the Middle East. The ports of the Kerala coast reprocessed broken bronze vessels into new bronze items, such as candlesticks and basins.[22] The Arabian Peninsula ports processed imported silver into jewellery. The Indian Ocean ports are, therefore, quite comparable as reprocessing sites to towns along the Mississippi River, the Nile, the Silk Road, and the Rhine. The expectation of such reprocessing formed part of the cognitive geography of such routes

Perhaps the highest value-added African export was ivory. Ivory decorated Egyptian mummy cases, domestic furniture, and sacred staffs. Some African ivory appears in objects manufactured even as far away as China in the first century CE. Masses of ivory went to Rome.[23] Ivory was both exotic and practical. It was very hard, yet workable into exquisite detail. Its strength and smoothness made it ideal for knife and mirror handles, scabbards, book covers and frets of stringed instruments. Ivory could cover chairs, but tiny saws could also render it into combs or the most delicate leaves for inlay into boxes. Its deep white colour was not matched in any other known material.

Like every luxury material, ivory was sometimes in fashion and sometimes not. There was an explosion of ivory carving and use in tenth century Islamic courts—the caliphs of Baghdad, Central Asia, Egypt and other countries in North Africa, and Spain. Another surge in demand occurred in twelfth- and thirteenth-century Europe for the production of reliquaries, crosses, and book covers. Jewish traders at Aden were heavily involved with the ivory trade.[24]

Malik Ambar's owner took him with a group of a thousand Ethiopian male slaves via the Persian Gulf and the Indian Ocean to India and sold him. The buyer was a high noble of the Ahmednagar kingdom in western India, himself an ex-slave from Ethiopia.

Malik Ambar began his military career in about 1565 CE as a simple soldier in the service of the noble who purchased him. He showed his military prowess and became a leader of men. His commands increased from a few hundred to a thousand, eventually to more than ten thousand slave soldiers. He became adept at internal and external politics and eventually gained his freedom. He defeated Mughal armies every year from 1610 to 1616 CE. In 1617 CE, in the face of a huge enemy force, he ceded the capital of Ahmednagar and portions of the kingdom, but two years later recovered them and even besieged the Mughal regional capital. In 1628 CE, after marches and counter marches, treaties and sieges, Malik Ambar died in bed at age the age of 80, and passed his power and his army to his son. The beautiful tomb that his son built for Malik Ambar near Aurangabad in Western India survives to this day.

* * *

Overall, what, then, were the general characteristics—both mental and physical—of the Indian Ocean route? Monsoon was the overriding feature. The southwest winds of November to February carried sailing ships from ports such as Aden to the east coast of Africa and the west coast of India. From June to September the winds reversed, blowing northeast and carrying ships from Africa and India to Aden, Mocha, Muscat, and the island of Socotra. Ship captains, traders, producers of commodities all had the mental expectation of the yearly monsoon rhythm.

For a more than a millennium and a half, the basic commodities of trade remained much the same—slaves, ivory, cloth from western India, metal tools, and weapons. The trade supplied food and timber essential to the survival of the trans-shipping ports of the Arabian Peninsula. The route was famous for its steady supply of slaves to the markets of Baghdad, Cairo, and cities in western India. Information on local fashion, cuisine, and tastes moved along the routes and influenced far-distant production centres, especially port cities where value was added by commodities that became higher-value trade items.

Moving these commodities depended on shared mental expectations of all those involved along the route. The slave trade, for example, rested

Illustration 21 Delicate, Pierced Stone Window in the Tomb of Malik Ambar. Courtesy of Richard Eaton.

on the expectation that governments along the way would provide holding facilities for slaves, that demand for slaves would continue and prove profitable, that raiders in Africa would find slaves to capture, that ships with knowledgeable captains would arrive at ports on the Swahili Coast to buy slaves at the correct time to transport them north, and that all legal systems supported slavery and the slave trade. In similar fashion, the horse trade depended on the mental expectations of how war should be fought in India, plus detailed knowledge of what sort of horses were suitable and what kings were buying.

A third enduring feature of mental expectations of the Indian Ocean route was the competition between nearby ports. It was typical of the whole route—the Swahili Coast, the ports of the Arabian Peninsula, and the western coast of India. Ports consisted of little more than a protected refuge from ocean storms. Since the draft of ocean-going ships was shallow, almost any river mouth or lee side of an island could be a port. Residents in such a favourable location attracted trade by building warehouses, supplying the needs of ships and sailors, and perhaps developing the harbour with a sea wall for greater protection. This competition occasionally spilled over into warfare between two rival ports.

It was also part of both mental expectations and physical realities that endemic violence against trade was characteristic of the Indian Ocean. Piracy was rampant. It shows up frequently, for example, in the letters of twelfth-century Jewish traders, which were preserved in Cairo. The cognitive geography of such pirate dangers continued, as evidenced by early European maps, which termed the northern half of the west coast of India 'The Pirate Coast'.[25]

It is hard to overestimate the spread of Islam in the creation of a unified trading culture in the Indian Ocean world. The practice of Islam created cultural continuities from the coast of Africa north to the Arabian Peninsula ports and east to the coast of India. Nevertheless, the unified culture of the ports and traders of the Indian Ocean route went far deeper than the spread of Islam along both the African and Indian coasts. Loose, flowing, Arab-style, ankle-length robes were the rule along the route from India through the Middle East and down the African coast, whether the traders were Muslims, Jews, or Christians. This dress, in Africa and India, was quite different from that of people who lived in the interiors. Kings, whether Hindu, Muslim, or animist, held court under the same sort of umbrella and bestowed the same sorts of high-end luxury fabrics as robes of honour. Many kings chewed betel nut from India, prepared with elaborate ceremony that incorporated tropical spices. Tropical spices were also routinely found in cuisines all around the Indian Ocean.

It was only in the sixteenth century that the first attempt control the Indian Ocean was made, by the Portuguese invaders. The Portuguese attacked, captured, or burnt Muslim ships, carrying the Crusades into the Indian Ocean. They demanded that every ship carry and pay for a Portuguese pass. Modern scholarship rather downplays the overall disruption of Portugal's attempts to control the whole of the Indian Ocean trade.[26] Indeed, Portugal's superior shipboard cannon and the training of its gunners gave it great advantages. Nevertheless, the Portuguese were spread very thin and Indian shipyards were able to build faster boats that could often outrun a Portuguese ship cruising the coast. The trade in pepper, cotton cloth, and slaves continued to be primarily in local hands for centuries.

The monsoon-driven sailing ships of the Indian Ocean route continued well into the twentieth century. It is within living memory that diesel-powered ships have replaced the sailing vessels. The rise of long-distance container shipping has pushed the traditional ports to obsolescence. Trans-shipping points such as Mocha, Aden, and Zeila at the mouth of the Red Sea, Pembe Island, and Zanzibar on the Swahili Coast have all gone into decline. The small ports of the Kerala coast are too shallow to handle the huge container vessels. All have become fishing ports. Vast amounts of goods still move across the Indian Ocean, but it is now concentrated in fewer ports.

Perhaps it is worth suggesting a few of the ways that the legacy of the Indian Ocean route remains strong. Slavery defined a predatory relationship between the African coast and the interior from Ethiopia south all the way to Zanzibar. Hostility, distrust, and suspicion between peoples of the interior and the coast are still characteristic of the modern countries of east Africa. Islam still connects the people of the Indian Ocean trade, even though national boundaries and rivalries divide them. The tradition of cotton agriculture and cloth production in western India survived both adverse colonial policy—which sought to destroy all indigenous cotton varieties and indigenous weaving in favour of British cloth—and the shift from home looms to factories

1. In the 1970s, Arab dhows from Gujarat made the yearly direct crossing to the African coast, stopping at the island of Socotra off the tip of the Horn of Africa. The oral stories of ship captains and their navigation techniques were at the centre of a wonderful exhibition at the Prince of Wales Museum (now the Chhatrapati Shivaji Maharaj Vastu Sangrahalaya) in Mumbai, 1992.

2. See G.R. Tibbetts, *Arab Navigation in the Indian Ocean before the Coming of the Portuguese* (London: Royal Asiatic Society: 1971). See also G.F. Hourani, *Arab Seafaring in Ancient and Early Medieval Times* (Princeton: Princeton University press, 1951).

3. R.B. Serjeant, 'Hadramawt to Zanzibar: The Pilot-Poem of the Nakhuda Sa'id Ba Tayi of al Hami', *Paideuma*, 28 (1982), p. 119.

4. See *Encyclopaedia Islamica*, 'Abd', and Emeri Johannes Van Donzel, 'Ibn al-Jawazi on Ethiopians in Baghdad', in C.E. Bosworth et al. (eds), *The Islamic World: Essays in Honor of Bernard Lewis* (Princeton, New Jersey: The Darwin Press, 1989), p. 115.

5. A century later in Baghdad, of the 11,000 male palace servants, 7,000 were African, of which 4,000 were eunuchs. Jacob Lassner, *The Topography of Baghdad in the Early Middle Ages: Text and Studies* (Detroit: Wayne State University Press, 1970), p. 267.

6. Over many centuries, kings and their advisers came up with only a few solutions to the loyalty problem. One was to import a small army from far away, insuring that its soldiers had no ties at court and belonged to no faction. At the time of Malik Ambar, kings in Europe raised large mercenary armies for the same reason that Indian kings raised slave armies. This solution continues into our own time. Gurkhas from Nepal still guard the Queen of England. Another solution was to raise sons of various rivals in the king's household and form them into an elite corps. The hope was that their first loyalty would be to the king rather than their father. A third solution was to raise an elite guard from various factions and ethnicities with its own ceremonies and traditions. Think of the Roman Praetorian Guard. Such an army's symbols often connected the soldiers directly to the king. For example, Mughal commanders wore a necklace with the king's portrait.

7. Scholars have questioned this account. It seems unlikely that parents could sell a man of eighteen into slavery.

8. Francisco Alvarez, *Narrative of the Portuguese Embassy to Abyssinia during the Years 1520–1527*, translated by Lord Stanley of Alderley (London: Hakluyt Society, 1881), p. 149.

9. *The Fetha Nagast: The Law of Kings*, translated by Tzadua Paulos and Peter L. Straus (Addis Ababa, Ethiopia: Faculty of Law, Haile Sellassie University, 1968), p. 175.

10. Cited in Emeri Johannes Van Donzel, 'Primary and Secondary Sources for Ethiopian Historiography: The Case of Slavery and Slave-Trade in Ethiopia', in Claude LePage (ed.), *Études Éthiopiennes* (Paris: Société Française pour les Études Éthiopiennes, 1994), I, p. 187.

11. Mark Horton and John Littleton, *The Swahili: The Social Landscape of a Mercantile Society* (London: Blackwell, 1988), pp. 31–46. When al-Masudi travelled to the east African coast in 916 CE, he found only one Muslim community and the few scattered references in the following four centuries show a spotty and gradual conversion.

12. Horton and Littleton, *The Swahili*, p. 49.

13. *The Travels of Ibn Battuta, A.D. 1325–1354*, translated by H.A.R. Gibb (New Delhi: Munshiram Manoharlal, 1993), p. 376.

14. See Kirti N. Chaudhuri, *Trade and Civilization in the Indian Ocean: An Economic History from the Rise of Islam to 1750* (Cambridge: Cambridge University Press, 1985), p. 57.

15. Anthony d'Avray, *Lords of the Red Sea: The History of a Red Sea Society from the Sixteenth to the Nineteenth Centuries* (Wiesbaden: Harrassowitz, 1966), pp. 73–4.

16. Alvarez, *Narrative of the Portuguese Embassy to Abyssinia during the Years 1520–1527*, pp. 111–12. In the 1640s, when the ambassador from Yemen's entourage of one hundred (largely slaves and servants, with twelve musketeers) passed along the same route, it was equally dangerous. Bandits attacked. The entourage formed a makeshift fort of their baggage on a nearby hill and sent for help from the Ottoman administrator of the area. After a standoff of several days, Ottoman troops arrived and rescued the ambassador. Other enemies killed or captured the bandits and the ambassador recounts with some satisfaction that he saw the bandits and their women sold as slaves in the port of Massawa. Emeri Johannes Van Donzel, *A Yemenite Embassy to Ethiopia, 1647–1649* (Stuttgart: Steiner Vrlag Wiesbaden GmbH, 1986), pp. 217–23.

17. W.P.H. Coolhass (ed.), *Pieter van den Broecke in Azië* ('s-Gravenhage: Martinus Nijhoff, 1962), I, pp. 147–8.

18. Francois Bernier, *Travels in the Mogol Empire, AD 1656–1668*, translated by Archibald Constable and Vincent A. Smith, reprinted edition (Delhi: Low Price Publications, 1989), pp. 134–5. In the same period, the king of

Ethiopia sent an ambassador to Imam al-Mu'ayyad Billah of Yemen for help in establishing a new Ethiopian port not controlled by the Ottoman Turks. The Imam's reply documents that the Ethiopian king sent twenty slaves as a present. Donzel, *A Yemenite Embassy to Ethiopia, 1647–1649*, p. 47.

19. Battuta, *The Travels of Ibn Battuta*, p. 366.

20. Donzel, 'Ibn al-Jawazi on Ethiopians in Baghdad', p. 117. Kish had competed with Aden and Mocha since the thirteenth century as a major trading port, including the trans-shipment of slaves to Baghdad and to India. See Horton and Littleton, *The Swahili*, p. 81.

21. Hasim Beg Astarabadi, *Furuhat-I 'Adil Shahi* (London: British Library, Add. 26, 234) cited in D.R. Seth, 'The Life and Times of Malik Ambar', *Islamic Culture* 31 (1957), p. 142. Note the investment of his Baghdad owner in Malik Ambar's education.

22. Shlomo Goitein, *Letters of Medieval Jewish Traders* (Princeton: Princeton University Press, 1973), p. 194.

23. Ivory sent to Rome came from elephants found on the savannah north of the Sahara. These elephants were hunted to extinction by about the fourth century CE.

24. Horton and Littleton, *The Swahili*, p. 81. Both the Roman and Eastern churches were involved in the increasing production of ivory religious objects in the twelfth and thirteenth centuries.

25. So noted in an early eighteenth-century English map in the collection of the author.

26. See Michael N. Pearson, *The Portuguese in India* (Cambridge: Cambridge University Press, 1987).

The Trans-Sahara

Ibn Battuta, the most widely-travelled man of the Middle Ages, arrived home to Morocco in 1350, intending—as his memoir says—to 'put down the staff of travel'. He had, over the previous 25 years, traversed the known and unknown world, including Makkah, Constantinople, the Crimea, the East African coast, India, Southeast Asia, and China. He had been robbed of everything on the coast of India and observed the Black Death at its worst in Baghdad and Cairo. The road to adventure, however, still beckoned and, in February 1352, Battuta set out on his last journey, the caravan route from Morocco, south across the Sahara.[1]

To conceptualize this route, visualize Africa as a series of east–west strips.[2] At its northern edge is a thin strip of Mediterranean climate and agriculture, as Battuta described the city of Miknasa (today, the historical city of Meknes): 'the wonderful, the green, the many-flowered, which has gardens surrounding it and is in a sea of plantations of olive trees in all directions'.[3] The Mediterranean strip is widest exactly where Ibn Battuta described it in eastern Morocco, and is also found on the Tripoli peninsula. In most places along the southern shore of the Mediterranean Sea, the desert extends right to the water. South of the strip of coastal desert are mountains, grazing lands that receive some rain, and south of these is a strip of savannah, grassland that gradually shades south into the Sahara Desert. At the time of Ibn Battuta, the last well-watered city before the Sahara was Sijilmasa, where southbound caravans assembled.

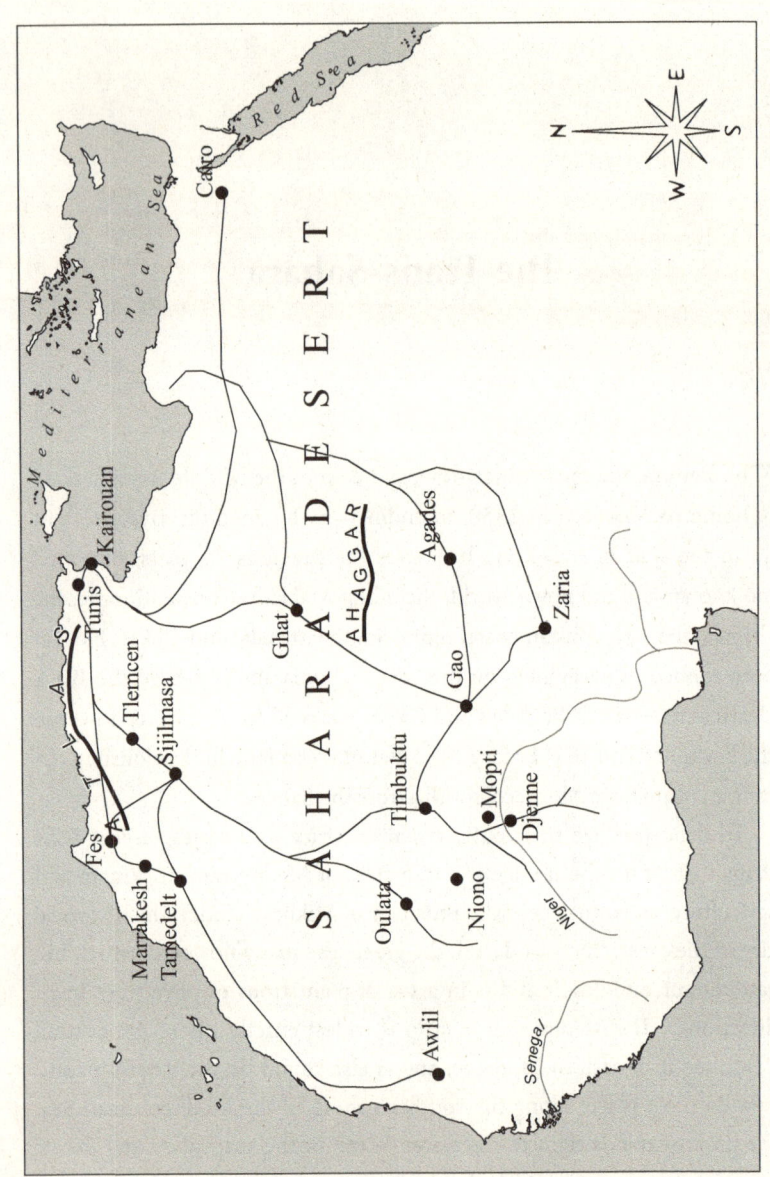

The Trans-Sahara

Illustration 22   *Camel Caravan in the Sahara Desert.* © Sergey Pesterev/ Wikimedia Commons/CC BY-SA 4.0

The Sahara is between 800 and 1,000 miles wide, and stretches across Africa, a place of rock, sand, very little water, and deadly heat. To get a sense of the scale of crossing the Sahara, consider that the route is roughly the same as Kashmir to Cape Cormorin—*and back*. It is about the same as from far northern Finland to southern Italy or the Mexican border of the United States north to the Canadian border. At the southern limit of the Sahara there is enough rainfall for a few thorny trees and, further south, a layer of savannah, suitable for grazing, traversed by the Niger River. Below the savannah is the rainforest of Western Africa.

Why would anyone risk travelling the Sahara to move anything across this gruelling stretch? In the long sweep of human experience in Africa, this is perhaps the wrong question. The Sahara is, in geological terms, quite new. Seven thousand years ago, it became a well-watered savannah containing a chain of lakes. In the subsequent centuries, herders raised animals. Early farmers raised grains and other crops. Sometime around 2000 BCE, rainfall began to decrease, lakes dried up, and only savannah grass and drought-resistant trees grew.[4] Rock paintings across the Sahara from around 1500 BCE show both Negroid farmers and hunters and a new sort of people—light skinned, long-faced, slender, and driving chariots pulled by horses. The paintings are similar to Egyptian ones of the time, showing men in beards and wearing kilts.

These new peoples, of whatever origin, were able to exploit the grasslands of a desiccating Sahara for raising horses and cattle and became a warrior elite. The Greeks knew the descendants of these peoples as Garamantes.[5] Carthage, Rome's North African rival empire, recruited them as cavalry units and profoundly influenced them. A written language, ideas, and symbols of kingship spread rapidly.[6] After Rome's defeat of Carthage (146 BCE), the Garamantes became a more practical problem. Cities along the south coast of the Mediterranean faced recurrent raids by these Saharan warrior nomads. To control them, Rome developed three strategies. The first was to sponsor Romanized client states among the warrior groups. The second was to recruit the warrior nomads into the Roman army. The third was to attempt to administer the warrior nomads from a few garrison oases deep in the Sahara. The introduction of the camel from Arabia at this time made feasible the movement of troops and supplies from cities on the Mediterranean coast, but such long-distance administration was a colossally expensive effort. None of these strategies was particularly successful. Rome abandoned its desert outposts as the empire declined in the third and fourth centuries CE.[7] The warrior nomads regained autonomy and control of the Sahara.

Geographers of the Roman Empire, such as Strabo and Pliny, thought no commodity worth the risks of crossing the Sahara.[8] The elephants and ivory of sub-Saharan Africa were readily available in the mountains north of the Sahara. Enslaved war captives were available in plenty around the Mediterranean. No one needed to bring them across the Sahara.

Even though Rome thought trans-Saharan trade economic madness, portions of the trans-Saharan route had long been central to life in sub-Saharan West Africa. Deep in the Sahara south of Morocco was a mine known as Taghaza, which produced salt that sub-Saharan people needed but did not have. Little is known of the ancient origins of this trade, except that the same warrior nomads feared by Rome ran the caravans.

Taghaza was at least a thousand years old by the time Ibn Battuta arrived there in 1352.

It is a village with no good in it. ... the construction of its houses and its mosques is of rock salt with camel skin roofing and there are no trees in it, the soil is just sand. In it is a salt mine. It is dug out of the ground and is found there in huge slabs, one on top of another as if it had been carved and put under the ground. ... Nobody lives there except slaves ... who dig for the salt and live on dates brought to them from Dar'a and Sijilmasa, and on the meat of camels, and on *anli* [an indigenous millet] which is brought from the land of the blacks.[9]

The trans-Saharan route in the time of Ibn Battuta functioned rather like an extended sea voyage. The captain and crew—a muslim Berber nomadic group, distant descendants of the Garamantes of Roman times—organized the overall logistics.[10] Ibn Battuta terms the leaders of the caravan 'massufa'. Passengers were responsible for their own food and supplies. A Berber guide kept the enterprise on its route. As with sea lanes, there were several alternate tracks across the Sahara. An easterly track began in Tripoli and crossed the desert to cities in the Lake Chad area. A far western track from Morocco paralleled the Atlantic coast and terminated in cities along the Senegal Valley. Just as a ship paid taxes at each port of call, a caravan paid a tax to each nomad group whose territory it crossed.[11] In return, the nomad group guaranteed the safety of the caravan and passed it to a representative of the next group on the route. Just as on the sea lanes, this system regularly broke down into warfare between nomad groups. Ibn Battuta's caravan, however, travelled safely. It averaged, as expected, somewhat less than 10 miles per day, and included two days per week for resting and grazing the camels.

Ibn Battuta did not actually describe the composition of his caravan. He had been in so many caravans in his decades of travel that this topic was perhaps no longer interesting to him. Caravans across the Sahara were different from those on the Silk Road. First, there were no oasis cities where grain and supplies could be re-stocked, so, as Ibn Battuta wrote, he had to carry everything needed for the whole three-month trip. The lack of oasis cities also meant that, in the face of sickness or fatigue, there was no opportunity to leave a caravan and recover. Second, water was scarcer than on the Silk Road, which meant carrying more for animals and men. A trader needed three to four camels to carry supplies and enough trade goods—various kinds of speciality cloth, beads, perfumes, horses, and, later, firearms— to make the crossing profitable. Saharan caravans, therefore, generally comprised a few hundred men and up to a thousand animals, rather than about 3,000 men and 10,000 animals observed on the Silk Road.[12] Third, the seasons of travel were quite different. The best time to travel the Silk Road was in the late spring and summer: the snow was off the mountain passes and winter's cold had eased; winter travel was not possible. Winter was, however, the time to travel in the Sahara. The summer months were so hot and so dry that everyone, even the nomads, shifted either north or south to the savannah. The result was that a caravan could make only one round trip across the Sahara per year. All of these factors meant that only very high-value goods, such as salt, copper, gold, ivory, and slaves, could be profitably traded across the Sahara.

South of Taghaza was a hazardous portion of the desert route. Ibn Battuta says it was normally a ten-day trek without water. His caravan was lucky. They found 'much water in it in pools left behind by the rains'.[13] The Sahara had more rain in Battuta's time than today, but rainfall was problematic from year to year. One year there might be rainwater in the rock pools, and the next year the pools would be empty. Over the course of a decade, the margin of the Sahara expanded or contracted, depending on the rains. Good years allowed savannah herders to expand their grazing area, just as bad years saw their grazing land shrink.

The gravest danger of caravan travel to an individual was separation from the group. The Sahara, of course, had no road markers, and much of the way was through stony ground with little visible track. Portions were over shifting sand dunes with no landmarks at all. Battuta knew this, but it took the death of a man in his caravan to remind him. Ibn Battuta routinely took his animals far ahead of his caravan to let them graze along the way. One day, one of the travellers argued with his cousin, and decided to walk far behind the caravan. He was never seen again though nomad trackers tried to find him. From that day onwards, Battuta 'did not go ahead … nor stay behind'.[14]

For the caravan as a whole, the last week in the Sahara was the most dangerous. Supplies and water would run out. The animals would be tired and there would be no grass for grazing. Caravan leaders knew this moment would come. They sent ahead a highly paid scout, termed a *takshif*, to notify the nearest city on the south side of the desert of the caravan's presence. If the scout succeeded in his mission, the city sent men with water and supplies for four days' travel into the desert to succour the caravan.

Ibn Battuta was relieved to see help from the city. 'On the night of the seventh day we saw the fires of those who came out for our meeting and we were happy about that. The desert is bright, full of sunlight, one's chest is dilated, the soul finds good in it, it is secure from robbers.'[15]

After packing critical supplies and water brought from the city on the camels, the caravan crossed the dry desert to Iwalatan, located in far south-east Mauritania and today known as Oualata. He had been in the caravan for two full months. Iwalatan was organized for caravan traffic. Ibn Battuta sent a message ahead of the caravan for a contact there to rent a house in the city. He stayed in Iwalatan for fifty days, finding a large Muslim presence that included mosques, judges, and religious teachers. The city's residents wore clothes of fine Egyptian linen. 'Its people were generous to me and entertained me.'[16]

Illustration 23 'Bound figure from the Jeno Civilization of the Middle Reaches of the Niger River at about the Time of Ibn Battuta's Journey'. Photo by Daderot. Courtesy Krannert Art Museum. Creative Commons. Wikimedia.

Let us pause while Ibn Battuta recovers at Iwalatan and consider the rich sub-Saharan trading cities in the vicinity of the great bend of the Niger River. One of the oldest of these cities was Djenné-Djenno, located on a large tributary of the Niger. The city was founded in approximately 250 BCE and was continuously occupied until abandoned in 1400 CE.[17] Recent archaeology suggests that the ancient city was neither a capital of a state nor a city that belonged to a chief, great man, or a king. There are no remains of a citadel, monumental architecture, defensive walls, or large group worship sites.[18] Instead the city consisted of clusters of craft specialists who produced things to trade with a dense population of herders and farmers in hundreds, if not thousands, of villages in the surrounding countryside. Even in the oldest layer, there is evidence of smelting non-local copper and iron ore into tools, ornaments, and objects.[19]

The centuries before Ibn Battuta's trip produced a variety of good-sized states in West Africa (such as Ife and Zimbabwe), and the large, culturally sophisticated Ghana Empire of the Soninke people, which stretched from the mountainous headwaters of the Niger and Senegal Rivers eastwards beyond the great bend of the Niger. The Ghana Empire, thus, controlled the terminus cities of the north-south trans-Saharan route (Walata, Timbuktu, and Djenné-Djenno), as well as the western terminus (Gao) of the eastern route to Lake Chad and Egypt. Trade to the north and east made the Ghana Empire rich.

About a century before Ibn Battuta's adventure, the Ghana Empire succumbed to factional conflict and broke up into smaller kingdoms. This did not stop profitable trade. In the oral epic of King Sundiata (ruled c. 1240–55), for example, when he, as a child, and his mother were forced into exile a second time, they travelled in a large, well-organized trading caravan.[20] In the king's years of integration of smaller states into the large kingdom of Mali, the trade still flourished. Ibn Battuta arrived at Iwalatan at the height of the power of the Mali Kingdom, which extended from near the Atlantic coast more than a thousand miles inland. It included a bewildering variety of peoples living in cities, on mountains, in the savannah, along the Niger River, and in the Sahara.

At the time, the ruler of Mali was perceived across the whole of the Islamic world as fabulously wealthy. The kingdom received tribute of gold from a mine in a region known as 'Wangara', somewhere between the Niger River and Lake Chad. Arab geographers knew about this fabled mine as early as 900 CE and referred to the lands south of the Sahara as the 'Kingdom of Gold'.[21] This perception was one of the most widely shared pieces of the cognitive geography about sub-Saharan Africa. The epithet 'land of gold' appears in virtually all of the Arabic geographies of the time. The mine's actual location was a well-kept secret in the time of Ibn Battuta. Its location today has been lost.

There was good reason for this widely shared perception of sub-Saharan Africa as the 'land of gold'. Two decades before Ibn Battuta arrived in Mali, the kingdom's ruler, named Mansa Musa, performed the Hajj to Makkah via Cairo with an entourage of such jaw-dropping size and splendour that literati were still writing about it decades later. He carried quantities of gold never before seen, which he dispensed with monumental largesse to scholars, clerics, and officials.[22] So much gold stayed in Cairo that it depressed the price for several decades. By the time of Ibn Battuta, gold was at the centre of the trans-Saharan trade. A trader could carry enough of it in a saddlebag to make the six-month trek profitable. Its value steadily rose in sub-Saharan Africa because of trans-Saharan demand, and rose even more dramatically during the four centuries of the Atlantic slave trade.

So what were the main items of trade across the Sahara? The cities on the great bend of the Niger could not provide three critical items: iron, salt, and copper. Iron ore came to the cities from relatively nearby high-grade deposits. Salt, as we have seen, came from the central Sahara. It was dividable into smaller and smaller units and, even as late as the time of Ibn Battuta, was used as a currency. From Ibn Battuta's description of the salt mine, it seems clear that the trade in this commodity formed part of his mental map of the Sahara and the trans-Sahara trade. Copper, which came from mines in both the Sahara and what is today central Zambia, was vitally important to status and ritual power in sub-Saharan Africa. We will take up this topic when Ibn Battuta visited a copper mine on his return journey.[23] The main trade item travelling north across the Sahara was gold, in addition to iron weapons and tools, and slaves.

After fifty days at Iwalatan, Ibn Battuta and his three companions headed south towards the Niger River. The roads were safe. The area now receives only 4–8 inches of rain per year but there was certainly more rain in 1352, when Battuta travelled there. He and his companions travelled through open grassland savannah with trees 'tall and of great girth: a caravan can find shade in the shadow of one tree'. These trees were certainly the famed baobab, able to survive fire and drought. Ibn Battuta tried many fruits unknown to him. Chickens, milk, and millet were readily available.[24] After 24 days of pleasant travel, the companions arrived at the Niger River, which flowed east. Ibn Battuta assumed that it was a tributary of the Nile, the only known African river to the east of the Niger region. It would be several centuries before anyone outside the Niger region was sure that the large river near Timbuktu was the same river that produced the huge delta on the coast of Nigeria that became the hub of the trans-Atlantic slave trade.

Most towns along the Niger, by the time of Ibn Battuta in the middle of the fourteenth century, had a sector occupied by what he terms 'white' Muslim traders from North Africa. For half a millennium, Arab traders had crossed the Sahara to trade in the sub-Saharan cities and kingdoms. Some settled. They built mosques, received local converts, and established madrassas for teaching. Ibn Battuta quite rightly anticipated that these cities would contain the basic institutions that he had found in Islamic cities across the world, such as a mosque, caravanserai, courts of Islamic law, public baths, and Muslim schools.[25] He was surprised, however, that local men from Inwalata, Timbuktu, and other towns along the Niger River had performed the Hajj. At Timbuktu a local man had a copy of a book Ibn Battuta knew well. He even met a slave girl brought from Damascus.[26]

The southern terminus of the trans-Saharan route was either Mali or Timbuktu. Both provided markets for the goods brought across the Sahara.

There were two good reasons that traders on the trans-Saharan route did not go further south or east of Mali to deal directly with the gold miners. First, the sultan of Mali would have prevented the trip. Second, Mali was just north of the zone plagued by the tsetse fly. Traders from north of the Sahara were well aware of the deadly sleeping sickness transmitted by the tsetse fly bite. They, therefore, exchanged their goods for slaves and gold (later ivory) at the capital, Mali, and formed a caravan to head north.

Ibn Battuta stayed at Mali, where the courtly ritual caught his attention and revised his mental map. Fine fabrics were prominent. Ibn Battuta recognized the silk of the sultan's pillow, the 'splendid robes of zarkhana' (a high-end fabric likely from Persia) worn by the official who spoke for the king, the imported woollen robes of the pages, and the soft red robe

of 'Roman cloth called *mutanfas*' (perhaps from Constantinople) worn by
the sultan. He well understood the language of the king presenting robes
to those he wanted to honour and how these high-value fabrics 'marked'
a man as belonging to the sultan. Ibn Battuta had seen just such fabrics
perform just such functions at courts from Spain through the Middle East,
Central Asia, India, and China.[27] These robing practices meant for Ibn
Battuta that Mali fulfilled his expectations not just for a basic Islamic city
but also for a sophisticated Islamic court.

Other royal symbols also connected this kingdom in sub-Saharan Africa
to a much larger world. The Sultan's name was read in Friday prayers just as
the names of kings were across the whole of the Muslim world. The Sultan
of Mali sat under a silk umbrella, just as kings from Spain to Southeast Asia
and China. The custom was a recent acquisition in Africa but had a long
history in Asia. A round and pointed umbrella shades King Ashurbanipal
of Assyria (668–27 BCE) in bas-reliefs at Nineveh. Slightly later texts from
India describe kings under the royal umbrella.[28] The point of this excursion
into royal symbols is to emphasize that important intangibles besides Islam
travelled the trans-Saharan route. No one knows who introduced ceremonial robes to the court of Mali, just as no one knows where the Sultan of
Mali saw a royal umbrella. The sultan decided, however, to adopt both royal
customs. Kings were entrepreneurs, looking for symbols and customs to
enhance their authority. Men on the trade routes brought ideas and customs to most distant places. Travellers returning to North Africa reported
on what they saw and reinforced a shared mental map of Islamic kings and
their elegant practices.

The worth of a widely accepted currency is also an intangible that
travelled the trans-Saharan route, the result of myriad exchanges for
goods over time. It is a measure of the connection of sub-Saharan Africa
along the north–south route that strings of cowrie shells were accepted as
payment.[29] The shells came, in the millions, from the Maldive Islands off
the coast of India. They were an accepted currency across India, Southeast
Asia, Southern China, and much of Africa.

A second accepted currency across sub-Saharan Africa was copper,
treasured in many different kingdoms for its red-gold colour. Craftsmen
worked and cast copper into bracelets, beads, masks, jewellery, ritual
weapons, drums, and ornamentation on weapons and furniture. Alloyed

with tin or nickel, it became the brass and bronze of vessels and bells. Iron, in contrast, was for used for tools and weapons, but deep cultural associations connected copper with wealth, status, and magic power. Its shining surface was a mirror and, therefore, a gateway between the material and spiritual worlds.[30]

On his return trip from Mali to Morocco, Ibn Battuta looped east along the Niger to Timbuktu, which had grown into a substantial city based on the caravan trade, then to Gao even further east on the Niger River, then joined a caravan headed for Egypt.[31] He wanted to see the famous copper mine at Takadda, current-day Atelic, in western Niger.[32] Copper had been found in the form of malachite, a copper carbonate. Recent radiocarbon dating shows copper smelting at the site from the first millennium BCE, and continuous operation until the mine and city were destroyed about 1450 CE, a century after Battuta's visit.[33]

> The people dig for it in the earth, bring it to town, and smelt it in their houses. This is done by their man and women slaves. When they have smelted it into red copper, they make it into rods about the length of a span and a half: some are fine gauge and some thick ... it is their means of currency.[34]

The mines produced great wealth for the owners:

> The people of Takadda carry on no business but trading. Every year they travel to Egypt and bring from there everything in the country by way of fine cloths and other things. For its people ease of life and ample condition are supreme; they vie with one another in the number of slaves and servants they have.[35]

Ibn Battuta turned north from Takadda because a messenger from the king of Morocco arrived with a command for his return. He kissed the order, bought two camels, provisions for seventy days, and commenced the journey in September 1355. He travelled with a large caravan north and west through a region known as Hakkar to the Berber town of Buda.

Between Takadda and Buda, Ibn Battuta's caravan included six hundred women slaves. They were likely bound for the slave market at Tripoli. Much has been written of the Atlantic slave trade of West Africa. It is, however, important to remember the size and longevity of the trans-Saharan slave trade. Modern scholars estimate, based on admittedly scrappy evidence, that between 6 and 20 million slaves crossed the Sahara to markets in North Africa between about 900 CE and 1900 CE.[36]

At Buda, Ibn Battuta shifted to another caravan bound for Sijilmasa and arrived at the court of Fez on 9 December 1355. He stayed in Morocco, dictated his memoirs as commanded by the king, and lived quietly until his death in 1368 or 1369 CE.

The clearest evidence that the routes across the Saharan were famous and formed a widely-shared mental map were their description, often in stock, repeated images and phrases, in centuries of Arab geographical literature. The geographies laid out the season for and difficulties of desert travel, the kinds of people along the way and the places and principal items of trade—gold, slaves, ivory, high-value cloth, salt, glass beads, and perfumes. These books described the Berber leaders of caravans, the risk of bandits and commonly accepted currencies, such as the *miqtal* of gold and cowries from the Maldive Islands. Some Arab geographical writing included discussions of the route by members of families who regularly traded goods along it.

Kings knew of the trans-Saharan route and sent royal gifts and emissaries along it. Down the route from North Africa, as Ibn Battuta noted, had come a variety of kingly customs, such as honorific robes made of fine imported fabrics and the royal parasol. Armies of the Roman Empire and the king of Morocco used the route for invasion, mostly with limited success. The Almoravids swept north from the Sahara on the same route with considerably more success.

Along the route moved the slow, patchy spread of Islam. Year by year, pilgrims from sub-Saharan Africa followed the trans-Saharan route to North Africa and then to Makkah. Kings, as elsewhere in the Islamic world, had their names spoken in Friday prayers. Most towns had an Islamic judge, cleric, and mosque.

The use and availability of paper spread slowly and haltingly along the route. Islam in sub-Saharan Africa did not have the kinds of institutions that utilized paper to transformative effect, as other societies that had become Muslim possessed.[37] Learned families, nevertheless, assembled whole libraries, several of which still exist today. Ibn Battuta found professional translators between Arabic and the local language, both in mosques and at court.

218

There and Back

The trans-Saharan route after Ibn Battuta was in no way diminished by either the Portuguese exploration of the western coast of Africa in the late 1400s or the developing Atlantic slave trade after 1600. The route flourished, though new cites replaced older ones. The great urban centre of Sijilmasa, from which Ibn Battuta entered the desert and to which he returned, was later destroyed and abandoned. It was the same with sub-Saharan kingdoms: The Songhai Kingdom replaced Mali and was itself replaced by a kingdom centred in Bornu, west of Lake Chad. In spite of these political changes, profits persisted in gold and slaves, salt and copper, European silks and glass beads, paper and arms. Timbuktu's great period of prosperity and patronage of learned men was from 1500 to 1800 CE, well after Ibn Battuta's visit.[38] In the nineteenth century the city of Kano bypassed even Timbuktu as the most important southern terminus of the route.

European colonialism ultimately ended the trans-Saharan caravan route. In the nineteenth century, European powers pressured North African states to end the profitable trans-Saharan slave trade. By 1900, Europeans controlled much of Africa and could enforce the ban, though, of course, the trade did not end until later in the twentieth century. The colonial powers also developed seaports on the west coast of Africa that drastically lowered transportation costs between North Africa and Europe. Moroccan traders set up shop at the port of Dakar in Senegal, bypassing the Sahara. The effective end of the trans-Saharan route came when the French built a railroad in 1906 that connected coastal Senegal to Bamako on the Niger. Everything to and from the Niger River valley and the sub-Saharan rainforest arrived at Dakar with such low transportation costs that the caravan trade could never again compete. What remained, however, over much of the trans-Saharan route was a warrior Arab elite dominating subordinated agricultural groups. Mauritania, for example, is one of the few remaining societies with widespread slavery, which supports the Arab elite.

Notes

1. Besides Ibn Battuta's record, there are only four eye-witness accounts of the trans-Saharan route between its known origins in perhaps 400 CE and the middle of the nineteenth century:

   (1) Leo Africanus, who accompanied his uncle on a diplomatic mission from Morocco to a sub-Saharan kingdom in 1510. He seems to have

gone again a few years later, possibly as a trader. The most accessible

version of the several volumes of the memoir is digital, Leo Africanus, c. 1492–1550, *A Geographical Historie of Africa ...*, translated by John Pory [Ann Arbor, Mich.]: Early English Books Online Text Creation Partnership [2002].

(2) The British government sponsored the Denham/Clapperton/Oudney expedition in 1822–4, which explored the more easterly route from Tripoli to Lake Chad. Oudney died on the trek. See Dixon Denham, Hugh Clapperton, Walter Oudney, Abraham V. Salamé, *Narrative of Travels and Discoveries in Northern and Central Africa: In the Years 1822, 1823, and 1824* (London: John Murray, 1826).

(3) Réné Caillié travelled up the Niger River to Timbuktu and north across the desert to Fez in 1828. See Réné Caillié, *Travels through Central Africa to Timbuctoo and across the Great Desert, to Morocco; Performed in the Years 1824–1828* (London: Henry Colburn and Richard Bentley, 1830).

(4) James Richardson led the second British expedition in 1850, which included Heinrich Barth and Adolph Overweg. Richardson and Overweg died en route. Richardson's diary entries of the Sahara crossing have been published. Barth wrote a full account. See Heinrich Barth, *Travels and Discoveries in North and Central Africa ...* (London: F. Cass, 1965, 1857).

There are a host of second-hand accounts of the trans-Saharan route, for example, those by Arab geographers, based on interviews with merchants or pilgrims who made the crossing. See Nehemia Levtzion and J.F.P. Hopkins, *Corpus of Early Arabic Sources for West African History* (Princeton: Markus Weiner Publishers, 2000). Many writers have described the Sahara from its margins. See, for example the memoir of George Francis Lyon, *A Narrative on Travels on North Africa in the years 1818, 19 and 20...* (London: Cass, 1966, 1821). He started from Tripoli but only reached Murzuq in what is today southern Libya.

2. In this geographical conception, I am following Edward William Bovril, *The Golden Trade of the Moors: West African Kingdoms in the Fourteenth Century* (Princeton: Markus Weiner, new edition, 1995), pp. 1–2.

3. Said Hamdun and Noel King, *Ibn Battuta in Black Africa* (Princeton: Markus Weiner Publishers, revised ed. 1994), p. 29.

4. See Michael Brett and Elizabeth Fentress, *The Berbers* (Oxford: Blackwell, 1996), pp. 14–15.

5. See Charles M. Daniels, *The Garamantes of Southern Libya* (Stoughton, Wisconsin: Oleander Press, 1970).

6. Brett and Fentress, *The Berbers*, pp. 39–41.

7. In the same period, Rome was using identical strategies against the Germanic tribes beyond the empire's northern border with equally limited success. See Brett and Fentress, *The Berbers*, pp. 53–7. The Vandals, a European 'barbarian' group crossed the Straits of Gibraltar, put an end to the Roman Empire in Africa, and ruled much of North Africa from 428 to 534 CE. See A.H. Merrils (ed.), *Vandals, Romans and Berbers: New Perspectives on Late Antique North Africa* (Aldershot, England: Ashgate, 2004).

8. Roman judgements of the relative worthlessness of lands south of the empire's African frontier echo the perceived worthlessness of the lands of the Germanic tribes west of the Rhine and the land of the Scots north of Hadrian's Wall.

9. Said Hamdun and Noël King, *Ibn Battuta in Black Africa* (Princeton: Markus Wiener Publishers, 1975, 1994), p. 30. The complete memoir is also found in *The Travels of Ibn Battuta, A.D. 1325–1354*, Volume IV (translation completed with annotations by C.F. Beckingham) (London: Hakluyt Society, 1994). A second salt mine, known as Sabkhat Ijjil, was located in what is today far western Mauritania, about 250 miles inland from the Atlantic Ocean. Caravans transported the salt south and east to Walatah (current-day Oaulata), where they joined the main north–south route from Fez to the Niger valley. See H.T. Norris, *Arab Conquest of the Western Sahara* (Harlow, Essex: Longman Group, Ltd., 1986), pp. 4–5.

10. Brett and Fentress, *The Berbers*.

11. Hamdun and King, *Ibn Battuta in Black Africa*, p. 67.

12. See Caillié, *Travels Through Central Africa to Timbuctoo and Across the Great Desert, to Morocco*, pp. 168–171.

13. Hamdun and King, *Ibn Battuta in Black Africa*, p. 31.

14. Hamdun and King, *Ibn Battuta in Black Africa*, p. 31.

15. Hamdun and King, *Ibn Battuta in Black Africa*, pp. 34–5.

16. Hamdun and King, *Ibn Battuta in Black Africa*, p. 37.

17. Roderick J. McIntosh, *Ancient Middle Niger: Urbanism and the Self-Organizing Landscape* (Cambridge: Cambridge University Press), p. 147.

18. Djenné-Djenno provides a contrary example to one of the most widely shared chestnuts of world history—that cities were the result of the emergence of kingship, with a necessary complement of bureaucracy, literacy, taxation of agricultural surplus, storage systems, and a priestly class. Put another way, as is written in virtually every world history textbook, you can't have cities without

states and all the apparatus they require. Djenné-Djenno was manifestly a city without any of the state apparatus. See McIntosh, *Ancient Middle Niger*, pp. 13–16. Arab geographers also generally did not notice these cities because, without kings or citadels or places of large-scale worship, they did not fit their expectations of cities any more than they fit the expectations of European observers a few centuries later.

19. Current day anthropology of craft workers in this region suggests that they settle and work at nodes of spiritual power necessary to their craft. The surrounding population recognizes these powers, such as the calling of spiritual forces in the smelting of iron or copper. It may be that the location of the early Niger cities was based on these perceived nodes of spiritual power, as much as any functional advantages. McIntosh, *Ancient Middle Niger*, pp. 188–91.

20. D.T. Niane, *Sundiata: An Epic of Old Mali* (Harlow, England: Pearson Education Limited, revised edition, 2006), p. 31.

21. See the translation of the relevant passage from Al-Masudi in Nehemia Levtzion and J.F.P. Hopkins, *Corpus of Early Arabic Sources for West African History* (Princeton, Markus Weiner Publishers, 2000), p. 32.

22. Al-Umari's interviews with members of the entourage are translated in Levtzion and Hopkins, *Corpus of Early Arabic Sources for West African History*, pp. 252–75.

23. Gold, about which both Muslim and European writers relentlessly sought information, was not a particularly important trade or ritual item. In sub-Saharan Africa, copper was preferred to gold. For example, gold jewellery did not appear at Djenné-Djenno until the centuries of contact with Muslim traders from north of the Sahara.

24. Hamdun and King, *Ibn Battuta in Black Africa*, p. 39.

25. See Nehemia Levtzion, 'Islam in the Bilad al-Sudan to 1800', *History of Islam in Africa*, edited by Nehemia Levtzion and Randall L. Pouwels (Athens, Ohio: Ohio University Press, 2000), pp. 63–8.

26. Hamdun and King, *Ibn Battuta in Black Africa*, pp. 64–5.

27. Transportation costs across the Sahara made these elite fabrics far costlier than in the remainder of the Islamic world. This is perhaps the reason that Ibn Battuta never received robes from the king during his stay in Mali.

28. Shielding the king with an umbrella remained a royal custom in India until well into the twentieth century. The few remaining kings of Southeast Asia still appear under one.

29. Hamdun and King, *Ibn Battuta in Black Africa*, p. 67.

30. See Eugenia W. Herbert, *Red Gold of Africa: Copper in Precolonial History and Culture* (Madison: University of Wisconsin Press, 1984), pp. 185–276.

31. There has been much recent scholarly interest in Timbuktu, including discoveries of several libraries of Islamic books held by private families. See the fine collection of essays in Shamil Jeppie and Soouleymane Bachir Diagne, *The Meanings of Timbuktu* (Capetown: HSRC Oress, 2008).

32. The desirability of copper as a trade item runs through early Arab geographical accounts of sub-Saharan Africa. See Herbert, *Red Gold of Africa*, pp. 113–14.

33. Herbert, *Red Gold of Africa*, pp. 16–17.

34. Hamdun and King, *Ibn Battuta in Black Africa*, p. 69.

35. Hamdun and King, *Ibn Battuta in Black Africa*, p. 68.

36. For the trans-Saharan slave trade, especially the better-documented eighteenth and nineteenth centuries, see John Wright, *The Trans-Saharan Slave Trade* (New York: Routledge, 2007). Arab geographers refer to the trans-Saharan slave trade as early as the ninth century. The question of what happened to the several million slaves transported to North Africa over the centuries vexes scholars. Their descendants are nowhere to be seen. Ralph A. Austen posits that the life expectancy of a black slave was so short that they did not reproduce. See Ralph A. Austen, *African Economic History: Internal Developments and External Dependency* (London: James Curry, 1987). Patrick Manning suggests that slaves were mainly female and their genes mixed with their owners. See Patrick Manning, *Slavery and African Life, Occidental, Oriental and African Slave Trades* (Cambridge: Cambridge University Press, 1990).

37. See Jonathan M. Bloom, 'Paper in Sudanic Africa', in Shamil Jeppie and Soouleymane Bachir Diagne, *The Meanings of Timbuktu* (Capetown: HSRC Oress, 2008), pp. 45–57.

38. See Timothy Cleaveland, 'Timbuktu and Walata: Lineages and Higher Education', *The Meanings of Timbuktu*, edited by Shamil Jeppie and Soouleymane Bachir Diagne (Capetown: HSRC Oress, 2008), pp. 77–84.

The Erie Canal

In cool, dry weather, boat travel on the Erie Canal could be glorious. Basil Hall, an Englishman travelling with his family soon after the canal opened in 1825, waxed poetic about the Mohawk River west of Schenectady.

> The day, fortunately for us, was cloudy, the air extremely pleasant, and the dust being well washed off the trees by two heavy thunder-showers of the day before, everything looked rich and green ... and as the windings of the canal brought us in sight of new vistas, new cultivation, new villages, new bridges, new aqueducts, rose at every moment, mingled with scattered dwellings, mills, churches, all span [sic] new. The scene was really one of enchantment.[1]

Reality, however, soon set in. All day long, passengers unceremoniously flattened themselves to the deck, as the boat passed under low bridges.

> Their height was barely sufficient for the boat to shoot through, and at first, when call to by the steersmen, 'Bridge—Passengers-mind the low bridge' it was rather amusing to hop down and then to hop up again; but by and by, this skipping about became very tiresome, and marred the tranquillity of the day very much.[2]

Night was rather worse. Canal boats were set up for the maximum number of passengers. There were no cabins, only lockers that folded out into tiny bunks. A heavy curtain separated the women's section from the men's.

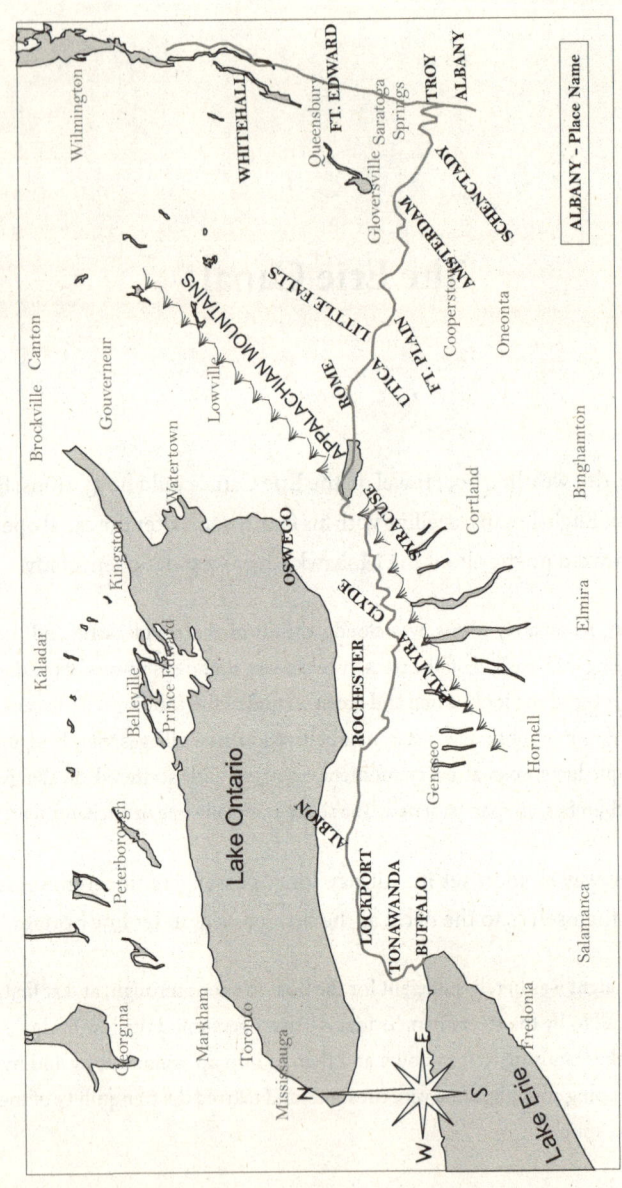

ALBANY - Place Name

The Erie Canal

These arrangements, which Hall originally found 'extremely ingenious', proved to be hot, noisy, and uncomfortable: 'By the time we reached Caughnawaga, we were so completely tired, that we resolved overnight [to return to their stagecoach]; as we had found one day of the canal was quite enough.'[3]

The story of the Erie Canal, justly treated as a 'miracle' in its own time, properly began ten thousand years ago when a glacier created a nearly perfect natural route from the Atlantic coastal plain through the Appalachian Mountains to the rich forested lands to the west. The glacier was more than a mile thick, covered all of eastern Canada, and fed a huge lake in the location of current-day Lake Ontario.[4] Runoff from the lake cut a channel east through the lowest point in the Appalachian Mountains. When the glacier receded, the channel remained, the only break in the Appalachian Mountains between Maine and Alabama. This post-glacier river no longer connected Lake Ontario and the Atlantic Ocean, but was fed by side streams from the Catskill Mountains to the north and the Adirondack Mountains to the south. The route rises only 450 feet from sea level (current-day New York City) to the summit of the Appalachians, and only another 200 feet to the level of Lake Erie at current-day Buffalo.

Around 1400 CE, five tribes both hunted the forest and cultivated cleared agricultural land along the route. From east to west they were the Mohawk, Oneidas, Onondagas, Cayugas, and Senecas. Among these tribes war was endemic and raids frequent. Around 1570 CE, under the visionary leadership of a Mohawk named Hiawatha, leaders of the five tribes swore not to wage war against one another and planted a Tree of Peace to commemorate the event. They formed a loose consultative government of elders, which met at Syracuse, adopted the central image of all five tribes under 'one longhouse', and named themselves the Haudenosaunee (termed the Iroquois by the French).[5]

In the middle of the nineteenth century, Lewis Henry Morgan, the father of ethnographic studies in the United States, recorded the customs and oral history of the remaining Haudenosaunee. He found that the route up the glacial river through the Appalachian Mountains and across the plains of Lake Ontario had been the backbone of the Haudenosaunee nation:

> These villages were so situated that the central trail, which started from the Hudson at the site of Albany, passed through those of the Mohawks and the

Oneidas; crossing the Onondaga valley and the Cayuga country, a few miles north of the chief settlements of these nations, it passed through the most prominent villages of the Senecas, in its route to the valley of the Genesee. After crossing this celebrated valley, it proceeded westward to Lake Erie, coming out upon it at the mouth of Buffalo creek, on the present site of Buffalo.[6]

From roughly 1625 to 1825 CE, the Iroquois Trail was a central component of four revolutionary changes. The first grew out of Haudenosaunee contact with white settlers. In 1616, the Dutch first moved from the Hudson River Valley into the Mohawk Valley, founding a small settlement at Schenectady. Both the Dutch and the Indians quickly figured out the benefits of large-scale trade based on the Iroquois Trail. The Dutch had connections that knew that beaver pelts were especially desirable in European markets. Along the entire length of the Appalachian Mountains, Indian trappers could only use canoes on the river-based Iroquois Trail to transport large quantities of pelts. For the Haudenosaunee the first revolution was as much social as economic.[7] They traded furs for cloth, alcohol, and especially guns. Within two generations of the beginning of trade with the Dutch, the Haudenosaunee used firearms to decimate nearby tribes and emerged as the most powerful and warlike tribe of the region.[8] Dutch documents suggest that the Haudenosaunee mental map became strongly anchored to the annual trade with the Dutch. They also lost skills in gathering and cloth weaving, and became dependent on the fur trade for many necessities of life.[9]

The second revolution connected the Iroquois Trail to worldwide political events. By the eighteenth century, few beaver remained along the Iroquois Trail, and the Haudenosaunee sought sources west into what is now Ohio and Michigan. This expansion provoked war with their competitors, the French. Centred in Montreal, and using the all-water route down the Great Lakes and the St Lawrence River, the French claimed all lands west of the Appalachian Mountains and backed up this claim with a chain of forts that ran through what is today Ohio, Pennsylvania, the Great Lakes, and the Mississippi Valley.[10] The French controlled the western end of the Iroquois Trail by means of Fort Niagara on Lake Ontario and Fort Le Boeuf on Lake Erie and claimed a border that cut right across the Haudenosaunee lands and the Iroquois Trail on the plains south of

Lake Ontario. The Haudenosaunee became implacable enemies of the French and, therefore, staunch allies of the British.

In the second half of the 1700s, the worldwide war between the British and French came to the Iroquois Trail. Fought in India, Europe, the Caribbean, and North America, it went by many names: the Maratha Wars, the Seven Years' War and, in North America, the French and Indian War. The terms of the French surrender in 1763 drastically increased England's overseas power, land, and commitments, nowhere more so than in North America. France ceded all its forts and cities along the St Lawrence River, through the Great Lakes, the upper reaches of the Ohio River and the Mississippi basin. In the short run this was, of course, good news for the Haudenosaunee because it opened all the western lands to their fur trade.

This worldwide war and subsequent overseas commitments, however, virtually bankrupted the British government and set off a desperate search for more taxes and revenue. This 'taxation without representation' was a central motivation for the revolution in the American colonies that began in the 1770s.

Only three years into the revolution, the Americans attacked the Haudenosaunee, allies of the British. In 1779, George Washington ordered the Clinton-Sullivan expedition; its 6,300 soldiers constituted almost a quarter of the colonial army. The expedition burned the site of the council fire, more than forty Haudenosaunee towns, and more than a million bushels of stored grain. The Clinton-Sullivan expedition shattered the Haudenosaunee Confederacy and its tribes. Some remnants retreated to Canada. Others were forced onto small reservations in upstate New York.[11]

The destruction of the Haudenosaunee Confederacy by American troops set off the third revolution along the Iroquois Trail—a land rush from 1790 to 1810. A mental expectation of 'open land' spread astonishingly quickly both in the East Coast colonies and in Europe. Settlers came up the Mohawk River and over the Appalachian Mountains on a rough wagon track that used the same gap in the Appalachian Mountains as the Iroquois Trail. They cut and burned the forest for farms on the broad plain south of Lake Ontario and Lake Erie. Many villages sprang up, such as Syracuse, Utica, Rochester, and Buffalo.

Almost immediately, farmers along the route realized they had a serious problem. The 'natural' market for their grain, timber, and pork was via the Iroquois Trail to New York and on to Europe. Wholesalers in New York quickly realized that the farmers along the Iroquois Trail were a large potential market for cloth, tea, sugar, and spices. The problem was that travel along the overland wagon route along the Iroquois Trail through the Appalachian Mountains was simply too expensive. It cost as much to move bulk goods the few hundred miles from the plains of Lake Ontario and Lake Erie to New York as it did to ship them all the way from New York to Europe. Faced with these hard economic realities, farmers in the new settlements shipped goods via the St Lawrence River to Montreal, or overland to Pittsburgh for transport down the Ohio and Mississippi to New Orleans.[12]

The solution to prohibitively expensive transport from upstate New York to the East Coast was the Erie Canal, the fourth revolution along the Iroquois Trail. The idea of an all-water route from Albany to the Great Lakes had been discussed for decades. As early as 1724, the surveyor-general of the colony of New York saw great potential for an all-water route to the Great Lakes, arguing that it could undercut the French route via the St Lawrence to Montreal. English traders would meet Indian trappers on the shores of Lake Erie, return east up rivers of the coastal plain, carry the boats and furs some miles to the headwaters of the Mohawk River, and travel downstream to Albany.[13]

After the American Revolution in 1784, George Washington became interested in canals, wrote of their economic potential, and worried that, without easy, reliable communication across the Appalachian Mountains, American settlers would be persuaded to join with the British to the north. He was a founding member and investor of a company that attempted to develop an inland canal based on the Potomac River. He fully understood the potential of a canal that would follow the Iroquois Trail.[14]

In 1796, Robert Fulton, inventor of the steamboat, wrote an essay in which he argued the general benefits of canals. Note his mixture of concrete economic benefits and the more subtle mental mapping that connected the places along a canal into a nation.

> ...an easy communication brings remote parts into nearer alliance, combines the exertions of men, distributes their labors through a variety of

channels, and spreads with greater regularity the blessings of life.... Easy communications to the different districts of a nation, also renders it more independent of its neighbors, by collecting and bringing forth its internal resources...[15]

By this time, Fulton and the literate elite of the United States knew that European engineers had already solved the technical problems of sophisticated canals. Fulton's essay discussed a French canal that crossed Languedoc, which, like western New York, had bulk products to sell and no convenient river on which to ship them. The canal connected the Mediterranean and the Atlantic, and avoided the 2,000-mile treacherous ocean voyage around Spain. Though it took 20 years to complete, a local baron named Pierre-Paul Riquet had planned, privately financed, and built just such an audacious 150-mile canal. He solved the three essential problems of a canal: how to raise and lower boats in both directions; how to close and seal lock doors; and how to maintain the necessary water level throughout the canal, which requires adding water to the flow. The canal rose more than 800 feet through more than a hundred complex locks, passed through a tunnel cut through solid rock, used aqueducts over rivers, and had a large reservoir at the top to add water to the system. Completed in 1681, the canal was justly considered a miracle of the age.[16]

Fulton also knew of the Bridgewater Canal in England. Though only 7 miles long, the canal demonstrated stunning economic benefits. It ran from the interior of a coal mine owned by a local noble directly to the mills of Manchester, crossing a boggy valley on an enormous aqueduct. An untutored engineer developed a system of lining the canal with layers of dirt and clay that successfully prevented water seeping out. Immediately on completion of the canal, the price of coal in Manchester dropped by more than half—and the mine owner still made a handsome profit. The success of the Bridgewater Canal set off a flurry of canal building in Europe that lasted for half a century. More than a hundred were built in England alone.[17]

Fulton's essay even discussed the Grand Canal of China, though he had few details. He noted that it moved immense amounts of grain from the south to the north and tied the country together.

From 1800 to 1815, mainly through essays in local newspapers, proponents made their case for the broad economic benefits of a canal, which would connect the Great Lakes and New York. The plan gained credence and followers.[18] They also made military and security arguments. After the United States negotiated the end of the War of 1812 with England, those who favoured the construction of a canal argued that troop transport to the Canadian border had been slow and very expensive, and that a canal would make future troop movements more efficient. They also argued that transport down the St Lawrence River could be stopped at any time by a hostile Britain. The United States, therefore, needed a wholly controlled interior route from the developing west to the East Coast.[19] Note that these arguments were really about cognitive geography, a mental map of the security of the borders of the United States.

It quickly became clear that neither local initiative nor private capital would turn the Iroquois Trail into the Erie Canal. The canal's most politically powerful champion was De Witt Clinton, governor of New York. He lobbied Washington for federal money for the project, but was rebuffed by Thomas Jefferson, who had narrowly won the presidency on the idea of minimal central government taxation or initiative.[20] Sceptics pointed out that the canal would be over 300 miles long, three times the length of any canal in Europe. With considerable support from both New York City and upstate towns, Clinton pushed a bill through the New York State legislature authorizing 17 million dollars in state bonds to build the Erie Canal, by far the largest capital project undertaken in the United States. The bonds would consume a third of the entire capital market in New York City.[21]

The canal legislation also set up a commission to survey and decide the route, design the locks, plan construction, and administer the whole project. De Witt Clinton chaired the canal commission and staked his political future on its success. Sceptics and political opponents lost no time in castigating Clinton. A political ditty of the day went like this:

Clinton, the federal son-of-a-bitch,
Taxes our dollars to build him a ditch.[22]

More than 3000 young, single men, recruited as contract labourers from Ireland, hefting pick and shovel for fifty cents a day, dug the canal in eight years. Someone invented a screw mechanism that quickly felled trees and someone else attached cutting blades to a steel plough to grub out underbrush. A third worker invented a giant horse-drawn winch that quickly pulled the stumps of first-growth trees.[23] The canal commission sent a young civil engineer to Europe to study canals there. He came back and discovered a local vein of suitable limestone for the hydraulic cement needed for building the locks.[24] As work progressed and the canal developed, many workers died in the malarial swamps west of Syracuse.[25] Ultimately, the workers cut a canal that was 363 miles long, 40 feet across at the top, 28 feet across at the bottom, 4 feet deep, and lined with compacted clay to prevent water seepage. Eighty-three locks replaced the portages where the Haudenosaunee had carried their birch bark canoes and furs.

One bank had the towpath on which teams of horses and mules pulled the boats. Several hundred low bridges connected farms to villages separated by the canal. In spite of a lack of civil engineering knowledge among those planning and executing the canal, it was completed far under budget and ahead of schedule.[26] The first flotilla passed through the canal in October 1825 and inspired local celebrations from New York City to Buffalo.

The canal immediately entered popular imagination and the famous, the rich, and the new class of professional travel writers booked trips. Lafayette, the revolutionary war general, travelled on the Erie Canal, as did the American authors Nathaniel Hawthorne and Hermann Melville. Of the dozens of memoirs and essays produced in the Erie Canal's heyday, one of the earliest and most thoughtful was by a Scot named Basil Hall, whose observations open this chapter. He had a distinguished career as a captain in the British navy, serving both in war and on voyages of exploration. During his official travels, Hall kept journals, which formed the basis of several of his books, including ones on Peru, Mexico, Java, and the first English account of Korea. He retired from the navy in 1823, married, and, in 1827, took his wife and young daughter on a long trip through North America.

At the first of the canal's locks, west of Albany, he noted the expanding commerce: 'I have seldom known a more busy scene. Crowds of boats laden with flour, grain, and other agricultural produce, were met by others as deeply laden with goods from all parts of the world, ready to be distributed over the populous regions of the west.'[27]

Hall could not have been more correct about the canal's immediate economic success. Transport prices for grain, timber, and other bulk products of the western lands dropped by 90 per cent.[28] Sale to the growing East Coast cities and export to Europe became profitable. Travel time between Buffalo and Albany dropped from over three weeks to ten days.

Boom times began the whole length of the Erie Canal. Grain wholesalers and land speculators made fortunes. Forty thousand passengers,

Illustration 24 *Erie Canal in Western New York State Crossed by Newer Bridge*. Photograph by the author.

the vast majority settlers heading west and speaking a welter of European languages, travelled the canal in its first year. Shops opened to serve them. Boat builders could not keep up with orders, which doubled and doubled again within five years. The populations of Buffalo, the western terminus of the canal, and Syracuse, with its massive underground salt deposits, grew tenfold in a decade. The rapids at Rochester proved ideal for milling grain into flour. Its population jumped from 300 to 8,000 within a decade.[29] Canal boats provided regular mail service to these new cities. In the first year, there were 160 boats. Within a decade, there were 3,000 boats, and, by the 1860s, more than 7,000 boats.[30] Settlers in side valleys built canals to connect to the Erie Canal.

Tolls on the canal allowed New York State to pay off its bonds well ahead of schedule. Trade on the Erie Canal insured that New York—not competing Boston, Philadelphia, or Baltimore—would become the dominant port and financial centre of the United States.[31]

The Erie Canal emerged so immediately famous that it initiated 'canal fever' across the nation, a profound change in the cognitive geography of how various regions of the United States would relate to each other. Projects were completed or under construction in Pennsylvania, Maine, Massachusetts, New Jersey, Virginia, Connecticut, Delaware, Maryland, and Ohio, as Basil Hall noted:

> By means of canals stretching from the very centre of that fertile region [Ohio], they can now send their produce to Lake Erie; from whence it may enter the grand canal at Buffalo, and so find its way to Lockport, Rochester, and Albany: and from thence its course to the sea at New York down the Hudson, is an affair of a few hours.[32]

Everywhere along the route of the old Iroquois Trail, the new canal brought profound local changes. Land values close to the canal soared. Towns on the canal prospered, while those away from the canal languished. Some farmers had their farms cut in half, while others gained access to new markets. The canal often altered natural drainage, creating swampy areas. New agriculture, cities, and mills sought the water that supplied the canal.

As a route, the Erie Canal generated its own ethos, quite different from that of either the Iroquois Trail or the 'upstanding citizen' image fostered by towns along its banks. The rough Irish who built the canal gained a reputation as drinkers, gamblers, and brawlers. The long workday had its daily ration of liquor. Canal workers continued the tradition of gambling, drinking, and brawling. The Erie Canal was somewhat the victim of its own success. Too many boats and long waits at locks generated bare-knuckle boxing bouts as entertainment, as well as general dustups between crews. Prostitutes were often aboard.[33] The canal also inspired legendary characters and folk songs with the usual topics of hard work, hard drinking, thwarted love, suicide, and murder. Canal workers were known as 'canawlers'.

> Canawler–Canawler
> You son of a bitch
> You'll die on the towpath
> You'll be buried in the ditch
> Canawler–Canawler
> You work on Sunday
> You'll never get rich.[34]

A verse from another ballad about work on the canal suggests the alcohol use and abuse:

> We were loaded with Star Brand Salt:
> The Cap he was loaded too.
> I wouldn't say it was his fault
> But what was a man to do.[35]

The 'degraded' moral condition of canawlers, especially the large number of young boys who led and maintained teams of horses, inspired missionary efforts to save their souls and mend their ways.[36] The missionaries were not notably successful.

For Romantics, like Victor Hugo on the Rhine, the Erie Canal provided access to Nature. According to the Romantics 'wild places' of singular beauty should and would deeply affect those who saw them. Basil Hall, ever the practical military man, was sceptical:

> All the world over, I suspect that the great mass of people care mighty little about scenery, and visit such places merely for the sake of saying they have been there ... On board the steam-boats on the superb Hudson, and in

when noticed at all, was looked at by our companions with indifference.[37]

Even the Romantics had to concede that canals were far from 'natural', but were, after all, the product of enormous human alteration of rivers and the countryside. As Hall noticed, every settler felled dozens of first-growth trees for every acre opened to agriculture. '... there prevailed a most uncomfortable appearance of bleakness or rawness, and a total absence of picturesque beauty in these villages: whose dreary aspect was much heightened the black sort of gigantic wall formed of the abrupt edge of the forest, choked up with underwood, now for the first time exposed to the light of the sun.'[38]

Illustration 25 'Erie Canal Locks at Lockport, NY'. Photograph by the author.

236

In contrast with the Romantic concept of the canal as a glorification of Nature, many people in the United States wrote of the Erie Canal as a triumph of Progress—Man in his ingenuity conquering Nature.[39] Man had a role in revealing god's plan for the betterment of mankind and the earth. The replacement of the Iroquois Trail by the Erie Canal was man's part in god's plan.

The lands along the old Iroquois Trail in western New York attracted every sort of visionary and idealist. Some preached various forms of evangelical Christianity. Others founded utopian communities based on their vision of god's plan for humanity. Some of these communities included the Mormons, the Oneida Community, Shakers, the Fox sisters, and the Millerites. Western New York was so dense with preachers and utopian communities that it was known as the 'Burned Over District' because so many were trying to burn out the sins of the people.[40] In this radical atmosphere, it is no surprise that the first convention to assert the rights of women was held at Seneca Falls, right on the Erie Canal.

In the second half of the nineteenth century, towns along the Erie Canal specialized in processing and combining goods shipped on the route. At Schenectady, General Electric manufactured products for the new electric industry as did, at the same time, towns on the Rhine. In Rochester, Kodak developed new photography technology, bringing its chemicals along the canal. Syracuse mined and shipped millions of tons of salt, in addition to sodium carbonate, much of it used in regional glass making businesses. Gloversville made gloves and sent them all over the world, Albany produced iron castings and shirt collars, Buffalo made steel from Lake Superior iron, and Pennsylvania, coal. Utica had large cotton mills.

Virtually from its debut, railroads were the principal competition to the Erie Canal all along the route. In 1826, a short rail line connected Schenectady and Albany, allowing passengers to avoid the time-consuming locks on the canal. More rail sections were built parallel to the canal in the 1830s and 1840s. In 1853, an industrialist brought together all these small lines into the New York Central Railroad, which ran from New York to Buffalo. The economic logic of railroads was inexorable. Railroads ran all year round while the Erie Canal froze for six months in the winter. The trains moved faster than the walking pace of horses. Railroads delivered goods directly to the centre of cities without unloading and reloading.

From the 1850s onwards, the Erie Canal steadily lost passenger traffic and freight tonnage to the railroad that paralleled it. The rail line on the old Iroquois Trail thorough the Appalachian Mountains became the dominant east–west rail connection from the eastern seaboard to the rest of the country. It remains so today.[41]

By 1900, the Erie Canal had been deepened, widened, somewhat re-routed, and re-named the New York State Barge Canal. Like the Mississippi River, this new version of the Iroquois Trail specialized in transport of heavy materials for construction and industry.[42] Portions of the old canal, however, remain. Tourist boats carry travellers both east and west from Lockport, New York, and the towpath has become a popular trail for both bicycling and hiking.

The old and new uses for the Erie Canal are not the end of the story of the Iroquois Trail as a trade route. Its natural advantages were evident to the planners of the Interstate Highway system in the 1950s, and they chose it to be the main artery connecting the Northeast and the Midwest. Today, the I-90, an intercontinental highway connecting the East and West Coasts of the United States closely parallels the New York Central tracks and the Erie Canal through the Appalachian Mountains from Albany to Buffalo. The relentless truck traffic connects Boston and New York with all points west.

As a route, the Iroquois Trail has both a long-term physical presence and changing complex mental definitions by the many groups that lived and travelled along it. The natural glacial cut through the Appalachian Mountains gave it an overwhelming advantage over all other routes from the eastern seaboard to the lands of the west. Native Americans knew of the route for millennia, and it became the backbone of the powerful Haudenosaunee. They envisioned their confederacy as 'one longhouse'. The Iroquois Trail was the means by which the 'eastern door' connected to the 'western door'. Along the trail came the birch-bark canoes filled with furs that forever changed the economy and social structure of the Haudenosaunee.

The French and the English well understood the Iroquois Trail's strategic importance and fought over it in the eighteenth century. For newly independent America, the Iroquois Trail was the route of thousands of settlers to rich western agricultural land.

With the building of the Erie Canal, the route gained a new wealth, a new ethos in songs and stories, and a new fame. It was the model for a wave of canal building across eastern America. In the late nineteenth century, the route once again shifted as the railroad tracks along the Iroquois Trail displaced the Erie Canal as the main carrier of goods. By the closing decades of the twentieth century, trucks carried the goods and cars carried passengers along I-90, the latest incarnation of the Iroquois Trail.

The Iroquois Trail suggests that there has always been a complex relationship between governments and routes. Like the building of the Grand Canal of China, establishing Chinese watchtowers along the Silk Road, removal of rocks on the Rhine, building the Roman roads, and dredging the Mississippi, it was often government *initiative* that turned a slow, expensive route into a cheaper, more efficient, more profitable one. Traders and private capital simply could not build the expensive but necessary infrastructure. Improvements to routes were frequently built in spite of considerable scepticism.

The Iroquois Trail also demonstrates the effects of technology on trade routes. The process started early with the use of birch-bark canoes to bring out large quantities of furs. Through all the rest of the route's history—the settler road, the Erie Canal, the railroad and I-90—newer incarnations did not necessarily completely replace older ones. The old Erie Canal has become a tourist destination. Its replacement, the New York State Barge Canal, specializes in bulk goods. The railroad tracks and I-90 now carry heavy goods to single destinations. With all these changes in technology and use, the basic natural advantages of the cut made by that ancient glacial river remain.

Notes

1. Basil Hall, *Travels in North America*, vol. 1 (Edinburgh: Cadell & Co., 1829), pp. 118–19.
2. Hall, *Travels in North America*, p. 120.
3. Hall, *Travels in North America*, p. 121. Nathaniel Hawthorne also lasted only one day on a canal boat. Unable to sleep because of the snoring around him, Hawthorne tried to get up, fell out of bed, paced the deck for a while, got off the boat at a lock, and happily walked through the night to Syracuse.

4. Basil Hall travelled both the Erie Canal and the plains leading to the Great Lakes, and was absolutely certain that the whole plains had once been the bed of an ancient lake. See Hall, *Travels in North America*, pp. 168–9. Also see Gerard Koeppel, *Bond of Union: Building the Erie Canal and the American Empire* (Cambridge, Mass.: Da Capo Press, 2009), pp. 14–15.

5. See the useful brief introduction to Iroquois history in Lawrence H. Leder, *The Livingston Indian Records, 1666–1723* (Gettysburg, PA: The Pennsylvania Historical Association, 1956), pp. 15–27.

6. Lewis Henry Morgan, *League of the Ho-dé-no-sau-nee or Iroquois* (New York: Dodd, Mead and Company, 1904), p. 80.

7. Gender roles significantly shifted as commodities produced by women were replaced by trade items. See, for example, Karen Anderson, 'Commodity Exchange and Subordination: Montagnais-Naskapi and Huron Women: 1600–1650', *Signs*, vol. II, no. 1 (Autumn 1985), pp. 48–62. Women also resisted conversion to Christianity because it undermined their rituals and spiritual power. See Carol Devens, 'Separate Confrontations: Gender as a Factor in Indian Adaptation to European Colonizations in New France', *American Quarterly*, vol. 38, no. 3 (1986), pp. 461–80.

8. For a French view of the off-again, on-again wars with the Iroquois see Anthony P. Schiavo and Claudio R. Salvucci (eds), *Iroquois Wars: Extracts from the Jesuit Relations and Primary Sources from 1535 to 1660*, vols. I and II. (Bristol, PA: Evolution Publishing, 2003).

9. The interchange between the Haudenosaunee and whites was not simply the adoption of 'advanced' white technologies. In medicine, for example, whites generally noted many successful Haudenosaunee remedies and their skill in setting bones. Haudenosaunee used European medicines when they were available. See William F. Fenton, 'Contacts between Iroquois Herbalism and Colonial Medicine', in Elizabeth Tooker (ed.), *An Iroquois Source Book*, vol. 3: Medicine Society Rituals (New York: Garland Publishing, Inc, 1986), pp. 503–26.

10. Detroit was founded in 1701 with 80 families and, with incentive of free land, soon grew to be the largest French settlement between Montreal and New Orleans.

11. The Haudenosaunee Confederacy was well known along the eastern seaboard, and its form of government influenced the framers of the American Constitution. See Arthur G. Adams, *The Hudson through the Years* (New York: Fordham University Press, third edition, 1996), pp. 3–4.

12. The Cumberland Gap rises to more than 1,500 feet, and was originally an Indian route. It was widened by Daniel Boone and a work crew, who created

a difficult but passable wagon road. It could not be used for bulk transport but only for transporting settlers in and high-value goods, especially whiskey, out. The Cumberland Gap and the Wilderness Road never created a great port (like New York) at its eastern terminus.

13. See the 'Memoir of Cadwallander Colden' (1724) as reprinted in full as appendix N in David Hosack, *Memoir of De Witt Clinton: with an Appendix, Containing Numerous Documents, Illustrative of the Principal Events of His Life* (New York: J. Seymour, 1829). Available online at galegroup.com, *The Making of Modern Law* (Gale, Cengage Learning, 2010), accessed on 10 June 2010.

14. Peter L. Bernstein, *Wedding of the Waters: The Erie Canal and the Making of a Great Nation* (New York: W.W. Norton & Company, 2005), pp. 65–76.

15. Robert Fulton, *A Treatise on the Improvement of Canal Navigation* (London: I. and J. Taylor, 1796), 1–10. The treatise is digitally available free at Google Books.com

16. Fulton, *A Treatise on the Improvement of Canal Navigation, 11–19*.

17. Lionel D. Wyld, *Low Bridge! Folklore and the Erie Canal* (Syracuse: Syracuse University Press, 1962), p. 12.

18. Bernstein, *Wedding of the Waters*, pp. 77–88.

19. Wyld, *Low Bridge! Folklore and the Erie Canal*, p. 12.

20. Jefferson would, of course, purchase Louisiana from Napoleon in a deal too good to pass up. The price was considerably smaller than the cost of the Erie Canal.

21. Gerard Koeppel, *Bond of Union: Building the Erie Canal and the American Empire* (Cambridge, MA: 2009), p. 8. More analysis and detail will be found in Carol Sheriff, *The Artificial River: The Erie Canal and the Paradox of Progress, 1817–1862* (New York: Hill and Wang, 1996), pp. 2–9.

22. George E. Condon, *Star in the Water: The Story of the Erie Canal* (Garden City, New York: Doubleday & Company, 1974), p. 65.

23. Condon, *Star in the Water*, pp. 56–7.

24. Condon, *Star in the Water*, p. 58.

25. Condon, *Star in the Water*, pp. 70–3.

26. Wyld, *Low Bridge! Folklore and the Erie Canal*, p. 9.

27. Hall, *Travels in North America*, p. 114.

28. Wyld, *Low Bridge! Folklore and the Erie Canal*, p. 12.

29. Wyld, *Low Bridge! Folklore and the Erie Canal*, p. 44.

30. Condon, *Star in the Water*, p. 110.

31. Boston, Baltimore, and Philadelphia all recognized the threat to their business posed by the Erie Canal. Canals to the west were proposed in all three

cities, but none were viable projects. None had the natural advantage of a glacial cut through the Appalachian Mountains.

32. Hall, *Travels in North America*, pp. 174–5.

33. Wyld, *Low Bridge! Folklore and the Erie Canal*, pp. 61–74.

34. Wyld, *Low Bridge! Folklore and the Erie Canal*, p. 83.

35. Wyld, *Low Bridge! Folklore and the Erie Canal*, p. 85.

36. Condon, *Star in the Water*, pp. 130–1.

37. Hall, *Travels in North America*, pp. 123–4.

38. Hall, *Travels in North America*, p. 128.

39. There is no more complicated nor freighted a term in the nineteenth century than 'Nature'. The Hudson River School of landscape painting, for example, emphasized wild hills and gorges as 'natural'. Modern scholars have had rather a field day analysing the term in various political, ecological, and literary contexts. See, for example, William Cronon, *Nature's Metropolis: Chicago and the Great West* (New York: W.W. Norton and Co., 1991) and Barbara Novak, *Nature and Culture: American Landscape and Painting*, 1825–1875 (Oxford: Oxford University Press, 1981).

40. Sheriff, *The Artificial River*, pp. 166–7. The scholarly literature on religion and utopianism in upstate New York is large. Two useful books are Curtis Johnson, *Islands of Holiness: Rural Religion in Upstate New York, 1790–1860* (Ithaca: Cornell University Press, 1989), and Marianne Perciaccante, *Calling Down the Fire: Charles Grandison Finney and Revivalism in Jefferson County, New York* (Albany, State University of New York press, 2003).

41. Another problem of the canal was technological. In spite of a large prize offered by New York State, no inventor came up with a viable design for a steam-powered canal boat. Both a cable system and electricity were tried, and both were unsuccessful. Nothing competed in reliability and cost with mules and drivers. Only deepening the canal and the internal combustion engine finally made animal power obsolete.

42. By the 1950s, much basic export tonnage from the mid-West was lost to the new St Lawrence Seaway.

Conclusion

Routes are an important means of understanding the broad-scale ebb and flow of the past. Many of the great routes had a name—such as Compostela, Hajj, Erie Canal, Grand Canal, Appian Way, and Rhine River—and were justly famous in their heyday, celebrated in songs, stories, poems, and geographical writing. Routes did far more than connect a source of some commodity with the areas that demanded it. They were places where millions of people lived, worked, travelled, wrote, married, fought, and created.[1] A route brought together people and ideas in a way that no other large-scale structure could. Along the Silk Road, Buddhism spread from city to city and eventually to China, changing and developing along the way. The rise of Sufi Islam was also largely a product of the western reaches of the Silk Road, preached first in caravanserais and hostels. The emotional spiritualism of western New York in the first half of the nineteenth century was directly linked to groups moving westward along the Erie Canal in search of land and the freedom to practise their various radical forms of Christianity.

This book has argued three main points. The first point is that each route was a complex mixture of the physical and the mental, but that cognitive geography generally preceded and provided the basis for the route. The belief in the safety and reliability of an internal canal route relative to a sea route from south to north, thus, underlay the Chinese imperial effort expended on the Grand Canal. The belief in the potential for vastly expanded agriculture underlay the construction of the Erie Canal. The belief that joint action would make a safer and more efficient Rhine underlay the establishment of the multi-country commission that took over the management of the river in the nineteenth century. Copper was indeed a trade item in Africa, but it was the notion of copper as a portal into the magical and spiritual world that fuelled the desire to possess it. What brought thousands of pilgrims to a shrine was its reputation for working miracles and fulfilling prayers. Returning pilgrims built this reputation as they recounted their experiences in a thousand towns and villages.

The book's second point is that routes were places of a variety of mental maps. A route, as perceived by a pilgrim, was almost entirely different from that of a trader, though they travelled in the same caravan. Within a government one faction might perceive a route as primarily a source of government tolls, while another promoted low tolls to stimulate trade. The military perceived a route as primarily a strategic artery, but caravans and pilgrims wanted unfettered use of it. Traders wanted the water to stay in a canal for transportation, but farmers perceived its importance in irrigating fields. Cognitive geography could also change quickly. Steamboat companies, for example, rapidly and successfully promoted the perception of the Mississippi, the Rhine, and the Nile as safe places for tourists.

The third point is that routes were places of conflict. Major battles were fought along routes, such as during the Great Roman Civil War, fought after the assassination of Julius Caesar, or the Battle of Shiloh in the American Civil War. Let us turn to some conclusions about aspects of the cognitive geography of routes.

Ecology

Routes generally connected different climatic regions, and each route had its season—a yearly rhythm dictated by ecology and climate. The annual grain tax moved up the Grand Canal only once per year. Transport had to follow the harvest, but precede the drop in the Yangtze and Yellow rivers, which made them too shallow for grain boats to cross. Similarly, travel on the Indian Ocean route was carefully arranged to take advantage of monsoon winds. Only for a few months could ship captains sail north, and there were only a few months when they could return on the reversed winds. The transportation of the grain supply from Egypt to Rome was also a yearly phenomenon. The grain had to be harvested and the ships loaded to reach Brindisi before the winter storms began. No one, except under extreme duress, sailed on the Mediterranean in the winter. The same sort of yearly rhythm was typical of the Silk Road. All passes over the Himalayas closed in the winter. No one risked the deep snow, extreme cold, and lack of fodder for the animals. The Erie Canal, the Mississippi above St Louis, and the Rhine froze in winter.

On land, typical patterns of influence radiated outward from the road. The central strip was the road itself and the towns and cities along it, characterized by connections up and down the route, such as caravanserais, intellectual networks connected by letters, and the processing of raw materials into goods for export along the route. Cincinnati, for example, made barrels for the shipping of cured pork down the Mississippi River. Towns along the Nile specialized in turning flax into linen for shipment downriver. Immediately outside of the chain of towns was often a strip of valuable agricultural land, which provided food, firewood, and fodder for the cities and travellers. This strip was at most a few miles wide, the distance a wagon could traverse in a day. The next strip outward from the route would likely also be agricultural land, which produced goods for processing and export, such as vineyards in side valleys off the Rhine River and wheat production along the Nile. Beyond this strip used for agriculture was generally a strip of agriculture mixed with herding, which provided products for trade, such as hides and wool. This arrangement was typical of the Silk Road, but also true of the western tributaries of the Mississippi.[2] Beyond the strip of agriculture and herding was a broad region in which naturally occurring resources were gathered. Timber, for example, was logged in the mountains above the Rhine and came downriver to shipyards in the Netherlands. Hill folk in Southeast Asia collected spices and medicines for export to China and the Middle East.[3] Such a pattern must have formed part of the mental map of those living and working along routes.

Routes had two additional important ecological impacts. First, routes brought serious disease. The Nile was such a vector for the deadly mosquito-borne Rift Valley Fever. Towns along the Mississippi saw connected outbreaks of malaria, cholera, and yellow fever. On a larger scale, the Black

Death followed routes through the Middle East and into Europe. Second, some routes profoundly affected drainage. Canals produced swamps where none had been before and altered the flow of rivers. Dredging and straightening rivers resulted in more rapid flow, but also produced floods in the lower reaches of the river.

Government Institutions

A government's role in routes varied from absolute control to quite minimal involvement. The expectation of government presence and its efficacy in providing safe travel formed a central part of the cognitive geography of all who used the route. At one extreme, the trans-Sahara route had no overarching government, no way stations, no road signs, and no well keepers. Caravans merely paid a tax to each tribe whose territory they crossed in return for their agreement not to attack the caravan and for some degree of protection from attacks by others while in their territory. Small kingdoms along the Rhine also provided virtually no services in return for the tolls they charged. Pilgrims on the Compostela road complained of the extortionate tolls charged by small states along the way, which provided no services.

At the opposite extreme was full end-to-end government control of the route. For example, labour impressed by the Inka built the trunk road in the Andes. Tight government control included staffed warehouses, way stations, teams of runners, and military outposts. Governments also prohibited traders from using the route. The Grand Canal of China had a very high degree of government involvement and control. Officials posted along its length examined cargoes and stopped boats lacking the necessary passes to travel. Periodic reports came to Beijing from dozens of sites along the canal. Government troops protected the canal and cleared traffic for the yearly grain shipment. From early times, the Grand Canal required massive amounts of corveé labour for maintenance. The ability to mobilize this labour was a measure of the efficacy of a dynasty and its retention of the Mandate of Heaven. By the end of the nineteenth century, the Mississippi River reached levels of government control approximating the Grand Canal. The Army Corps of Engineers assumed responsibility for licensing pilots, maintaining lighted markers, locks, and dams, and guaranteeing a minimum depth of water.

246

Conclusion

Many routes fell between these two extremes, for example, the Mississippi in the first half of the nineteenth century. The government did not license the boats, pilots, or goods. Nevertheless, there were military outposts, government agents, and a common legal code. The Nile during the same period had somewhat more government control, including government-staffed toll stations and military posts. Kings along the Silk Road provided somewhat fewer services, perhaps a military escort to the next city or caravanserais for storing trans-shipped goods. The Roman route to the East provided watchtowers only on the most dangerous portions of the Appian and Egnatian Ways. On these routes, with middling government involvement, there was still a need for a post system. Although privately carried and fragmented, letters often reached their destinations more reliably and speedily than one might expect. Such correspondence was usually among members of an ethnic, religious, or family network, and the expectation of such regular contact with distant members formed part of the participant's mental map.

Part of government involvement in a cognitive geography of a route was its sponsorship of a legal structure to mediate relations. Roman law prevailed along the Appian Way and east to Byzantium and Egypt, as well as to the northern frontier along the Rhine. The Grand Canal was controlled by an elaborate legal system that took its cues from the court at Beijing. On other routes, however, governments did not control the legal system. Dozens of different kingdoms along the Rhine enforced differing legal systems, with Catholic states upriver and Protestant Holland at the mouth of the river. Similarly, the Mississippi crossed both slave and free states. Some peoples on the Indian Ocean route followed Sharia law, but not everyone involved with trade followed Islam or recognized its laws.

Flow of Material Goods

Across the world, all traders shared some features of a common cognitive map. They understood that it was fundamentally more expensive, ten times more expensive even, to transport goods by land than by water. To be profitable all caravan trade, therefore, had to consist of high-value goods, such as spices, medicines, slaves, sugar, salt, luxury fabrics, carpets, gems and beads, feathers, aromatic oils, books, religious relics, and craft goods. Water transport made it profitable to trade heavier items over longer distances, such as oil, grain, timber, stone, hides, preserved meats, bulk metals, and raw cotton.

They all understood that local desires for fashion, adornment, and luxury were just as powerful as those for basic needs, such as food, health, or shelter. Luxury goods from the east, such as frankincense and tropical spices, were virtual necessities for upper-class life in Rome. Routes carried information about these local desires back to the producers, such as what were the favoured colours in cities along the route, what medicines might be sold, and when the goods needed to arrive. Along routes, commodities gained reputations, for example the softness of silk loomed in a certain city or the medical efficacy of cloves from a single island. Some of the most persistent desires defined prominent places in widely shared mental maps, such as the 'land of gold' in Arab geographies of sub-Saharan Africa, or the 'land of frankincense' in Roman geographies.

Some goods were high value because they connected the material and the spiritual worlds. In sub-Saharan Africa, copper warded off not only disease, but also evil spirits and spells. Native Americans along the length of the Mississippi traded for copper for much the same reasons. Prayers and sayings of the Prophet Muhammad were woven into carpets along the Silk Road. Beads traded in Southeast Asia, such as carnelian and lapis, were said to possess magical properties. Every pilgrim who returned from Compostela had a clamshell. Many believed that the shell was a talisman that had powers arising from its association with the shrine of St James. The incense trade from Southeast Asia to China was based on a scent's power to honour both ancestors and Buddhist deities.

The flow of material culture also reflected the degree of integration of a route with a capital city. In the case of the Inka, the pottery, cuisine, urban architecture, and spatial layout of outlying cities must have affected the cognitive geography of conquered peoples, emphasizing the reach and power of the empire. In the Roman Empire a military camp along the Appian Way was similar to one in the farthest reaches of England. Archaeologists have found evidence of wine, olive oil, even dates in the ruined Roman camps along the Rhine.

Routes often depended on widely accepted currencies. A *miqtal* of gold and the silver *dirham* were known and accepted across the Islamic world, which included the Indian Ocean route, the Nile, and the trans-Saharan route. The cowrie shell, as a small currency, spread across India, China, Southeast Asia, and Africa. Silk cloth was considered currency in China, along the Silk Road, and in India. Pepper could be traded through all of the Middle East, Russia, and Ethiopia. Salt had a relatively stable exchange rate across Africa. Each of these commodities across a wide area had an agreed upon exchange value for horses, camels, slaves, food, housing, and caravan costs.[4] These expectations of relative value in appropriate places were an integral part of the cognitive geography of routes.

Networks

Very, very few people travelled a route alone. They went with friends, colleagues, relatives, or people from their village, and shared food, alcohol, songs, stories, boasts, and jokes. Whether pilgrims, tourists, traders, or soldiers, all travellers were part of a larger network based in towns and cities along the route. Traders in Rome corresponded with compatriots in Alexandria. An Arab or Turkish trader's reputation preceded him up and down the Nile. Along the Silk Road, kings wrote letters of introduction to other kings further ahead for travelling Buddhist monks. Pilgrims, both men and women, on the road to Compostela or Makkah, met and formed friendships with others on the trek. Women traders in Southeast Asia exchanged news of local markets as they travelled. Kings kept in touch through royal emissaries. The expectation of finding members of one's network was certainly part of the mental map of a route.

The sheer variety of networks meant that various languages co-existed along a route and became part of diverse mental maps. Arabic was usable on the trans-Saharan route because of the availability of translators, but in no way displaced local languages. If networks of Arabic speakers spread north and south along the route, local language networks spread east and west within the Sahara. On the Nile, Turkish was the language of the government, but Arabic was the local language. On the Roman route to the East, Latin was the language of officials and upper-class landholders, but Greek was spoken throughout the countryside. Boatmen, professional caravan drivers, and sailors typically used specialized languages and slang incomprehensible to outsiders. Their stories and songs often featured a

hapless and clueless traveller. The Erie Canal, for example, passed through
country in which the settlers saw themselves as pious representatives of
Christianity. They perceived the network of boatmen on the canal as a
drunken, brawling, immoral lot, to be converted if possible and avoided
if not. Travellers on the Mississippi had much the same reputation—
gamblers, drinkers, and flashy dressers.

Every route had its network of bandits or pirates bent on stealing
goods and enslaving or ransoming travellers. The opportune places for
theft were mountains, forests, coasts with isolated coves, the open ocean,
and deserts. All were places beyond easy government patrol, well known
to travellers, and part of their cognitive geography. Travellers made judg-
ments of risk based on the best information available from their network.
Pirates and bandits tapped their own networks to devise escape routes for
eluding pursuers. Bandits and pirates figured prominently in the mental
maps of the routes discussed in this book, such as the Japanese pirates
who plagued the coast of China, the bandits in the central mountains of
Roman Italy, marauders along the caravan route in Ibn Battuta's Morocco,
and brigands in the mountains between the Nile and the Red Sea.

In the eighteenth century assembled a new network, that of tourists
and the professionals who served them. The idea of tourism began in
England in the eighteenth century in response to the Romantic Movement
that encouraged the viewing of ruins and saw Nature as edifying. The first
travel agent appeared in London in about 1750 to book tours on routes
that had become relatively safe and inexpensive. The Rhine River hosted
masses of tourists, many of them women, by the end of the eighteenth
century, as did the Mississippi and the Nile during the heyday of steamboat travel in the nineteenth century. The network of professional guides,
ship captains, and hotel owners passed information essential to serving
the needs of tourists.

Armies were among the most important networked groups along routes.
The large Roman roads were built primarily for rapid military deployment
and known as viae militaris. (military road). Many major battles were
fought along routes because they were generally the only means of moving
large armies. This was as true of the campaign along the Roman road to the
East as it was for the campaign for control of the Mississippi River during
the American Civil War. Steam riverboats were crucial in ferrying troops to

the North's victory in the battle of Shiloh. The Rhine was the site of major European battles from Roman times to World War II.

Some networks produced results that were quite unintended by the builders of the route. Whole populations used roads to emigrate, especially as an empire began to decline and lost control of its routes. Bulgarians moved south into Greece and west along the Roman route. The invaders of Rome used the same routes along which the conquering legions had marched two centuries before. One reason to build the Erie Canal was military. In the War of 1812, it had proved slow and expensive to move troops north to the Canadian theatre. The canal, some argued, would make such deployment easier, speedier, and less expensive. A far more important network along the Erie Canal, unintended by its builders, consisted of new spiritual Christians who built communities in western New York. These communities were central to the emerging abolitionist and feminist movements in the nineteenth century.

Technology

The relationship of technology to a route was complicated. Often, transport technology and route technology developed together in a series of incremental steps. Roman road-builders, after much experiment, developed a roadbed and stone surface that were capable of handling large and heavy carts, drained well, and were suitable for large marching armies. Roman carts evolved to a standard-axle width for wheels to fit in standard spaced grooves on the roads. Inka technology, in contrast, did not include wheeled vehicles, so their routes had stairs built to the human stride. The Inka, nevertheless, developed miles-long inclines and roller systems for moving enormous building blocks hundreds of miles along their routes.

Technology could be comfortable with quite different underlying politics or ideology. Centuries of steady development in China in water management technique and boatbuilding saw no serious challenge to the basic ethos of Confucian taxation to achieve stability, prosperity, and order. The Chinese Imperial court took the lead in constructing infrastructure and giving out tax incentives for land development. The principle purpose was not trade but balancing the south's capacity to grow surplus grain with the north's chronic grain shortage. The Erie Canal had much the same technology as the Grand Canal as well as the government initiative in building it, but its dominant ethos was quite different from China's. The canal was to promote trade, increase private wealth, and thereby expand the tax base for the state. The Confucian ethos of the Grand Canal and the development ethos of the Erie Canal seem equally comfortable with the same canal technology.

Technology did, however, make a major difference on some routes. The introduction of the camel, for example, as a transport technology, made the trans-Saharan route feasible. The steamboat radically changed the predictability and comfort of travelling on the Mississippi River, the Rhine, and the Nile in the period during 1820–50. The main function of the Rhine River changed in the nineteenth century with the development of heavy industry along it. The need for transportation of heavy, bulky raw materials made the Rhine an ideal route for profitable barge traffic.

***

In the long sweep of history, routes were profoundly important. They did not simply connect empires or civilizations, but influenced the human population far beyond a road, sea lane, port, or caravan city. Routes were the conduit for ideas and religions, fashion and architecture, medicines and cuisine. They mixed peoples and languages. Demand for raw materials directly affected agriculture along the route and reached deep into the grazing and gathering lands beyond the farms. As materials were processed along routes, new designs, motifs, and products appeared. Plants moved along routes far from their native habitat to become important sources of food, medicines, and fabrics. Whole populations relocated along routes.

Routes also figure prominently in cognitive geographies. The trans-Saharan route appeared in centuries of Islamic geographical literature. The Rhine was the setting for stories, songs, poems, and opera. The Grand Canal was a subject of paintings and literature. The Mississippi generated folk songs, as well as novels and stories by authors like Mark Twain. The Erie Canal inspired folk songs, some of which are still sung. The Appian Way figured in the satires of Horace. Poems about the Compostela pilgrimage and music composed at the shrine were undoubtedly carried back with returning pilgrims.

Some of the advantages of older routes are still important in our modern world. The Erie Canal was reborn as the Barge Canal, as well as the New York Central Railroad lines, which still carries the majority of the freight between the eastern seaboard and the rest of the United States. Its advantage as the only level pass through the Appalachians will continue into the foreseeable future, and even the I-90 follows the same route. Transport by water is still less expensive than by land, making bulk transport along the Rhine and the Mississippi likely, well into the future. As a route, the pilgrimage to Makkah is far more popular now than at any time in its long history.

Along routes people lived, worked, spread religions, created, and learned in exciting, if not always predictable, ways. In their mental maps, producers looked to distant markets, needed up-to-date information, and often had to understand more than one language. Traders needed to establish and believe in relationships of trust over long distances. Some formed alliances based on kinship, common religion, or shared ethnicity, but others, like those of today, experimented with new business forms. They had to calculate risk and make the best decisions they could. Spiritual quests, then as now, motivated seekers on pilgrimage routes.

Technology continues to evolve along routes. The truck with a double trailer makes more efficient use of the I-90, just as the maglev reinvents the train. Tourism today still follows some old routes, such as the Nile and the Rhine, and the Erie Canal, and rediscovers others, such as the Silk Road and the pilgrimage to Compostela. Just as in the past, we cannot predict the unintended consequences of a route. Plants, people, food, disease, music, architecture, and cuisine still move along them in ways that no one can foresee. Now, routes connect the whole world. We live along them and fruitfully continue to imagine them.

Notes

1. My study of routes is aligned with historical studies of large regions, such as Indian Ocean research. It makes much sense to study, for example, all the port cities of the Indian Ocean together, regardless of the nation to which they currently belong. The port cities were part of a route that spread ideas, cuisine, religions, fashion, and commodities.

2. Jonathan Skaff, 'Survival in the Frontier Zone: Comparative Perspectives on Identity and Political Allegiance in China's Inner Asian Borderlands during the Sui-Tang Dynastic Transition (617–30)', *Journal of World History*, vol. 15 no. 2 (June 2004), pp. 117–53. See also Mahnaz Ispahani, *Roads and Rivals: The Political Uses of Access In the Borderlands of Asia* (Ithaca, NY: Cornell U. Press, 1989).

3. Where the agricultural strips were not present or inadequate, such as the high Andes, Northern China, the transit islands of the East African trade, or the mines in the Sahara, particular efforts had to be made to ensure the food supply.

4. Any assumption that the establishment of a route and trade necessarily benefited those along the route is simply incorrect. The appearance of the Europeans along the Mississippi meant the speedy ecological extinction of the beaver and buffalo the and rapid decimation of several tribes by disease and war initiated by the Europeans. It's not clear that the Greeks benefited from the Roman road across the peninsula. It was a military road and the beneficiaries were the new Roman estate holders along it. The establishment of the Grand Canal probably did not benefit the farmers in the south of China. They merely paid the same burdensome taxes in grain. The Erie Canal benefited settlers, but not the Native Americans who were displaced.

Index

About the Author

Stewart Gordon is an independent research scholar connected to the South Asia Center of the University of Michigan. Gordon is best known for his extensive writing on Marathas, including *The Marathas, 1600–1818* (recently translated into Marathi) and several dozen articles on South Asian and World History. He has served as a consultant for the History Channel, the Discovery Channel, and the Walt Disney Company. His recent book, *When Asia Was the World*, is a bestseller and has been translated into seven languages. He has rambled by bus across Turkey, Iran, Afghanistan, Pakistan, and India. He has struggled up Inka paths in Peru, and boated up the Mekong and the Mississippi.

Gordon is also a professional restorer of fine antique furniture and has owned shops in Ann Arbor, Los Angeles, and London. He currently lives in Ann Arbor and has recently built a full-sized, fully equipped horse-drawn gypsy wagon. For more on Gordon's talks, workshops, new publications, artwork, and photos of his travels, visit stewartgordonhistorian.com